Praise for *Pathways to Peace* . . .

"Victor's book is filled with the voice of discovery and healing. The discovery of the peace that lies just beneath our fear and aggression. The peace that is our birthright. He encourages that inner wisdom with skillful means and heart-fed insight. This is a menu for the banquet of peace we all hope someday to sit down to together."

—Ondrea and Stephen Levine

"An essential tool kit for all who want to do something to reduce violence and create a kinder world."

—Sam Keen

"We all know the problems. Victor LaCerva has solutions. *Pathways to Peace* is a practical, inspirational book that effectively combines research and resources with authentic activities and exercises for deep personal and societal change. Victor has always had a gift for working with men. Now his work extends to the larger community, with a book that is unique and genuinely helpful."

—Peggy O'Mara
Editor/Publisher of *Mothering*

"A clear, readable manual of useful insights and information that will be helpful to anyone working to reduce the level of violence in our society."

—Starhawk

PATHWAYS TO PEACE

Forty Steps
To a Less Violent America

Pathways
to Peace

Forty Steps to a Less Violent America

Victor La Cerva, MD

Foreword by Ashley Montagu

HEAL

PUBLISHED BY:
HEAL FOUNDATION PRESS

HEAL

Business Offices:
Executive Director
Stephan McLaughlin Jr.
1770 North Germantown Parkway
Suite 3-162
Cordova, TN 38018
(801)-947-0317
www.healfoundation.org

Editorial Offices:
P.O. Box 120969
Nashville, TN 37212

Pathways to Peace
Edited by Ellen Kleiner
Book Design by Richard Harris
Index by Elizabeth Wolf

Packaged by
Spiridon Press, Inc.
P.O. Box 120969
Nashville, TN 37212
Visit our web site at www.spiridon.com

Publisher and Editor: Randall Bedwell
Managing Editor: Carol L. Boker
Cover Design: Pat Patterson, Patterson-Graham Design Group

Permissions: "Thirty Developmental Assets" reprinted with permission from Peter L. Benson, The Troubled Journey: A Portrait of 6th-12th Grade Youth (Minneapolis, MN: Search Institute, 1993); "Rainbows" reprinted from Talking From the Heart: An Anthology of Men's Poetry (1990), with permission of Hank Blackwell and Men's Network Press, Albuquerque, NM; "Ten Recommended Attitudes About Technology" reprinted from In the Absence of the Sacred by Jerry Mander (1991) with permission of Sierra Club Books; and "I Am Me" by Virginia Satir used with permission of Avanta, The Virginia Satir Network, 310 Third Avenue NE, Issaquah, WA 98027. All rights reserved.

Publisher's Cataloging-in-Publication
(Provided by Quality Books, Inc.)

La Cerva, Victor.
        Pathways to peace: forty steps to a less violent America /
        Victor La Cerva; foreword by Ashley Montagu --2nd ed.
        p. cm.
        Includes bibliographical references and index.
        ISBN 0-9661575-0-8

        1. Violence-United States-Prevention. I. Montagu, Ashley,
        1905-II. Title

HM281.L33 1997   303.6'0973
                                       QB195-20594

(previously) ISBN# 0-9649104-0-3

Notes of Gratitude

Deepest thanks to Laura, for her openness and willingness to rediscover our friendship, and for her dedication as a mother.

Mille grazie to the circle of men in my life, who enrich my being beyond measure and who always provide encouragement and feedback so that I might keep on keeping on: Barry, Gaylon, Hank, Harold, John, Len, Michael, Mitch, Rick, and Tim; Juan, a wise and generous amigo; and Steven, a strong and gentle friend for more than forty years. They are always there when I need them most.

Heartfelt thanks to Ellen Kleiner of Blessingway for her editing. She gently took a rough-hewn piece and sculpted it to create something more beautiful and useful. Richard Harris moved like the wind to complete the wonderful graphics and layout in record time. Also, thanks to Peg Shanahan for her past artistic contributions.

Deep appreciation to my grandparents and parents, who gave me a solid foundation of encouragement and caring from which to move forward in my life.

Mitakuye oyasin to many, many other important friends. You know who you are, and I am honored and blessed by your ongoing love.

No one writes a book alone. Some of the ideas expressed in this book are from sources carefully cited; others are from sources long forgotten. I acknowledge these people's contributions to my life by sharing freely from their own founts of wisdom.

Thank you, dear reader, for your interest. I sincerely hope and desire that you will benefit from the ideas contained in these pages and that you will pass your insights on to others. May this book bring you light and peace, give voice and guidance to discovering who you really are, and encourage you to act upon your inner wisdom and personal truth.

This book is dedicated to my daughters, Rosa and Gina.
Their beings constantly fill me with love, wonder, and appreciation.
Teaching me gently and with compassion, they bring forth my light
as they help to heal my darkness. May they inherit a less violent world.

CONTENTS

FOREWORD

To be human is to be in danger, because with the loss of our instincts we, unlike other animals who retain their necessary share of them, have to learn everything we come to know and do as human beings *from other human beings*. Our socializers, beginning with our parents, generally mean well, but if their teachers have failed to give *them* the love and encouragements needed for healthy development, we shall not prosper as healthy human beings. Health, in terms of our species, implies the ability to love, to work, to play, and to think critically. Such a failure will indeed be catastrophic, will for many of us constitute the most disastrous of all tragedies: a vast difference between what we were capable of becoming and what we have been caused to become.

My scientific studies of the nature and development of human behavior, based on more than seventy years of research, as well as the studies of literally thousands of other scientists, have made it unequivocally clear that human beings are born to live as if to live and love were one. It would appear that we are programmed to follow the basic pattern of what the loving mother does for her child, which results in the reciprocal benefits they confer upon each other in their nurturing bonding relationship. Here the operative signal is *love*.

Because we live in a world in which there is a great deal of *un*loving behind the show of love, and in which the meaning of love is rarely understood, let me describe what love is. Love is the communication, through demonstrative acts, of your profound involvement in the welfare of others, such that you give them all the encouragements, supports, sustenance, and stimulation they require for their unique development and fulfillment. It lets them know that they are precious to you; that you will always be standing by; that you will never commit the supreme treason of letting them down when they are in need of you; and that you will help them become all that is good and loving.

In this wonderful book, Victor LaCerva succeeds in setting out in a most readable and practical manner the criteria for the achievement of healthy development among adults and children. It is indeed a book that should be widely read, and as becomes its importance, it is beautifully and memorably written.

In a world as devastatingly violent as our own America, we stand very much in need of solutions that will enable us to prevent the future development of the socially destructive practices from which we all suffer. Toward that end, this book offers us much wisdom and practical guidance. In a sick society we need healers like Victor LaCerva, who can help us cure ourselves of the destructive effects of the brutality in which we are held like so many apathetic prisoners.

Many years ago F. Scott Fitzgerald described America as a willingness of the heart. It still could be, if we were to take to heart and follow the guidelines that Victor LaCerva so clearly and persuasively sets out before us in this admirable book.

Ashley Montagu
Princeton, New Jersey

OPENING THOUGHTS

THERE EXISTS A WONDERFUL COMMUNITY CELEBRATION KNOWN AS FOUR-CIRCLE dancing. The outermost circle in this dance is composed of loving witnesses: the musicians, the audience, and, extending beyond physical parameters, everyone connected to those who are present. The next circle inward is the male yang dancing circle; closer to the center is the female yin dancing circle. The innermost circle is a place of creative abandon. As the rhythms begin, the dancers are told, "Don't dance until you feel like you have to be tied to a tree *not* to."

Writing this book has been a similar experience. Speaking about violence prevention before hundreds of groups across the country, I became inundated with requests for more information. It turned out that many people were working day and night to decrease violence, and many more would join the effort if given appropriate knowledge and skills. This discovery was exhilarating. I let the energy build until I felt compelled to write down everything I knew about peacemaking.

Sailing on the river of my imagination—often from 3 am to 5 am, in what Shakespeare termed "the dead vast and middle of the night"— I began to distill the essence of what I was learning. I was playing victor at the edge, pulling together the scattered pieces of myself, tapping into some archetypal source of clarity and energy while watching my own fears, listening to the silence, and embracing its fertile ground.

Good teachers don't have a monopoly on truth; they simply have the ability to *frame an issue* so that truth emerges. The issue here is violence in America—a threat to survival on many levels. Framing the problem in terms of pathways honors where we have been, what our current situation is, and where we are headed. It also acknowledges the diversity of trails leading to nonviolence. The truth that emerges is quite simple. If we continue with what we have been doing and, more importantly, refusing to act upon what we know is possible, we will generate more suffering. If we set forth along any one of these pathways, however, we can help create a place of safety and peace for ourselves, our children, and generations to come.

The First Path

THE WAY OF REALITY

WHAT THEY DON'T TELL YOU ON THE
EVENING NEWS, WEATHER, SPORTS, AND RAMPAGE

We cannot begin to solve the significant problems we have with the same level of thinking with which we created them.
—Albert Einstein

MOST OF US ARE BOMBARDED DAILY BY MEDIA ACCOUNTS OF SEEMINGLY random, senseless, and out-of-control violence. We are left with vague feelings of anger, sadness, anxiety, guilt, fear, concern, hopelessness, and a sense that *some*one should do *some*thing about it. Part of the conversation we have with ourselves when we hear an evening news flash or read a morning headline is that violence is everywhere, that little can be done about it, and that our only option is to protect ourselves and our families from it. The media acknowledge the terrible shape we are in, but offer few solutions.

While growing up, I was personally victimized by violence. As a frontline emergency room physician for many years, I witnessed terrible suffering. More than once, I have been in a room with a hundred men crying and grieving the violence done to them by other men. Listening to the stories of battered women, watching the faces of abused children, and protesting with mothers who lost children to gun violence, I came to understand that most violence is preventable.

One definition of health is "having the same disease as your neighbors." And the disease most prevalent in our culture is violence. The propensity toward violence is within us all. So, too, is the antidote of choice: an attitudinal shift that arises upon acknowledging that at any given moment we are either compounding the problem or contributing to the solution. This first path is a trail map of the overall terrain, a navigational guide to the distribution of violence.

STOP THE VIOLETS!

It's the cry of children in a culture that is just beginning to listen. After centuries of glorifying and celebrating violence, adults in the United States are declaring that they, too, have had enough—that today's levels of violence are unacceptable.

National statistics reveal a shocking picture. Homicides number about 24,000 a year.[1] Over the course of an infant's first year of life, child abuse is the leading cause of death.[2] By eighteen years of age, one out of three girls and one out of six boys are subjected to some form of sexual assault ranging from inappropriate fondling to repeated acts of incest by a parent, stepparent, foster parent, relative, or close friend of the family.[3] One out of two women is physically assaulted by a male partner at least once in her lifetime.[4]

Fatal shootings are also commonplace. One out of every ten children who die in the United States is killed with a gun.[5] In fact, more handgun deaths occur within our borders in a year than occur in most other industrialized countries in a century.[6] Between 1985 and 1992, handgun deaths in the United States increased by 61 percent.

HANDGUN DEATHS: 1985–1992

	1985	1990	1992
United States	8,092	10,567	13,220
Japan	46	87	60
Switzerland	31	91	97
Great Britain	8	22	33
Australia	5	10	13

Reprinted courtesy of the Center to Prevent Handgun Violence, Washington, DC

Gradually, our nation is coming out of denial. We first acknowledged the existence of child abuse in the 1960s, after a series of medical and popular press articles alerted health professionals to the magnitude of the problem. In the 1970s, with the creation of community-based shelters, we brought domestic violence out of the closet. With the 1980s came open discussions about sexual assault, date rape, and incest. The 1990s may be the decade for addressing elder abuse, an emerging concern from coast to coast.

The evening news, while replete with footage of violence here at home, rarely informs us that life is not like this everywhere. The fact that it is not offers a promising perspective. If people in other countries manage to avoid killing themselves to the extent we are accustomed to, and succeed in raising their children without corporal punishment and other forms of physical abuse, then perhaps we can learn some lessons from them. If people in other cultures can alleviate or release sexual tensions so as to avoid high rates of sexual assault, and can honor women rather than view them as targets of male aggression, then perhaps we can as well.

The point in looking abroad is not to glamorize other societies, or to suggest that only the United States has a problem with violence. Nor is it to doubly victimize Americans by implying that we not only experience such tragic outcomes but are somehow bad, and that's why they are happening to us. The purpose is simply to remind us that the violence need not continue. We become part of the solution when we learn about other cultures and traditions that support nonviolence.

VISUALIZE WHIRLED PEAS

Many of us have been led to believe that violence strikes out of the blue, or in "bad" neighborhoods at the "wrong" time of day. We perceive acts of wanton cruelty as accidents, strokes of bad luck—in short, incidents that cannot be prevented.

We have been handed erroneous information and a distorted view of reality. The truth is that women in the United States are more likely to be injured, raped, or killed by a boyfriend, spouse, or ex-partner than by a stranger. At least 65 percent of all homicides are committed by people who know their victims, and do not take place in the course of another crime.[7] The most common form of sexual assault is acquaintance rape, in which the individuals involved have a prior relationship. Young children who are sexually abused are most often molested by their fathers, stepfathers, foster fathers, moms' boyfriends, uncles, coaches, counselors, babysitters, or other trusted friends or relatives. Even elder abuse is committed primarily by friends or relatives who provide support outside of nursing homes.

Of course, some violence *does* occur at random, and some people *are* attacked by strangers. Aware of this fact, community groups are beginning to offer courses that help people reduce their chances of being victimized by strangers. The large majority of violence casualties, however, continue unchecked because we are blind to the reality that such incidents occur between people who know each other.

We are aware that a teenager who goes to a party, gets drunk, drives home without wearing a seat belt, and crashes into an embankment has not been subjected to an act of God. At many points along the way, this tragedy could have been prevented. But is a teenager who goes for a ride with a young male she just met (who believes the difference between a no and a yes is a six-pack), gets high, and is then raped truly the victim of an accident? Is it mere coincidence when the mother of two young children is lying dead at her boyfriend's feet after law enforcement officers have been to the address many times over the previous six months to quiet down a "domestic disturbance"?

The fact that most violence occurs between people who know each other gives rise to a favorable outlook. By providing the skills needed to cope with conflict and the strong emotions it arouses, we as a culture can dramatically reduce the number of perpetrators in our midst. At the same time, by offering training in avoiding victimization and by making it safe for people to speak the truth during a crisis, we can decrease the casualties of aggression.

WOMEN WHO SEEK TO BE EQUAL TO MEN LACK AMBITION

Most violent perpetrators and most victims of fatal violence are males between the ages of fifteen and twenty-four. The leading causes of death in this age range are motor vehicle crashes, suicide, and homicide, with a different order of rank reported in different parts of the country.

Why are young men at greatest risk of killing others and being killed? No doubt because of gender training, which starts early in our culture. To get a sense of what is involved, take a few moments to do the following exercise. Fill in both boxes, answering each question with the first words that come to mind.

ACT LIKE A REAL MAN

How do we train boys to behave in our culture?

What qualities do we expect them to demonstrate?

What words do we use when they deviate from these expectations?

ACT LIKE A REAL WOMAN

How do we train girls to behave in our culture?

What qualities do we expect them to demonstrate?

What words do we use when they deviate from these expectations?

In aspiring to manhood or womanhood, one must express certain emotions and repress others. For males in our culture, anger is the most allowable feeling. For females, fear and sadness are more desirable.

The Act Like a Real Man training manual we abide by prepares young boys to be tough and in control, to not cry or be afraid, to hide feelings, be daring, and make money. Boys are expected to fight, tolerate being ignored, play sports, and "take" various forms of harassment to become more manly.

The Act Like a Real Woman training manual grooms young girls to play counterpart to the male; for men to be heroic, they must have someone relatively helpless to save. Hence, girls can be smart, but not too smart. They can make money, but not more than their male companions. As adolescents, they must accept the fact that they will be whistled at, catcalled, pinched, and accused of having a bad reputation if they seek the same sexual outlets as young men. Women are supposed to be sexy, but not too sexy—passive caretakers who are sweet and polite and more interested in others than in themselves. To enhance these qualities, we give little girls dolls and train them to be nurturers. (The dolls our boys play with are most often Ninja Turtle or Power Ranger varieties designed to beat the heck out of each other.)

In response to this cultural training, we all lose. A man who does not conform to the masculine guidelines is called a wimp, pussy, sissy, or queer. A woman who fails to live up to feminine expectations is labeled a whore, bitch, slut, dyke, or butch.

Although traditional gender roles are beginning to dissolve and the training manual boxes are losing their rigidity, we have not fully altered the way we raise our girls and boys; too often, the small actions we take each day continue to support box thinking. As a result, young men are still acting out violently. They are desperately seeking a diploma in masculinity, which the larger culture suggests can only be achieved by exhibiting risky, aggressive behaviors.

Because of their inexperience in recognizing, allowing for, and expressing a wide range of human emotions, many young men channel all their uncomfortable feelings into anger, the approved emotion for males. This scenario begins in childhood, when the expansive keyboard of feelings—including guilt, shame, rejection, anxiety, loneliness, hurt, fear, depression, and even joy, wonder, and enthusiasm—are ignored, denied, suppressed, or medicated away with drugs. By adolescence, the accumulation of unexpressed feelings, augmented by body sensations of frustration and tension, translates into anger. In some individuals, this anger seeks release in rage or violent actions. In others, the hostility is directed inward.

Regrettably, the youth suicide rate has quadrupled over the last thirty years, with males bearing most of the increase. In view of our cultural encoding, it is easy to understand why a teenage girl attempting suicide may take five aspirin, leave the bottle on the table, and call three of her friends, while a male in a similar state of mind may simply take the family gun and blow his brains out.

INSTANT FOOL: JUST ADD ALCOHOL

How would you respond to the following situations?

★ Your eight year old wants a sip of champagne at a birthday celebration.
★ Your fourteen year old tells you a friend's parent smokes dope.
★ You smell alcohol on your fifteen-year-old daughter's breath when she returns from a party.
★ You find an empty beer can in the back of your teenager's car.

Are you concerned about your child's use of alcohol or other drugs (AOD)? Are you worried that people under the influence of these substances will act abusively toward your child? If so, you can put your fears to rest by understanding your child, knowing the people your child is with, and having a sense of their behavior patterns.

Violence causing injury or death is linked to the illegal drug trade in two ways: through the business of dealing drugs and through the economic needs of addicts. Violence is infrequently a direct result of buying or selling drugs, as is commonly portrayed in the media.

The reality is that homicide à la *Miami Vice* accounts for less than 10 percent of homicides in most areas of the country, and a slightly higher percentage in a few large inner-urban areas. Most of these casualties are attributed to rival drugsters who know each other.[8] Only occasionally do homicides occur during the course of a burglary to obtain money for illegal substances. Hence, even in the drug trade, violence is rarely stranger directed. Drug-related violence, like violence in general, arises largely *between people who know each other.*

Because alcohol is the substance easiest to measure in dead bodies, it is the one for which we have the best data. Current statistics reveal that alcohol is associated with 50 percent of suicides and 50 percent of homicides nationwide;[9] the proportion of homicides linked to alcohol would no doubt be higher if the alcohol levels of the killers were known. Most law enforcement officials agree that when they respond to domestic violence calls, well over 80 percent involve AOD. Child abuse and sexual assault involve lower, yet still significant, AOD levels.

Self-abuse with AOD, however, does not automatically lead to violent behavior. Many alcoholics, rather than looking for bar fights, pass out in front of the television set at home. It is important to remember that although AOD significantly impairs one's ability to make appropriate decisions and judgments, it does not always bring on aggression. And when it does, the chemical often serves as an excuse for acting out, a vehicle for shifting blame and avoiding responsibility. "It wasn't the real me that broke my wife's arm," said one remorseful husband. "It was the me that drinks too much. The alcohol made me violent."

Many people who dissociate in this way are reenacting strategies they learned in childhood. One of the means by which children survive abuse is by "splitting"—a psychological response that is reinforced by the environment. Just as a boy has a nice dad and a dad who beats him up, he himself may someday split, in his own version of Dr. Jekyll and Mr. Hyde.

Alcohol use, particularly at very low and very high doses, does not predict aggressive behavior. Between these extremes, in the presence of peer encouragement or perceived attack, it can enhance aggressive tendencies. Aggressive behavior, on the other hand, *does* predict alcohol use.

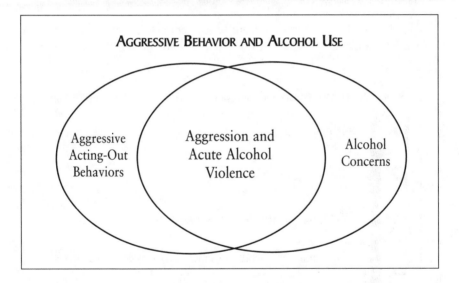

People who act aggressively often have problems with alcohol. In this diagram, the circle on the left represents people who have aggressive tendencies and no alcohol problems; the circle on the right denotes those who consume alcohol and do not exhibit combative behaviors. The area in which the circles overlap—representing individuals who have aggressive tendencies and consume alcohol—illustrates the population in which drinking problems combine with acting-out behaviors.

These individuals have a similar profile: they tend to be male, under age thirty, unemployed or working at a blue-collar job, and to have a history of impulsive behaviors and often a failing marriage. In addition, they are apt to have personal ideas and adhere to supportive cultural norms that allow them to avoid taking responsibility for the violence they commit. Their usual response is: "It was just the alcohol."

We each have a set and setting that influence whether or not our relationship with a drug will be abusive. The *set,* or mind-set, is what we expect will happen when we take the drug. The *setting* is the larger cultural expectation. A villager in South America, for example, may have a set that chewing locally grown cocoa leaves will give him the stamina needed to perform hard physical labor. A city dweller in the United States, in contrast, may have a set that snorting a gram of cocaine will help him feel high instead of depressed. The setting in Ethiopia, where coffee was first cultivated, was that a strong brew of coffee would help religious leaders stay up all night to discuss spiritual matters—a far cry from needing two cups in the morning to function well. When we are aware of set and setting, and of how these change across time and continents, we become more conscious of our drug use.

A substantial number of Americans have a set that alcohol will loosen them up socially, and our cultural setting—that alcohol boosts the success of a

---

WHY DO PEOPLE USE DRUGS? PRIMARILY FOR THE FOLLOWING PURPOSES:

R Religious experience

E Exploring the self

A Altering a particular mood or feeling

L Loosening up socially or enhancing physical pleasure

I Increasing performance, either physically or artistically

T Treating dis-ease

Y Youthful rebellion, expressing individuality, or affiliating with a group that is "different" from the norm. Peer pressure can be instrumental in initiating drug use for this purpose.

party—reinforces this belief. The result is that many people have a negative relationship with the drug; they believe they need it to enjoy themselves. One in ten Americans has a significant problem with alcohol, and one in eight is an adult child of an alcoholic, struggling with the consequences of having grown up in an alcoholic family.

Humans seem to have an innate tendency to alter their consciousness through drugs and other means. Because this is so, the operative question to ask is not "What is a good or bad drug?" but rather "How do we know if we (and our children) are in a good or bad relationship with a drug?" The relationship is good if it adheres to the A B L E model.

OUR RELATIONSHIP WITH A DRUG IS GOOD IF WE HAVE:

A   **Awareness of the drug's effects.** We know what we are taking, what its basic pharmacological effects are, what the prevalent setting is for the drug, and what our own set is.

B   **Behavioral and health consequences that are not adverse.** Available information indicates that both long- and short-term effects on our bodies and general functioning are not compromised.

L   **Liking for the drug.** One of the first signs of being in a *bad* relationship with a drug is our need to take more of it to get the same pleasurable effects. After a while we stop enjoying it as much, and it begins to dominate our lives. Another sign is increasingly troublesome aftereffects.

E   **Ease of separation from the drug.** We can take it or leave it. Having the drug around is no problem because we don't feel compelled to use it.

These insights open the door to an impressive array of prevention and treatment options. We need to be discussing drugs in R E A L I T Y terms, focusing on good and bad relationships as well as set and setting. In addition, we must suggest healthier ways of altering consciousness, such as meditation, yoga, visualization, rock climbing, martial arts, kayaking, and other sports. When talking to teens about alcohol, how can we not mention its relationship to acquaintance rape? When treating domestic violence offenders for anger management, how can we ignore their alcohol problems or send them elsewhere for treatment?

Alcohol is the drug of choice for most teenagers, and the one most implicated in violent acting-out behaviors. Moreover, despite declines in teenage AOD use, the rate of teenage alcoholism is on the rise. Consequently, when speaking with teens, we need to spend about 85 percent of our time discussing alcohol, and the remaining 15 percent reviewing other available drugs.

The media compounds the plight of our young people by providing conflicting messages about AOD use. We become part of the solution by clarifying our own values regarding chemical use and by stating clearly our expectations of the young people we are close to.

I Have PMS and a Handgun . . . Any Questions?

The presence of a firearm in any potentially violent situation increases the possibility of an injury or a death. Because most violence is between people who know each other, and because all men and women get angry and irritated at times, a "potentially violent situation" would have to be *any circumstance involving a human being alone or in the company of one or more acquaintances or loved ones.*

Firearms contribute significantly to violent death and disability. Every two years the number of Americans killed by handguns surpasses the total number of Americans killed in the Vietnam War. Children bring guns to school; gang members use them regularly; and young people are maimed or killed by accidental (aka negligent) shootings. Altogether, 60 percent of suicide and homicide cases among young people involve firearms.[10]

How are all these guns obtained? A 1993 report on gang activity states that, in the words of gang members who were interviewed, "getting a gun is as easy as getting a pack of cigarettes."[11] Often, the guns used in these tragedies are obtained from home—our homes. According to a landmark study recently conducted in Washington, DC, of the 398 firearm deaths that occurred over a six-year period in residences where the weapon was kept, only 2 involved an intruder shot during an attempted entry. For every 10 self-protective shootings attributed to a firearm kept in the home, there were 13 accidental deaths, 46 criminal homicides, and 370 suicides; handguns were used in 70.5 percent of these incidents.[12]

This study and others show that if you keep a gun in your home, you or another family member are more likely than an intruder to be killed or injured by it. Yet, despite the results of these surveys, we have 200 million guns in the United States. About 67 million of them are handguns which, although amounting to only 34 percent of firearms, are responsible for 80 percent of all deaths due to firearms.[13] At least 1 million additional guns enter legal circulation each year. Clearly it is time, while haggling over the registering of firearms, to voice our common agreement on the larger issue: we are *all* against gun violence.

SOME MEN BREAK MORE THAN THEIR GIRLFRIENDS' HEARTS

Domestic violence is at the center of today's web of violent behavior.[14] At least 25 percent of all female suicide attempts are preceded by battering.[15] At least 50 percent of murdered women are killed by their male partners, most of whom have a previous history of battering.[16] Between 30 and 50 percent of rape victims seen in emergency rooms have been battered.[17] Forty-five percent of mothers of abused children are themselves victims of battering.[18]

Domestic abuse streams outward into every imaginable domain. Child abuse may lead to child homicide. An early history of sexual abuse may pave the way to self-abuse through alcohol or other drugs, early promiscuity, adolescent pregnancy, or aggressive acting-out behaviors. A large percentage of women in prison for homicide are there because they killed an abusive partner whom society was unable to protect them from. Many more women are doing time for writing bad checks in an attempt to provide for their children while fleeing from domestic violence. A large percentage of juveniles incarcerated for murder killed an abusive relative.[19]

Imagine that you are a five year old watching your father beat up your mother, or destroying her favorite things, or killing a family pet, or threatening to kill himself along with the entire family. Whenever a child witnesses domestic violence of any sort, child abuse is occurring. Yet society does not recognize it as such. When law enforcement officials go to an address to calm down a domestic disturbance, they check the children for signs of physical abuse. If none are found, no report is made to social services. In the eyes of the outside world, as far as the children are concerned, *nothing happened!*

The truth is that children who live amid domestic violence are abused in one of three ways:

* **Intentionally.** Of all mother battering, 30 to 50 percent extends to the children as well. Additionally, domestically abused mothers are eight times more likely than nonabused mothers to discipline by way of corporal punishment.
* **"Accidentally" (through parental negligence).** While trying to protect their mothers, children often get in the way of a blow, or get hit by objects flying around the room.
* **Invisibly.** Children, like combat soldiers, experience post-traumatic

stress disorder effects such as nightmares, hyperalertness, or flash-backs.[20] Children exposed to a family culture of violence tend to run away, get involved with drugs, become pregnant, or form abusive households of their own at much higher rates than other children.

We as a society can no longer afford to tolerate the unacknowledged abuse of children. Refusing to report domestic violence involving children to social services keeps the problem a secret, denying families the help they need and leaving children exposed to destructive patterns.

The patterns themselves extend across a broad spectrum of behaviors, as indicated in the chart below.

POWER AND CONTROL ELEMENTS

Isolation. Controlling what she does, who she sees and talks to, where she goes.

Emotional abuse. Putting her down, calling her names, or making her think she is crazy.

Economic abuse. Trying to keep her from getting a job, making her ask for money, or taking her money.

Threats. Suggesting he will harm her emotionally, commit suicide, or take the children.

Using male bravado. Treating her like a servant; acting as master of the castle who makes all important decisions.

Intimidation. Provoking fear through the use of looks, actions, gestures, or a loud voice; smashing things; or destroying her property.

Using the children. Inducing guilt about her parenting approaches; using visitation to harass her.

Sexual abuse. Making her perform sexual acts against her will; attacking the sexual parts of her body; or treating her like a sex object.

Physical abuse. Punching, kicking, grabbing, slapping, choking, pulling hair, pushing, twisting arms, beating, or using weapons.

Domestic abuse tends to cycle, progressively damaging children and disempowering women. In some relationships, physically violent phases increase in severity and nonviolent periods shorten. In others, the physical violence as well as the power and control elements remain stable at relatively low levels. In still others, the violence escalates rapidly, and the degree of power and control becomes evident in stalking behaviors; women in these situations are often harassed and threatened for years, even after leaving the relationship.

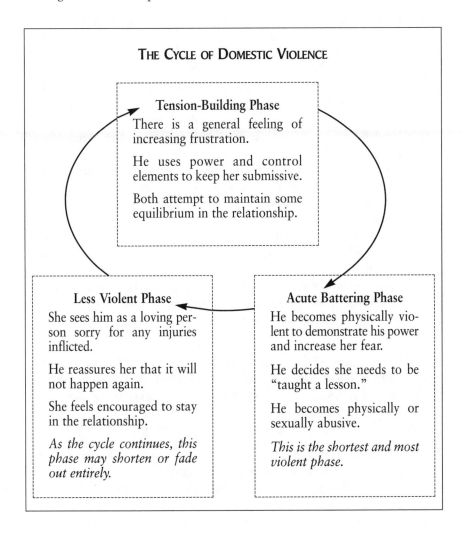

THE CYCLE OF DOMESTIC VIOLENCE

Tension-Building Phase

There is a general feeling of increasing frustration.

He uses power and control elements to keep her submissive.

Both attempt to maintain some equilibrium in the relationship.

Less Violent Phase

She sees him as a loving person sorry for any injuries inflicted.

He reassures her that it will not happen again.

She feels encouraged to stay in the relationship.

As the cycle continues, this phase may shorten or fade out entirely.

Acute Battering Phase

He becomes physically violent to demonstrate his power and increase her fear.

He decides she needs to be "taught a lesson."

He becomes physically or sexually abusive.

This is the shortest and most violent phase.

Why would a woman stay in a household governed by violence? Here are some of the more common reasons:

- ★ **Leaving is dangerous.** The departure period is when a woman is most likely to be injured or killed.
- ★ **Lack of information.** Women, especially teens, may not know where to go for help.
- ★ **Lack of resources.** Money, transportation, and other means of seeking independence may not be available.
- ★ **Fear of losing the children.** Splitting up often threatens a mother's custody of her children. Her abuser may have the economic power, social status, or emotional control needed to make her look bad in court. If in protecting her children from further violence she refuses him visitation rights, she may be accused of custodial interference—an outcome that frequently arises. In such instances, the violence often remains unattended to.
- ★ **Legal issues.** Pressing charges and seeking a protective order can complicate an already menacing situation. The woman may lose the support of her mother-in-law and others who have helped keep the violence to a minimum.
- ★ **Bad advice.** Relatives and members of the clergy may have the woman convinced that staying married is the "right" thing to do, no matter what the cost.
- ★ **Love.** The power of love that binds the woman to her partner may keep her riveted to the relationship. Who has not been hurt by a loved one, or not hung on to a relationship in hopes that the other person will change?

Although getting out is far from easy, staying in is disastrous. A mother who remains in a domestic abuse situation may inadvertently chain her children to the wheel of violence, for her home has become a training ground for a new generation of victims and victimizers.

Immediate action is essential on all fronts, including:

- ★ Universal screening for involvement in domestic abuse any time a client presents to a health or social service institution (see next page).
- ★ Reporting to social services any child who is present in a domestic violence household because, by definition, child abuse is occurring and the family needs help. Child protection workers need considerably more training in appropriately managing these referrals and in collaborating with existing resources.

QUICK HISTORY-TAKING TOOL

To screen for domestic abuse, healthcare and social service workers can incorporate into the routine office visit the following questions:

S

A

F

E

Stress/Safety. Do you experience a lot of stress in your relationship? Should I be concerned about your safety?

Afraid/Abuse. Are you afraid of your partner? Has he ever abused you in any way?

Family/Friends. Are your family and friends aware of the situation? Is there someone you can confide in? Who is your primary source of support?

Emergency plan. Do you have an emergency plan to use when things get really difficult? Do your children know how to dial 911?

★ Removing weapons and ammunition from the hands of criminals involved in domestic violence.

★ Increased use of electronic monitoring devices as soon as protection orders are established. These devices assist law enforcement officials in protecting women who have decided to leave or trial separate.

★ More support groups for men who batter. Networking opportunities help prevent batterers from finding other people to victimize after their partners leave. Extending the period of time allotted to court-ordered counseling is needed as well.

The desire to reduce levels of violence in our country will remain only a wish unless we offer effective assistance to families trapped in the cycle of violence. As we move toward creating a more family-supportive society and reducing the general acceptability of violence, we will begin to see decreases in all forms of violent expression.

YOUR PERSONAL SAFETY PLAN

Safety during an Explosive Incident
- ✓ If an argument seems unavoidable, try to have it in a room that can be easily exited. Stay away from the bathroom, kitchen, bedroom, or any other room likely to contain a weapon.
- ✓ Practice getting out of your home safely. Identify the best doors, windows, elevators, or stairwells to use.
- ✓ Pack an overnight bag, and keep it at a relative's or friend's home.
- ✓ Tell one or more neighbors about the violence, and ask them to call the police if they hear a disturbance coming from your home.
- ✓ Devise a code word to alert your children, family, friends, and neighbors to the need for police intervention.
- ✓ Decide where you will go if you have to leave home. Make a plan even if you don't think you will need to get out.
- ✓ Use instincts and judgment. If the situation is very dangerous, consider giving the abuser whatever he wants to help calm him down. You have the right to protect yourself until you are out of danger. Always remember, you don't deserve to be hit or threatened.

Safety While Preparing to Leave
- ✓ Open a savings or credit card account in your own name to increase your independence.
- ✓ Leave money, an extra set of keys, copies of important documents, extra medicines, and clothes with someone you trust, so that you can leave quickly.
- ✓ Determine where you can stay and who might be able to lend you some money.
- ✓ Keep close at hand the shelter or hotline phone number, as well as loose change or a calling card.
- ✓ Review your safety plan often so that when it comes time to leave, you will know exactly what to do. Remember, *leave-taking is the most dangerous time of all.*

Safety in Your Own Home

✓ Immediately after the batterer has left, change the locks on your doors and secure your windows with additional locks and safety devices.

✓ Discuss a safety plan your children can use when you are not with them.

✓ Let your children's school and daycare know who has permission to pick them up.

✓ Tell your neighbors and building manager that your partner no longer lives with you and that they should call the police if they see him near your home.

Safety with a Protective Order

✓ Keep your protective order on you at all times. Give a copy to a trusted neighbor or family member.

✓ Call the police if your partner breaks the protective order.

✓ Think of alternative ways to find protection if the police do not respond right away.

✓ Inform family, friends, neighbors, and your physician or healthcare provider that you have a protective order in effect.

Safety on the Job and in Public

✓ Let someone at work know of your situation, including security personnel. Provide a picture of your batterer if possible.

✓ Arrange to have an answering machine, caller ID, or a trusted friend or relative screen your telephone calls at home.

✓ Each time you leave work, have someone escort you to your car, bus, or train, and wait with you until you are safely en route. Vary the ways you travel from work to home.

Emotional Safety

✓ If you are thinking of returning to a potentially abusive situation, discuss your options with someone you trust.

✓ If you must communicate with your partner, determine the safest way to do so.

✓ Maintain positive thoughts about yourself, and assert your needs with others. Read books, articles, and poems to help you feel stronger.

✓ Decide who you can call if you need to—someone you can talk to freely and count on for support.

✓ Plan to attend a support group for at least two weeks to learn more about yourself and the relationship.

CHECKLIST: WHAT TO TAKE WITH YOU WHEN YOU LEAVE

Identification
- [ ] Driver's license
- [ ] Children's birth certificates
- [ ] Your birth certificate
- [ ] Social security card
- [ ] Other forms of identification

Financial Items
- [ ] Money or credit cards
- [ ] Bank books
- [ ] Checkbooks

Other
- [ ] House and car keys
- [ ] Small salable objects
- [ ] Toiletries (diapers)
- [ ] Change of clothes
- [ ] Phone card

Legal Papers
- [ ] Your restraining order
- [ ] Lease, rental agreement, or house deed
- [ ] Car registration and insurance papers
- [ ] Health and life insurance papers
- [ ] Medical records (vaccinations, prescriptions)
- [ ] School records
- [ ] Work permits, green card, visa, passport
- [ ] Divorce and custody papers

- [ ] Medications
- [ ] Jewelry
- [ ] Children's small toys
- [ ] Address book

- [ ] Pictures of you, your children, and your abuser

Adapted from material compiled by the city of Cambridge, MA

AQUI ESTAMOS, AQUI QUEDAMOS, NON NOS VAMOS
(WE'RE HERE, WE'RE STAYING HERE, WE'RE NOT LEAVING)

In an eloquent sermon delivered at the National Cathedral in Washington, DC, Canon Kwasi A. Thornell described the following situation: "In the courtyard, a few stand around his body, police sirens are in the background, but it is too late. The blood from the shot to his fifteen-year-old head drains out, and with it his life. It stains his Adidas jacket, symbol in the community of making it—being somebody in America. He sold crack to make the quick and easy money to buy American. We told him, 'Just say no!' . . . His underpaid and overworked teachers just said no, I don't have time to help you with your class work. The manager at the store just said no, he didn't have a job to give him. The preacher at the church just said no, he could not hold a dance for youth in his church. His parents said no, they didn't have the money to buy his clothes, his school books or . . . the little extra things he needed. So when the crack dealer came along and had the answers, he just said yes, because everyone was just saying no. No to his future and to his hope and to his being."[21]

Violence, like every other form of disease, occurs in all ethnic groups and across all socioeconomic levels. However, just as the poor bear a disproportionate burden of negative outcomes from cancer, high blood pressure, and diabetes, they are also prone to a prodigious amount of violent, acting-out behaviors. This is due primarily to the adverse effects of poverty: poor education, lack of financial or public-transport access to mental health or substance abuse facil-

---

DAMAGING EFFECTS OF POVERTY

Family Stress
Parental depression and conflict
Less effective parenting
Marital strain and breakup
Child aggressiveness and
delinquency

Lack of Food
Low birthweight
Related birth defects
Anemia and learning problems
Stunted growth and lower
test scores

Neighborhood Problems
Exposure to crime
Post-traumatic stress symptoms
Inferior schools
Fewer job opportunities
Lower achievement

Fewer Resources for Learning
Inferior child care
Fewer books
Fewer stimulating family trips, hobbies,
and extracurricular activities
Home and work responsibilities
take priority over schoolwork
Financial barriers to college

Housing Problems
Homelessness
More asthma, chronic diarrhea, lead poisoning
Frequent moving
Utility shutoffs
Crowded conditions, providing more stress and less rest
More play-related injuries

Adapted from material provided by the Children's Defense Fund

---

ities, a sense of helplessness and hopelessness about the future that generates an acceptance of day-to-day risk taking, as well as stress-filled lifestyles that leave little room for preventive healthcare practices.

Another pivotal factor is the relationship between crime in the suites and crime in the streets. Some corporations heavily target alcohol and firearm distribution to low-income neighborhoods. And, because large corporate banks control the flow of economic development dollars, it is almost impossible to acquire loans for establishing businesses that will improve these neighborhoods. While corporate tax breaks and subsidies remain unchallenged, we as a nation continue to reduce support services and increase the number of children living in poverty.

Who are the nation's poor? A small segment of this population is composed of welfare recipients who, contrary to major media implications, are not happy with their lot. Eighty percent of the welfare budget goes to tackling the problem of adolescent pregnancy, leaving recipients with an average benefit of $215 apiece per month—not a desirable income by anyone's standards. With little wonder, the large majority of people on welfare do *not* want to remain there.

Most of the poor in this country work at low-paying jobs with inadequate benefits while trying to feed their children and give them a decent place to live. Twenty-five percent of these children live in poverty—that is, in households earning less than $14,800 for a family of four.[22] On any given night, more than 100,000 children are homeless.[23] These figures stand as testimony to how hard it is for families to survive in today's economy.

In speaking of the correlation between poverty and violence, it is therefore important to avoid doubly victimizing the poor by suggesting, "Not only do you experience more violence, but it is your fault." Poverty is in some ways self-defining: in a culture in which money is important, there is little dignity in being poor, and children born into poverty begin to see themselves through the lens of failure before even entering the larger world. Yes, a rising tide, as we like to believe, carries all boats—but to rise with the tide, you must be in a boat to begin with!

The Children's Defense Fund delineates a number of ways in which poverty damages children:

- ✶ Five year olds who have lived in poverty have significantly lower IQs than those who have not known poverty. IQs at this age are affected more by family income than by any other factor, including maternal education, ethnicity, and growing up in a single-parent family.
- ✶ Poor growth affects up to 15 percent of children living in poverty. An estimated 3 million young children, most of whom are poor, have elevated blood lead levels that put them at risk for impaired mental and physical development.
- ✶ Every year of living in poverty significantly increases a child's risk of falling behind in school by sixteen to eighteen years of age.

✷ Poor children are about three times more likely than nonpoor children to die during childhood.[24]

No racial or ethnic group is more violent than any other. Some do, however, experience greater levels of poverty. Most prisoners, for example, are young minority males, reflective of the poverty conditions in which they were raised.

Why are more black men in prison than in college? Why are 25 percent of American Indian men dead by the age of thirty? How many middle-aged Hispanics can remember being punished for speaking Spanish in grade school, or can recall stories about their ancestors' land being sold for almost nothing to European immigrants to the Southwest?

We must acknowledge the historical violence that has been committed against the nation's minority populations. African Americans have not fully recovered from the disruption caused when 60 million of their ancestors were taken by force from Africa, herded onto slave ships on which many of them died, transported across the ocean, and unloaded into marketplaces where their children and mates were sold to separate plantations. Nor has our culture ever apologized for the systematic breakup of these immigrant families. Where is the monument in Washington, DC, honoring the lives of those who died in slavery while helping to build the wealth of this country?

By the same token, how many treaties with Native peoples have been broken? Where is the compensation for, or even acknowledgment of, the enforced relocations, the uprooting of children from family and culture so that they could be raised in boarding schools, the attempt to destroy Indian traditions and beliefs while appropriating their sacred lands?

My response to these types of questions used to be something like this: "Well, it is not *my* fault. *I* did not do any of those things. My ancestors came here with nothing and worked hard so that their children could have more than they did." Then, a few years ago, in a multicultural men's group, I began listening to the pain etched in the hearts of the now grown children of minority ancestry. A forty-five-year-old black professional spoke of being watched in a record store for fear that he might steal something. An American Indian talked about his childhood anguish after seeing his father, brothers, and uncles succumb to violent alcohol-related deaths. Hispanic men recounted their mounting frustration as higher positions and better-paying jobs seemed to be going continually to Anglos.

As soon as we felt safe enough to explore our differences, we discovered that we had more in common with one another than we did with the uneducated, ethnically matched peers we grew up with who, for various reasons, remained trapped in the destructive patterns we all knew as children. Today when I hear questions about historical injustices, I say: "I understand the importance of historical violence. Let's focus together on what needs to be done now."

Only by confronting the racism rampant in ourselves and in our culture can we begin to understand the critical role it plays in continuing the cycle of violence. Accustomed to living in our own cultural soup, we may not even be aware of the biases we carry. We may assume that the reality we abide by is, or ought to be, the same for everyone in our culture.

To put racism clearly on the table, we need to talk through the dilemmas. We also need to prioritize the building of trust and relationships over goal setting and tasks, and open ourselves to the diverse perspectives human beings have arrived at in the following areas:

* **Time.** Do you almost always know what time it is and how much time you have left to finish a task? Do you expect others to as well?
* **Mobility.** Do you expect others to be as mobile as you are?
* **Independence.** To what degree does your extended family influence your life decisions?
* **Relationship to the natural world.** Do you believe that humans are a superior life form or part of the web of life? Do you view the natural world as an accumulation of resources to be exploited or as a multiplicity of life forms that share the planet with us and have an "intelligence" of their own?
* **Housing.** Do you require living space designed for solitude or for communal activity?
* **Sense of history.** Are the laws and stories that you look to for guidance written in books, or are they transmitted orally?
* **Decision making.** Are you accustomed to hierarchical forms of management, majority rule, or consensual practices?
* **Lineage.** Is your ancestry patriarchal or matriarchal? Did your progenitors revere their young? Did they honor their elders?

Racism is not the only "ism" that interferes with our ability to be fully present with other human beings. We are equally limited by ageism (What do you think old people are like? How are they "supposed to" act?), sexism, nationalism, religious dogma, and preconceptions about body size, gender orientation, abilities, and disabilities—all of which contribute to the often subtle phenomenon of "othering." The belief underlying this approach to life is: "We are better than them. They should act differently."

Isms, by their nature, create separateness and conflict. Unacknowledged isms, the most insidious of them all, fuel judgments and tensions we do not even know we are harboring till they burst into expression.

Turn It Off and Tune In

The media damage us in many ways. First, there is the sheer amount of time we spend watching television and videos—time that is not devoted to nurturing our relationships, listening to our children, or attending to our personal growth and development. Second, the messages we receive consistently reinforce our othering tendencies and mold the perceptions of our young, who are trying desperately to understand gender roles and societal expectations. Third, the media train us to be good consumers, to buy more than we can afford, in a frantic effort to fill the emptiness left by our lack of community.

In addition, the media limit our imaginations. Did you ever read a book and then see the movie version of it? If so, you are probably aware that movies do not quite live up to their literary counterparts; what we envision while reading the book is not sparked by the film. When we first see the movie and then read the book, the main character in the novel keeps looking like Robert Redford or Elizabeth Taylor. Seeing the movie at the outset limits what we are free to imagine while reading.

Three independent presidential commissions have outlined the adverse effects of televised violence on young people, yet the broadcasting of violent resolutions to problems persists. The average child sees 16,000 televised murders by the end of high school, and spends more time in front of the tube than in the classroom.[25] Saturday morning cartoons are extremely violent, and are little more than sales vehicles for the latest war toys.

Movies and videos are no better, despite the rating systems that have been devised to protect our young from the insensate brutality. A youngster of any age can rent a *Chainsaw Massacre #3* variant without parental permission and spend two hours watching the gratuitous cutting up of bodies. A movie that shows an ax being raised and then a head rolling on the floor is rated Parental Guidance. If it shows the ax striking the neck, it is rated Restricted.

Violent rap/rock lyrics have joined the brainwashing. Guns 'n' Roses, for example, sing: "I had to kill her. . . . She bitched so much she drove me nuts. . . . Now she's dead and I'm happier this way."

Where are we on the awareness wave of violent programming? At the same point we were at for alcohol twenty years ago, when drunks on television were funny and alcohol was commonly featured on prime-time family shows.

The Second Path

THE WAY OF CONFUSION

How Did We Get Here? What Will Lead Us Forward?

And now here is my secret,
A very simple secret:
It is only with the heart that one can see rightly.
What is essential is invisible to the eye.

—Antoine de Saint-Exupéry

ANY DEDICATED PEOPLE ARE WORKING TO INCREASE THE PEACE. MANY MORE would like to lend their energy, but are searching for a sense of direction. It is as if our society is lost in the woods, wandering around, bewildered about which moves will make a difference. We are tired and confused, and the darkness of violence and self-abuse resulting from alcohol and other drugs, poverty, and racism seems to be spreading. No longer confronted by a major world enemy, we must finally face the enemy within our borders. This is a scary and difficult encounter, yet just what is needed to find our way home again.

MY, HOW TIMES HAVE CHANGED!

Large bursts have been appearing on the sociocultural Richter scale over the past twenty years. As patterns emerged, many of them left their mark on the most recent generation of children. The following shifts have made a major impact:

* ★ Women entered the workforce in large numbers; all the while, men spent at least as many hours as before working outside the home. The impetus for prioritizing work over home was twofold: expanded career choices and economic survival. This shift away from home and family has resulted in increased numbers of latchkey children who return to television or to empty houses at the end of the school day, and whose after-school activities remain largely unsupervised.

  Whereas family life supported one set of values, work life supports another. Most parents have difficulty reconciling the two perspectives, and the majority of young children feel the resulting tension. No longer are they free to patiently learn to tie their shoes by repeating the motions twenty-nine times a day. They must lace them up once, quickly—or more likely, press together two strips of Velcro.

* ★ The divorce rate swelled, and with it the rise of single-parent families. Many children growing up without their fathers have been living in economic poverty, deprived of male nurturance.

Differences between Family Life and Work Life

Family Life	Work Life
Time at home	Long hours away from home
Stability	Mobility
Tolerance for chaos	Insistence on efficiency
Focus on the needs of others	Focus on one's own needs
Process based	Goal based
Present oriented	Future oriented

★ Mobility increased, weakening the extended family structure. As family members began leaving their hometowns for better educational and job opportunities, neighborhoods started breaking down as well. Today, with adults relocating on average every four years, it is difficult to achieve community stability, and neighbors have ceased striving for lifelong friendships.

★ The Wal-Mart phenomenon emerged, dappling the landscape with large convenience stores. Corporate entities that gobble up smaller, less competitive mom-and-pop operations contribute further to the loss of traditional neighborhoods.

★ Television and media became dominating social forces, replacing the front porch or the kitchen table as heart of the household.

★ Spiritual deficit disorder reached epidemic proportions. With the loss of spiritual connectedness came a de-emphasis on service, forgiveness, kindness, and other qualities and values promoted by major religions.

★ Money attained godhood. Joseph Campbell, the world's foremost authority on myths, once pointed out that the highest structures around reflect who our gods are. In prehistoric times, the tallest mountains and the rainforest canopy were sacred sites. In the Middle Ages, towering Gothic cathedrals, turreted castles, and mountaintop temples were revered dwelling places of the divine. Today's highest structures are bank buildings and centers of commerce.

★ Consumer madness rose to remarkable heights, ushering in a new religion (consumerism) and staunch devotional practices (trips to the mall). The bumper sticker "I owe, I owe, it's off to work I go" proclaims the essential malaise of a culture intoxicated with purchasing power and steeped in debt.

★ 24/7/365 sprang forth as a symbol of human purpose. Soon afterward, hurry sickness became a predominant social ill, as exhibited in fast

Do You Have Hurry Sickness?

	Always/ Usually (3 points)	Sometimes (2 points)	Seldom/ Never (1 point)
Do you rush your speech?			
Do you hurry other people's speech by interrupting them or completing their sentences for them?			
Do you hate to wait in line?			
Do you seem to be short of time to get everything done?			
Do you detest wasting time?			
Do you eat fast?			
Do you drive over the speed limit?			
Do you try to do more than one thing at a time?			
Do you become impatient if others speak or act too slowly?			
Do you seem to have little time to relax and enjoy yourself?			
Do you jiggle your knees or tap your fingers?			
Do you feel overcommitted?			
Do you think about other things during conversations?			
Do you walk fast?			
Do you hate dawdling after a meal?			
Do you become irritable if kept waiting?			
Do you detest losing in sports and games?			
Do you clench your fists or tense up your neck or jaw muscles?			
Does your concentration sometimes wander into the future?			
Are you a competitive person?			

Total Score: _____

45–60   High potential for hurry sickness
35–44   Medium potential for hurry sickness
20–34   Low potential for hurry sickness

Adapted from Walt Schafer, *Stress, Distress and Growth* (Davis, CA: International Dialogue Press, 1974)

cars, fast food, and fast relationships. Amid the chronic lack of time arose a hungering for downtime—breaks reserved for doing nothing or for gorking out in front of the tube to recover from the day's hectic pace. With hurry sickness, tasks took precedence over relationships. Getting the job done, most often with an eye toward the bottom line, took precedence over *how* it was done or the human suffering it incurred. Schools expanded to enhance their "efficiency," student-teacher ratios enlarged, and community support diminished.

✱ Human connectedness with nature progressively declined. Freeing up time to watch a sunset or take a morning walk became difficult. Outdoor pursuits turned into big business, requiring expensive equipment and "expertise." Trekking off into beautiful landscapes required scheduling, so much so that national parks became as crowded as

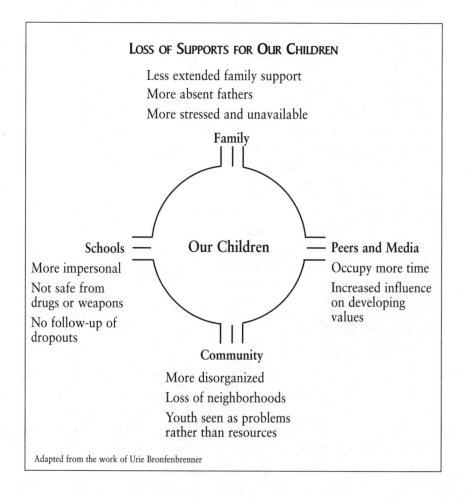

Loss of Supports for Our Children

Less extended family support
More absent fathers
More stressed and unavailable

Family

Schools — **Our Children** — **Peers and Media**

More impersonal

Not safe from drugs or weapons

No follow-up of dropouts

Occupy more time

Increased influence on developing values

Community

More disorganized

Loss of neighborhoods

Youth seen as problems rather than resources

Adapted from the work of Urie Bronfenbrenner

parking lots, due to reservations made months in advance. It is hard to protect what you don't love, and difficult to love what you don't know intimately. Nature as an expoitable resource is still a dominant theme.

★ The industrial economy gave way to an information economy. In the process, the number and variety of jobs available to relatively unskilled high school graduates or dropouts plummeted. Helplessness and hopelessness took hold of many young people as they discovered that they may not have a chance at the American Dream through traditional channels of endeavor.

★ The number of disenfranchised citizens mushroomed. Currently 1 million youngsters drop out of school[1] and admit to regular drug use; and unintended pregnancy is both frequent and widespread.[2] Our throwaway children outnumber our runaway children.

Homelessness, divorce, adolescent pregnancy, the self-abuse of teens through alcohol and other drugs, and other trying situations that arose from time to time a generation ago are now occurring with such frequency that societal support structures are overwhelmed. Assistance is sorely needed.

Due to the changes unleashed over the past twenty years, children in the United States are no longer assisted through the difficult passage into adulthood by the customary safety nets of family, school, and community. Instead, today's youth—increasingly influenced by the media and peers—approach this passage with more vulnerability than any previous group of children.

FROM THE 4-H CLUB TO THE 5-H CLUB IN ONE GENERATION

From	To
4-H club	5-H club: hungry, homeless, helpless, hugless, homicide victims
Hanging out with friends	Doing drugs on the corner
Asking, "Can I stay out late?"	Answering, "Sorry, my baby's sleepy."
Holding a job as a means of exploring power and independence	Carrying weapons or selling drugs as a statement of power and independence
Parents asking themselves, "Do I know where my children are?	Parents inquiring, "Do my children know where my gun is?"

CHILDREN SHOULD BE SEEN, HEARD, AND BELIEVED

Violence represents a multigenerational transmission of learned behavior patterns used to express emotion and resolve conflict. Some researchers are looking into a genetic component to violent behavior. Blood testosterone levels, extra Y chromosome studies, spinal fluid serotonin activity, as well as EEG, MRI, and CAT-scan patterns have produced hints of a genetic precursor to violence;[3] none, however, are definitive. The general consensus is that the propensity toward violence is passed on not through genetic material, but rather through *early behavioral modeling,* or through *physiological changes that occur while witnessing violence at an early age.*[4]

Society plays a role as well. Violence in our country operates within a cultural context that supports the use of force and aggression. The societal message is: It is okay to use force to get what you want.

In short, the ways in which we express our emotions, resolve conflict, and cope with adversity are all rooted in the personal and cultural imperatives we grew up with. These precepts have molded our understanding of normal behavior. If our early modeling incorporated the use of violence to resolve conflict, then we are "wired" to use it also, and to consider it justifiable. Even if our parents did not advocate violence, we may be culturally predisposed to rely on it in times of frustration.

In either case, as soon we add acting out to our own repertoire of behaviors, we join in the cycle of violence. And to the extent that we avoid critically examining what works and what doesn't, we get stuck in the old patterns. Practice makes *permanent*—not perfect, as is commonly believed.

To the extent that we recognize our infectious condition, on the other hand, we can rid ourselves of the insidious germs of violence. All it takes beyond awareness is the desire, understanding, and skills needed to alter our daily habits. The desire springs forth as soon as we see that acting out no longer delivers the results we want, or never was life enhancing, or that our approach to conflict was introduced by people who were themselves greatly stressed, if not confused.

Families come in many shapes and sizes. As family members we nurture, protect, support, and influence each other—*and* we experience tension and conflict. The understanding needed to change our acting-out behaviors arises when we recognize that during childhood, we received both gifts and wounds. As adults, we can choose to celebrate the gifts while going within to heal the wounds. The deeper they are, of course, the more time and support we will need to heal them.

Breaking the chain of violence is not about shaming our parents, blaming our parents, or holding them responsible for the unhappiness in our lives; it's about *healing the hurts inside us.* In reacquainting ourselves with these hurts, we will find that although we cannot change the past, we can change our relationship to it.

The way to begin is by uncovering the old patterns of destruction—specifically, the old family rules. Here are seven family rules that wound:

* **Authority of perfection.** Always be right, and insist on others doing the right thing. The message here is: If you can't do it perfectly (in my eyes), then you have failed. Give lots of negative feedback to be sure your children get it right.
* **Blame.** If something does not happen as planned, blame someone—either yourself or another family member. Assigning blame is more important than doing whatever is necessary to move on.
* **Control.** Be in control of all behavior and every interaction. Refuse to sanction differences or freedom of expression.
* **Deny.** Abstain from acknowledging needs and feelings, especially anxiety, fear, loneliness, grief, rejection, and vulnerability. When disrespectful, shameful, abusive, or compulsive behavior occurs, dismiss it or disguise it. Keep the family secrets.
* **Expect unreliability.** Assume that no relationship embodies constancy. Watch for the unpredictable. Avoiding conflict is more important than developing trust and honesty.
* **Foster nonclosure.** Refrain from bringing transactions to completion. Discourage follow-through. Differences of opinion cannot be resolved.
* **Grumble.** Refuse to talk openly and directly about joyful, uplifting experiences as well as shameful, abusive, or compulsive behavior.

These and other family rules—such as "Don't talk," "Don't feel," and "Don't trust"—interfered with our optimal development. We are, in essence, as sick as we are secretive.

FAMILY RULES EVALUATION

Take as much time as you need to answer the following questions:

What family rules did you grow up with?

Which of these are you passing along to your children and grandchildren?

Family rules that hurt, as we know, place children in an impossible turmoil. They become torn between truth and loyalty, blame and responsibility, overpowering rage and the "safety" of depression, grief, and numbness. Families that adhere to these rules are often called "dysfunctional"—a crippling term that alludes to weaknesses but no strengths. In reality, a "dysfunctional family" is an assemblage of competent, caring people stuck in difficult situations. As we come to terms with our childhood wounds, we would be wise to keep this in mind, and to regard our families of origin not as dysfunctional, but as positioned somewhere along the continuum of healthy functionality.

Injuries sustained in physical, sexual, or emotional abuse can be healed by acknowledging them and by realizing that we were not at fault, that these incidents did not happen because we were inherently bad children. We were good children with the capacity to exercise many more qualities than were permitted at the time. And as adults we can reach into this reservoir of goodness and develop new coping skills. With the healing comes the promise that we will not pass on similar wounds to our own children.

One father I know views his healing journey as a gift to his son. This man had gone underground as a child, simply to endure the suffering he experienced in his family of origin. All the while, his essence became "covered over" with layers of mandates and "acceptable" survival tactics. Willing to bring up old childhood pains as an adult, when he had more resources for coping with them, he was able to relieve himself of both the family baggage and the protective patterns of behavior that no longer served him. Awareness, patience, and compassion were his allies; and celebrating his parents' nurturance became his inspiration, for throughout these difficult months he was also fathering his young son. As he puts it, "We're held back not by the love we didn't get in the past, but by the love we're not giving in the present."

MINDS ARE LIKE PARACHUTES: THEY FUNCTION ONLY WHEN OPEN

One afternoon I received a call from a very upset school nurse. A ten-year-old boy, she said, had brought a knife to school and, while arguing with another boy during recess, had pinned him to the ground, with the blade at his throat. What can be done, she asked, for the children who witnessed this incident?

An eleven-year-old girl had terror in her eyes while explaining that her older sister was being incested night after night by their stepfather. She would lie awake for hours each night wondering if she was next. What can be done for her?

All children who witness violence, even those who don't see it but know it is transpiring, are victimized. Although they themselves have not been attacked, they carry the scars of abuse. And wounds of this sort, like those caused by overt abuse, do not magically repair themselves over time.

To the contrary, a history of direct or indirect victimization is one of the most important risk factors for subsequent violence. The majority of today's prison inmates were physically or sexually abused as children.[5] Young boys and girls who were sexually abused are at greatest risk of self-abuse through alcohol and other drugs, aggressive acting out, sexual addiction, or other destructive behaviors. Even a suicide attempt is the single most important predictor of a "successfully completed" suicide.[6]

The human spirit is forever moving in the direction of healing. To work through the wounds of childhood, it will re-create the familiar terrors and traumas in early adulthood. A child who grows up with an alcoholic, for example, is apt to engage in an adult relationship with an alcoholic. Similarly, a child who grows up with abuse is likely to enter into an abusive adult relationship. By re-enacting the trauma at a more advanced stage of development, one can learn to master the situation and awaken to a deeper level of being. A breakthrough of this sort requires multiple doses of ongoing support and encouragement.

A percentage of young adults in every town and city across the nation are *untreated* survivors of violence. Many suffer from one form or another of post-traumatic stress disorder and are seeking refuge from their pain in alcohol and other drugs, or in continuing the cycle of violence. Because most mental health dollars are directed at highly symptomatic individuals with chronic conditions, the mental health needs of these survivors of violence go largely unmet. We are in dire need of expanded twelve-step groups, peer support groups, and co-counseling programs to provide assistance to this portion of our population.

IF YOU DON'T KNOW WHERE YOU'RE HEADED, YOU'LL END UP SOMEPLACE ELSE

While searching for ways to turn our present situation around, we must remember that it took time to arrive at this juncture, and that it will take more time to create the changes we envision. There are no easy solutions, quick fixes, or politically expedient routes. This is slow work. It is akin to planting trees whose shade we may never enjoy.

The planting, nonetheless, can begin. For assistance, we can look to a variety of social movements that have taken root in recent years. The HIV/AIDS struggle, for one, illuminates ways to break out of box thinking. I am reminded of a story about an AIDS outreach worker in New York City whose target population was runaway teenage prostitutes. Instead of handing out educational brochures, she set up a storefront operation and offered makeup lessons and foot massages. Only after establishing rapport with the girls did she bring out the condoms and proceed to teach the teens how to use them without letting their customers know they were practicing safer sex.

Other creative departures from box thinking are also in effect. The Carter Center has issued a proposal for a company to design a needle that can be used only once. The objective is to help decrease the spread of AIDS among people who use IV drugs, thereby increasing protection levels in the overall population. Detroit now opens up many of its basketball courts from 10 pm to 2 am on weekends, giving teens a place for positive interactions on Friday and Saturday nights. In addition, nonviolence advocates are inviting people to trade in their guns for concert tickets or toys, and to exchange their toy guns for other playthings or books.

Driving While Intoxicated (DWI) initiatives reveal that an effective way to inspire change is to incite the anger of mothers and begin directing this energy in an organized way. Like Mothers Against Drunk Driving (MADD), a grassroots movement formed under an umbrella organization, a mother-based initiative that takes root in several small communities can help propel violence prevention from coast to coast. Groups started by mothers who have lost children to violence are already springing up. If these small coalitions join forces and collaborate in their efforts, there will be no stopping them.

From the war on drugs we can learn that the Just Say No strategy is ineffective. People respond better when they are given something better to say *yes* to. Yet they cannot say yes *or* no until they have been given information and skills.

"Just Say No" Doesn't Work

We can't just say no to:

Spanking	*unless we*	Use positive forms of discipline
Bringing guns to schools	*unless we*	Make schools safe for everyone
Violent videos	*unless we*	Offer nonviolent heroes and heroines
War toys	*unless we*	Create cooperative games that are exciting
Teens hanging out	*unless we*	Provide them with useful ways of directing their energy
Gangs	*unless we*	Offer effective mentors to young people who have not yet experienced a sense of accomplishment or belonging

Another lesson emerging from the war on drugs is the importance of stressing harm reduction in lieu of prohibitions. An approach based on harm reduction acknowledges a continuum of preventive behaviors and offers healthier lifestyle choices that correspond to each individual's unique set of circumstances. Can't go out and party without getting drunk? Call a cab, or arrange for a designated driver. Can't break your IV habit? Use clean needles.

Redressing violence by switching from a prohibition perspective to one based on harm reduction would look something like this:

OUT OF HARM'S WAY

Problem	Prohibition Model	Harm Reduction Model
Anger	"Don't be physical; talk it out."	"Hit walls instead of people."
War toys	Off-limits	Limit purchases
Loaded guns in homes	Not to be left loaded and unlocked; to be stored safely	Teach children what to if they find one
Violent videos or cartoons	Forbidden	Watch with children, discuss issues, limit viewing
Spanking	Taboo	Agree to never hit while angry
Weapons in schools	Not allowed	Install metal detectors, conduct locker searches, encourage students to report the presence of guns
Use of drugs or alcohol	Unacceptable	Insist on designated driver protocols
Sexual activity	Postpone; remain abstinent	Advocate use of a condom to prevent sexually transmitted diseases, and birth control to prevent pregnancy

We can also learn a great deal from the ecology, or Green, movement. How quickly powerlessness turned into action once guidelines were given for every-day environmental practices. It became relatively easy to switch off lights in rooms we were not using, carry cloth bags to the market at least some of the time, avoid buying styrofoam cups, purchase in bulk to reduce packaging, and turn off the running water while brushing our teeth. Although a bit more diffi-cult, it was still within our reach to keep the car tuned, plant some trees, and compost our organic leftovers. Now, just a few years after our environmental awakening, recycling is user friendly and is available in more and more areas of the country.

With practicalities guiding the rallying call to end human degradation, like the one to end environmental degradation, we are sure to triumph over the seemingly impossible odds of curbing violence. For starters, we might set beside each Reduce, Reuse, Recycle notice an equally memorable reminder: Time Out, Talk It Over, Touch Tenderly and Safely.

Each time we integrate a lesson learned from other social movements, we must remain focused on the goal at hand. This may sound like a tall order, con-

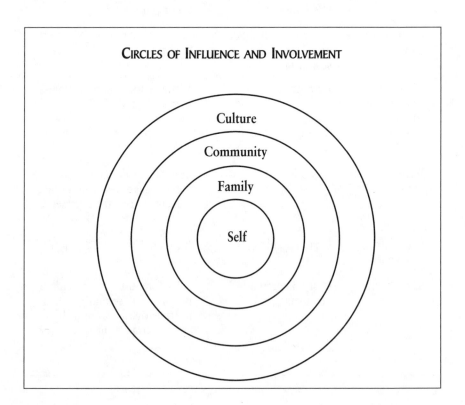

CIRCLES OF INFLUENCE AND INVOLVEMENT

Culture

Community

Family

Self

sidering the many faces of violence in our culture—the gender prototyping, alcohol and other drugs, firearms, poverty, media images, racism, personal histories of victimization, cultural shifts, and familial conditioning. Indeed, spokespeople in each of these arenas are likely to claim that their particular sphere of activity is *not* the cause of violence. Media advocates will speak of First Amendment rights, and will quickly point out that many people who watch violent programming do not become violent. Gun club members will cite Second Amendment rights, and will argue that guns do not kill people, but rather people kill people. Alcohol industry officials will state that they are simply providing a desired product, and that they are not at fault for the one out of ten Americans with a drinking problem.

Each of these statements is true; no single factor *is* responsible for all the violence we are experiencing. At the same time, individual factors do contribute to the puzzle of violence in America. And by improving any piece of this puzzle, we can dramatically alter the bigger picture. Our job is to focus on solutions at the levels of self, family, community, and the larger culture. These are the paths we must each walk to make a difference.

The Third Path

THE WAY OF ACCEPTANCE

TEN STEPS TO PERSONAL POWER

A	**A**ppreciate the anatomy of anger
C	**C**olor the flow of grief
C	**C**larify the cloak of fear
E	**E**xplore the essence of joy
P	**P**roduce less stress
T	**T**ame the wild horse of mind
A	**A**ttend to the spiritual
N	**N**urture your healing self
C	**C**ommit to communicate
E	**E**stablish a place of peace within

*For a long time it had seemed to me that life was about to begin—
real life, but there was always some obstacle in the way, something
to be got through first, some unfinished business, time still to be
served, a debt to be paid. Then life would begin. At last it dawned
on me that these obstacles were my life.*

—Father Alfred DeSousa

ONE OF MY FAVORITE BUMPER STICKERS READS: "WHEREVER YOU GO, there you are." It's true—yet our seemingly lifelong task of learning to embrace all of who we really are is shortened by leaps and bounds each time we manage to accept a small piece of ourselves. I remember cringing in disbelief the first time I heard my older daughter yelling at her sister with the same nasty tone of voice I use when *I'm* angry. There it was: a clear mirror of the behavior I had been modeling while spreading my stress around the family living room.

Soon afterward, during a discussion of sexuality at a men's conference, my body started shaking uncontrollably, shattering inner "walls" while releasing memories of teenage sexual abuse. I could not believe the amount of fear and pain that had been locked within me. Embracing the flood of remembrances, I began to heal from the trauma.

The journey toward wholeness and integrity begins from within. The more we let down our walls and call a truce to our inner wars, the more likely we are to become a river of peace for the young people we encounter. This path invites you to explore the territory of your own emotions, mind, body, and spirit.

APPRECIATE THE ANATOMY OF ANGER

In the way that a gardener knows how to transform compost into flowers, we can learn the art of transforming anger, depression, and racial discrimination into love and understanding.
—Thich Nhat Hanh

In our culture, men are encouraged to express their anger. Might makes right, we are told, and righteous anger is so sweet. Men are not encouraged, however, to admit to fear or pain. Big boys don't cry; they are like tough, sturdy oaks that feel no pain and fear no one.

If you have grown up male, these messages live in your body. They were passed on to you by your father and other men, more by temperament than by teaching. If you have grown up female, you may have been denied your anger, encouraged to disown it or, when faced with another person's anger, to withdraw, escape, or give in. Our families had many unspoken rules about anger and other strong emotions, and we as children learned them well. Our challenge now is to pass on more inclusive and less violence-provoking messages to the children *we* are teaching.

The basic violence prevention message about emotions is: *All feelings are okay, yet all behaviors are not.* Everyone is entitled to the full range of emotional experience. The more we accept our feelings and allow them to move through us, the richer and more peaceful our lives become. So let them flow, and let them go. Any behaviors they trigger in passing are yours to channel. How you express your anger is far more important than the fact that you have it—or, as is more likely, that it has *you*, firmly in its grasp.

Anger extends along a continuum ranging from irritation to annoyance to fury to rage. Each person has an internal anger meter that is set at a threshold somewhere along this continuum. A person whose meter is set at "rage," for example, will express anger by speaking, acting, or moving without restraint; mindlessly violating anything or anyone in the vicinity; or shaming others, if not physically wounding them. At this end of the continuum, anger seeks to dominate the brain, blurring all distinctions between right and wrong action.

Those most vulnerable to rage are children and adults who do not have well-established protective boundaries. Physiological conditions may also play a role. When we are hot, cold, hungry, tired, or in physical pain, our anger threshold shifts, causing otherwise congenial encounters to become a source of irritation.

Is anger good or bad? What one *does* with the energy of anger may be good or bad, but anger itself simply *is*. It lives in the body as a million-year-old survival response to life-threatening conditions. To defend itself against annihilation, the body gears up for action: the heart rate increases, respirations deepen, pupils dilate, blood shifts away from the digestive tract to major muscles, and stress hormones as well as blood sugar levels rise. In response, the person will either do battle or take flight. Curiously, the fight-or-flight response—a mechanism that initially helped our species survive— now threatens to destroy us. Our most promising option is to learn new ways of dealing with this energy.

When Anger Gets Stuck. When we hold on to anger, it tends to get stuck inside. More often than not, it surfaces in the form of resentment. Our resentments—which are nothing more than held-back anger that we keep reliving—feed an escalating cycle of vengeance. Here's what happens: we get angry at someone, keep it to ourselves, wait for the person's next move, then pull out our red-stamp resentment collection to justify our ongoing anger at this person.

Resentments hurt us; they wreak havoc in the body. They also hurt our offspring, because the unresolved, undirected anger is forever on the verge of exploding forth. With the passage of time, anger rooted in the unhealed wounds of one generation spills over onto the next generation.

Beneath most vented anger is a layer of fear or grief. A father I know lost his child in the supermarket and became furious upon finding him. Outwardly, this man expressed anger; inwardly, he had been terrified that something had happened to his child. If we, too, begin getting inappropriately angry, especially if this happens habitually, we would do well to explore the fear or hurt that keeps fueling the angry energy. Having identified the trigger, we will be able to focus on expressing the emotion that really needs attention, instead of continually venting.

Anger tends to arise from one of four causes: *an unmet expectation* (you ask your child to do something, and she does not respond), *an undelivered message* (you have something to convey, and the other person either does not hear it or does not permit you to say it), *a blocked intention* (you are looking forward to a long weekend, and the boss says you have to work, or the car breaks down as you are leaving), or *a perceived violation of personal boundaries* (you step outside and notice a bunch of teens sitting on your car, or a neighbor's trash strewn about your property). Never can another person "make" you angry. To the contrary, your feelings of anger are generated by your body, and are therefore *your* responsibility. The attitude most likely to set the stage for anger is an entitlement view of the world—a sense that other people, and life itself, "should" treat you in a particular way. This perspective, in conjunction with the stresses of daily life, is almost certain to send sparks flying.

When stuck anger comes to the fore, it is likely to target loved ones. Why? First, because we feel safer and more secure expressing anger to loved ones, as opposed to strangers. Second, frequent contact provides increased opportunities for venting anger. Third, the cumulative effect of a loved one's irritating behaviors can be encumbering and distressing, eventually registering "hot" on our anger meter. Then, too, we may be unconsciously motivated to have our loved ones alter their ways. Anger, in this instance, may signify a secret desire to "get them to change"—a desire that is not doing anyone any good.

To pick up on early signs of anger, tune into your body. You may feel a tightening of your jaw, or a sensation of heat in your abdomen, or tension in your shoulders or neck. Aware of the wake-up call, stop whatever you are doing and initiate a coping strategy to defuse this potentially destructive force.

Healthy Ways to Cope with Angry Energy. To develop a constructive expression of anger, allow the feelings to rise to the surface, all the while appreciating the energy of this emotion and your willingness to accept it. Greet it as you would an uninvited guest who has just made his way into your living room. Then right away articulate the anger as honestly as you can: tell the person you are upset with exactly what is bothering you. While explaining the situation, silently applaud your ability to be honest and direct.

Other healthy ways to cope with anger in the moment include the following:

* Positive self-talk to help you feel in control.
* Time out (see sidebar on page 63).
* Tensing and relaxing various muscle groups.
* Visual imagery directed at seeing the other person as a hurt child.
* Physical exercise, such as running, jumping rope, or walking the dog.
* Writing in a journal, drawing, painting, or working with clay.
* Using "I" statements, such as "I feel ——— when you ———. And I'd like ———."
* Sending a "heart flash"—a mutually agreed upon signal reminding the other person of your love.

The goal is to attend to the anger as quickly as possible. With practice, you can become so sensitized to the early signs of anger and so adept at responding to them that irritations and annoyances will no longer escalate into full-blown anger.

What to Do When Angry Energy Is Directed at You. When confronted with other people's anger, raise an inner shield or envelope of protective light, and stay centered. Get out of the way of the thunderbolts, and keep a safe physical distance at the first inkling of violence. Realize that the vehemence is *their* stuff, and tell them you *know* how

THE TECHNIQUE OF TIME OUT

These five steps can help transform the dynamics of a relationship from control to mutuality, from power to love.

1. Realize that emotions are rising.
- ✓ Notice when you feel angry or scared, or when your body registers a stress signal.
- ✓ Recognize when your partner looks angry or upset.

2. Quickly call a time-out.
- ✓ Say, "Time out," then stop talking and start walking.
- ✓ Make a T signal like the one referees use.
- ✓ Agree on a meeting time and place.
- ✓ Leave the room without slamming the door.

3. Let the other person go.
- ✓ Using your self-control, emotionally release your partner. (This is the hardest step of all.)
- ✓ Return the T signal to contract with your partner.
- ✓ Make sure your child is in a safe place.
- ✓ Go far enough away so that you can't see or hear your partner.

4. Take a two- to thirty-minute cooling-off period.
- ✓ Try mild exercise to work off the adrenalin.
- ✓ Deliberately distract your mind; think of pleasant events.
- ✓ Practice thought stopping. Avoid brooding over wrongdoings.
- ✓ Take your partner's viewpoint. What are his or her grievances?

5. Acknowledge your contribution to the problem.
- ✓ When you meet again, say, "I still think I was ninety-nine percent right, but I did make a mistake when I ———."
- ✓ If your partner will not admit to a mistake, take another time-out.
- ✓ Release your anger. (Holding on to it will only convince your partner that you were 100 percent at fault.)
- ✓ State clearly that you are more interested in finding a solution than in assigning blame or being right.

angry they are. This will at least prevent them from getting angrier to convince you of their ire.

When angry words come your way, listen without interrupting, seek to understand the cause of the upset, then reflect back what the person has said to you. Call a time-out if needed. Keep your boundaries, and refuse to carry the energy that has been released.

An angry person will often try to provoke anger to create a shared state of temporary insanity. And indeed, anger *is* infectious. But you can insulate yourself from it by realizing that just as the other person's thoughts generated the fury, his thoughts will dissipate it. All you can do is foster his desire to calm down, and then deal with the underlying practical issue. It is impossible to solve problems when anger is present. So, like Captain Picard in the television series *Star Trek* advocates, "Shields up, and open a channel!"

Some people mistake the energy of anger for that of life itself. They view hostility as a protective friend and source of vitality. A man consumed with personal grievances knows he is alive. Swept up in his rage, however, he does not know it is destroying his peace of mind and his ability to center on the injustices that exist *beyond* the confines of his mind.

You cannot fight your anger or control it. But you can, with time and patience, accept your anger, process it, treat it with tenderness and kindness, get to know it, and heal the pain and fears that give it life. Your anger will then be transformed into a more creative form of energy, or will gradually wither away.

Additional Resources

Books

Kivel, Paul. *Men's Work*. Center City, MN: Hazelden Publishing Group, 1992.

Lerner, Harriet Goldhor. *The Dance of Anger*. New York: Harper & Row, 1985.

Tavris, Carol. *Anger: The Misunderstood Emotion*. New York: Simon & Schuster, 1982.

Videos

Learning to Manage Anger: The RETHINK Workout for Teens (and Adults). Available from the Institute for Mental Health Initiatives, 202-364-7111.

COLOR THE FLOW OF GRIEF

There are griefs, but mine is different. It delights me; I delight in it. Thus grief is what I want, and this sorrow is my good health. I don't understand how I'm to complain. It is my will that brings my grief. It is my own will that turns into grief. I get such joy from willing this cry, that I am in pain acceptably. And I get such a delight from my grief that I am deliciously in bad shape.

—Chrétien de Troyes

There is pain in being human. Because we have loved, grief walks by our side. At times, life itself appears as a tragedy in endless acts. Acutely aware of the suffering in ourselves and in the world, we need a good cry every day to release the indwelling sadness.

We *cause* ourselves pain as well, by doing what is expected of us rather than following our own inner guidance. To the extent that our outer lives are not congruent with our inner ones, we experience helpless futility and loss of authenticity. Trapped within, the resulting pain separates us from one another. Shared, however, it can connect us in deep ways.

Sadness, like anger, is neither good nor bad; it simply *is*. It resides in the old pleasure and pain pathways of the limbic brain. There, it is acted upon by thousands of chemical messengers, or neurotransmitters.

The healing of an emotional injury is somewhat akin to the healing of a physical injury. When one has a physical wound, the body seals it off, then sends in cells to remove the dead tissue and clean up any remaining debris. The skin is gradually remodeled, often leaving a scar. The brain, which undergoes its own form of remodeling, is composed of billions of neurons, or nerve cells. A typical neuron has between 1,000 and 10,000 synapses, or reconnecting points, some excitatory and some inhibitory. At each of these junctions, a neurotransmitter is stored, released, and recycled. When we experience a strong emotion, these neurons release their chemical messengers, which dispatch the "news" throughout the brain, resulting in a cascade of feelings that in turn affect the entire body. Each cell then fires a new impulse in a thousandth of a second, either enhancing or diminishing the developing emotional symphony.

Any prolonged alteration in neurotransmitter activity can lead to depression. When this occurs, it is in the emotional limbic brain that antidepressant drugs restore chemical equilibrium.

The point to remember is that an emotional wound, like a physical one, is *self-rectifying,* provided that the natural flow of sadness is permitted to take place. With the release of sadness, we move through a process of emotional cleanup—from loss to isolation to eventual insight and resolution—stimulated by biochemical changes in the emotional limbic brain.

The Personal Blues Scale. Sadness extends across the darker end of the color spectrum. Some people get blue from time to time; others, more prone to shades of indigo, experience the deeper drawing inward known as clinical depression. Major depression, as opposed to situational depression, is present when that rotten, down mood invades every part of one's life.

Because sadness lives in the body, it is responsive to physiological cues. When you are tired, hungry, or physically uncomfortable, the world may seem bleaker than usual. Sadness also tends to hole up in different parts of the body. Where in your body do you hold emotional pain? Where do you feel most weighed down? The sense of heaviness occurs because you pull in at these sites to avoid feeling vulnerable, helpless, hopeless, and powerless.

Over time, we progress from enfolding our sadness to breaking down in tears, shattering the casing that has held it within. At this point, many people think they will drown in the ocean's depths, fail to regain functionality, fall apart, or never be themselves again; but in going with the flow of sadness, they get tossed back onto the shore. In short, surrendering to a good cry—if not a year of frequent sobbing— we are freed of our anguish. The most lifesaving measure of all is to be heedful of bodily indicators of sadness early enough to avert a full-blown depression.

The psyche has indicators too: sadness always comes on the heels of loss. Anyone sensitized to the suffering in the world will tell you of the pervasive sense of loss that is available to stir up human sadness. Triggers include the following:

Loss of the sense of meaning or purpose.
Loss of feeling loved in a primary relationship.
Loss of well-being or optimal functioning.
Loss of expected outcomes.
Loss of personal possessions.
Loss of loved ones through death or relocation.
Loss of people we don't know, but empathize with.
Loss of connection to the planet or its creatures.

Grieving Our Way through Sadness. Grief is a healthy response to sadness, sorrow, hurt, emptiness, and other expressions of loss. To work through grief, we need to unleash our buried feelings. This means releasing all controls and letting go to suffering, acknowledging that we cannot manipulate the events and circumstances life brings our way.

Many men, because of their conditioning, circumvent the grieving process by remaining silent (engaging in inexpressive secret grief), taking physical or legal action (resorting to aggression, anger, or violence as grief substitutes), or immersing themselves in diversionary activities (resisting the confrontation with grief through work, risk taking, sex, sports, or other addictive behaviors). Unable to surface, the anguish endures.

In truth, only you can relieve yourself of pain. So welcome it from the depths. Wallow around in it. Accept and be patient with it. Dance with it, and be grateful for the growth it brings. Feeling the wounds fully, admire the beauty of the hurt. If you have built walls to protect yourself from suffering, let those barriers dissolve in a cascade of tears. Enter the trail of tears, and let it guide you through your fears. Go down into the sadness, touch the deep loss, and know that you are suffering what you always needed to suffer but never before had the courage to face.

True grieving is nothing like neurotic suffering—the repetitious, compulsive complaints of an ego bound up in denial, resistance, and struggle. In neurotic suffering, we are moody, filled with self-pity, and quick to blame others for the weight we are carrying. We are in pain because we have failed to honor appropriate boundaries, or have assumed that life is "not fair" and that we never get "enough" of what we want. Of course, assigning blame to our pain, or judging it good or bad, prevents us from feeling it and, consequently, grappling with it.

True grieving is deep soul suffering. Moreover, it is the *conscious experience* of the woe of the soul. The word *grief* itself derives from the Latin *gravare,* meaning to be pressed down, to accept the weight of sadness. And having accepted this weight, we are relieved of it in our return from grief—a return marked by a throwing out of the old tapes.

When Sadness Gets Stuck. Unreleased sadness turns to regret. Each time the depths are stirred in the ocean of sadness, memories of past hurts well up. They, too, seek liberation.

A classical repository for our regrets is the emotional jukebox of sad songs we sing to ourselves. Over and over again we croon tunes of loss, of giving up, of damage to self-esteem or lack of confidence in our ability to cope with challenges. Busily reenacting our past regrets, we avoid *feeling the original loss.*

Most of us have difficulty owning our pain. We put on a happy mask, pretending everything is okay. But beneath the facade is a pipeline to shame and guilt. Our shame convinces us that we are inadequate and nothing can be done about it. Males in our culture carry a special burden of shame about wars, sins of the patriarchy, bureaucratic injustices, our fathers' failures. Females are burdened with the sense of never doing enough to nurture their relationships.

The journey out of shame begins the moment we look directly at our feelings of worthlessness and find beneath them a sense of value. Then the small daily steps of focusing on who we *are*, instead of who we are *not*, can take us wherever we want to go.

Guilt, on the other hand, keeps us clinging to offenses we have committed against ourselves or others, stewing over what we did or did not do in the past—the should haves, would haves, and could haves of our lives. If we feel guilty for a prolonged period of time, our grievances become part of our blue-stamp collection of regrets. To prevent the accumulation of guilt, we need only accept responsibility for each of our actions, apologize for any hurt we have caused, and, when possible, repair the damage.

Healthy Ways to Cope with Sadness. When you seem to be drowning in sadness, add enjoyable activities to your day. Try exercising, bathing, or spending time outdoors. Writing can inspire you to evoke, confront, explore, vent, and atone for a tableau of feelings. Drawing can be equally healing. Capture, if you can, the size, shape, and color of your grief; the feeling that is most dominant; or how you look inside.

Above all, accept support. Grief cannot be resolved in solitude, so consider it an act of healthy dependency to pierce through the envelope of silence and reach out to others. If you are concerned about your impact on others, remind yourself that, according to the *I Ching,* the Chinese *Book of Changes,* pain breaks open the shell of understanding. The more you go into your grief, the more spontaneous and alive you will be; the more you go into your wounds, the less likely you will be to inflict woundedness on others. Honor your pain by avoiding isolation: talk with an understanding and nonjudgmental person for as long as you need to, find five people you can call on night or day, volunteer for community activities, support your friends, and keep in touch with loved ones. For an extra measure of support, consider peer counseling or a twelve-step group.

COPING WITH SADNESS

Add special activities to the day. Exercise, draw, write, play music, or sing.

Accept support. Welcome outreach from friends, family, neighbors, co-workers, and more formal groups.

Allow for the expression of all feelings. Establish a private grieving time and place—a room, a personal altar, or a place in nature.

Attend to spirit. Connect with the great mystery through church, synagogue, the *I Ching,* tarot, personal power objects, meditation, tai chi, sleeping under the stars, or rituals at sunrise or sunset.

While engaging in activities and seeking out the company of others, avoid the inclination to bypass the abyss of sorrow by filling up your life with a barrage of excitement and desire. An I-want-to-get-it-over-with mind-set is ultimately self-defeating, for grief has a rhythm of its own. The best approach is to respect its inherent tempo and to give voice to your emotions. Allow for the expression of *all* feelings. Just as we need, in the words of family therapist Virginia Satir, four hugs a day for survival, eight for maintenance, and twelve for growth, so, too, do we need *a good cry at least once a week for clearing our sadness.* Tears are a biological stress reliever—nature's tranquilizer. Indeed, people who go for long spells *without* spilling tears feel exhausted, on guard, stifled, constricted, frustrated, bottled up, or physically uncomfortable.

To launch a regular practice of crying, seek out a private, secluded spot in which to let loose your wildest outbursts of grief. Then once a day, safely nestled in your place of solitude, reflect on memories of unresolved situations or unhealed wounds: visualize the other person, and say what needs to be said. In time, strive to feel at ease crying in the presence of others. Your tears will link you with your heart, revealing chambers that you never knew existed. Opening to pain expands the repertoire of the heart.

Above all, follow your spiritual yearnings. Trust the inner guiding hand that knows what you need for your emotional healing. Connect with whatever you conceive to be your higher power, the great mystery, or the essential principles of your life.

TEARS OF JOY

There is something about the sound of a man crying
that frightens me

those first moans of sadness that come
from the depths so unfamiliar for too long.

Perhaps the little boy in me cannot bear to know
that there is pain in being a man,
that those who hold my little hand and protect me from the darkness
are also vulnerable.

There is something about the sound of a man crying
that makes me want to shout

that catching of the breath as painful groans
emerge in spurts from the shaking body.

Part of me wants to scream, "Stop it . . . grow up . . .
be strong . . . we all know life is hard without you reminding us,"
and thus create a wall of words to keep my own grief away.

There is something about the sound of a man crying
that compels me to hold him

the waves of wailing sorrow that drown attempts to speak,
sentences broken apart by the storm's fury, his body
collapsing into the moment.

The father in me wants to comfort with my arm, simply being there,
saying nothing, offering a safe space of love and acceptance.

There is something about the sound of a man crying
that heals me

those soft snifflings as the face relaxes, the deep sighs
and the palpable calm of release that signal another part
of another wound is whole again.

And the man I am is filled with hope by all these sounds,
especially when they are my own.
My last tears fall in silence, joining those of other men,
to become a powerful, gentle rain
that washes away the violence among us.

When Someone Else Is Grieving. Because a person in grief is in pain, be sure to allow for as much expression of pain as is needed. Grieving is not a waste of time or an indication of impending collapse; it is a *direct ingress to renewal.*

Communicate nonverbally. Provide open-hearted empathy, a safe container that the grieving one can pour herself into, and lots of comfort through touch, home-cooked food, and other gestures of affection. In short, show her that you respect, value, and care for her.

In addition, speak openly and thoughtfully. Offer kind words and compliments. Tell the truth about a significant loss in *your* life, without giving unnecessary or disturbing details. Use an emotive vocabulary: say, "I feel," "I need," "I wish," or "I miss," rather than "I think." Point out distorted or negative thinking without being disapproving.

When visiting, don't ask her to open the door for you moments before you plan to dash off on errands. By the same token, don't overstay your welcome. Don't blame or criticize her for her condition. Don't compare her with others who are worse off. Don't demand that she "snap out of it," focus on tomorrow, or forget the past; depression, after all, is not a sign of weakness. Instead, *ask her what she'd like from you at this time.*

Imagine that you are the bereaved one. Like a bird in stormy flight, the vacant stare of your knowing eyes crosses the room effortlessly. Will you don a mask of denial by minimizing, analyzing, trivializing, fantasizing, or narcotizing your pain? Will you fly from the generations of sadness reflected in your eyes? Will you seek healing in endless acts of busyness? Holding back from the pain, you discover, may create greater unhappiness. Yes, the only way out is through. Hurt always instructs, and your wounds will teach you compassion.

Additional Resources

Copeland, Mary. *Depression Workbook: A Guide for Living with Depression and Manic Depression.* Fresno, CA: Harbinger Publications, 1992.

Knapp, R. L. *Beyond Endurance: When a Child Dies.* New York, Schocken Books, 1986.

Lukas, Christopher, and Henry Seiden. *Silent Grief: Living in the Wake of Suicide.* New York: Bantam Books, 1990.

Staudacher, Carol. *Men and Grief.* Oakland, CA: New Harbinger Publications, 1991.

Tittensor, John. *Year One.* Sydney, Australia: McPhee Gribble Publishers, 1984.

Clarify the Cloak of Fear

Come to the edge, he said.
They said: We are afraid.
Come to the edge, he said.
They came.
He pushed them . . . and they flew.
Those who love us may well push us when we're ready to fly.
                                                —Guillaume Apollinaire

Fear is the mind-talk that prevents us from hearing our intuition. Although it alerts us to the fact that we are in danger—of being either physically hurt, mentally incompetent, emotionally wounded, or spiritually lost—its walls of protection become a self-imposed prison. Fear constricts our consciousness, limiting the realities we are able to create. Try as we might to control it, we succeed only in producing more fear. Life is, after all, uncontrollable.

Fear, like anger and sadness, is not good or bad; it simply *is*. It announces itself as physical tension, and is especially susceptible to fatigue. Indeed, moving through this emotion requires enormous amounts of energy.

The continuum of fear ranges from concern to outright panic. Somewhere along this broad continuum is our individual comfort zone that determines how much money we need in the bank to feel secure, where we need to live to feel safe, and how much of ourselves we are able to invest in our relationships and our work. Each time we are pushed beyond the confines of this comfort zone, we experience fear, discomfort, and ultimately growth.

Bumping up against our limits, we not only expand them but also begin hearing the voice of intuition. After surviving several risks of this sort, we learn, very gradually, to trust ourselves.

The Many Cloaks of Fear. Fear comes dressed in a multitude of cloaks. Most often it arrives in a loss-of-self cape that billows in the wind. At such times, you may fear death—the ultimate loss of self. Every death you witness can arouse anxiety, for it may appear as a harbinger of your own. The fear of death is actually a fear of not living life to its fullest and is expressed in such questions as "Is that all I get?" and "Don't I have a second chance?" Or you may fear losing yourself in another person by being too close or by being dominated or overwhelmed. Loss of self is a frequent concern following physical, emotional, or mental injury.

Fear also comes rigged up in its you-are-not-good-enough mantle. In response to these appearances, you may begin playing the when-then game, which entails a series of thought patterns along the lines of "When I get one more skill (friend, car, client), then I'll really be ready for the big time." You may fear being rejected, condemned, abandoned, or alone. You may worry about being defective or inadequate, unworthy of being loved or wanted. You may interpret critiques of your actions or creations as direct hits on your inner being. Concluding that you are not good enough to experience success, you may decide to avoid taking risks for fear of confirming your feelings of unworthiness. In the end, you may be too intimidated to follow your dreams, terrified that you are incapable of fulfilling them or of adapting to the changes that will arise if you do fulfill them. To disguise this fear, you may adopt a stance of superiority, unaware that constantly judging others, like judging the self, merely drains away energy.

Wrapped in its you-will-not-get-your-needs-met attire, fear may convince you that you will be deprived of something essential unless you stay in control. In response, you may tighten your grasp on power, money, position, or health. Or you may rush around so driven in your search for satisfaction that you will fail to see the value in what you already have.

When fear dresses up in its you-will-not-be-able-to-handle-loss robe, you may tremble at the thought of illness, of losing a loved one, or of being fired from a job. You may decline an invitation to speak before an audience or to sign up for a championship event for fear of falling short of earlier victories.

In essence, fear can keep you in place, hold you back, stop you from taking risks, and undermine the risks you do take. In risking, we embrace our fear and adopt a more expansive mind-set—one that encompasses awareness of possible consequences and clarification of our goals. People who risk best are not fearless individuals; they are individuals who are motivated by their fear to take what they need and get where they want to go.

When Fear Gets Stuck. Unacknowledged and unmet, fear becomes magnified into anxiety, which expresses itself in loss of direction, inadequate reactions, and lack of intentionality. Anxiety is a pool of undifferentiated, unexpressed feelings that have amassed over the years—sentiments we did not want to face, impulses we were unwilling to admit to. Trapped in this maelstrom of anxiety, we are unable to concentrate on the details of what has gone wrong or what may go awry.

We dabble in "what ifs," a form of chronic disempowerment filled with energy leaks into a past that no longer exists and a future that has not yet come. Or we dwell in worry, an illusory belief that the outcome of past fears can successfully predict the future.

Anxiety keeps us locked in an unmediated tension between now ("Can I?") and then ("I should have" and "I ought to"). The vicious whirlpool of stuck fear squeezes out the present moment, which is where our power lies.

Healthy Ways to Cope with Fear. Losses of all sorts can be faced, analyzed, challenged, and endured. One way of acting upon fear is by collecting its energy. Denying, belittling, ignoring, or telling yourself you shouldn't be afraid will wall off your fear, separating you from the energetic resources needed to get through it. Instead, evaluate the power and usefulness of the fear you are feeling, and put it to work for you.

In times of danger, try visualizing an umbilical cord of will forces extending outward from your center, two finger-breadths below your navel, and follow it through the haze of fear to your desired destination. Let your sense of direction and purpose lead you through the confusion generated by fear. State your intentions clearly, and see yourself as having already moved through the present difficulty.

A third coping technique is to follow your breath. Breathing deeply and slowly will bring you back to the here and now—a command vantage point that can expand your awareness of options. Focus on *how*, rather than on *why*, you are afraid. Where is the tension in your body? Where is the holding and the constricting? Mentally direct your breath into these areas. Then as you inhale, bring in love and the basic goodness of the world; as you exhale, let go of fear.

In addition, tell the truth about your life, including how you feel about your present predicament. Accept what is not working, and get back on the road to your life goals. Regard your weaknesses not as deficits, but as sources of information—markers indicating areas that need strengthening. If you expect to be perfect in every way, you will have a great deal to be afraid of. If you instead admit to your mistakes, they will tell you where to go.

While deciding whether or not to take a risk, ask yourself these key questions:

* What would I attempt to do if I knew I could not fail?
* What am I most afraid of?
* What do I believe about myself?

★ What is the worst risk I ever took? What is the worst mistake I ever made? What was I hoping to achieve?

★ What risks have I taken in order to feel loved or accepted? How did I feel afterward?

★ When would I have been better off saying no?

Reframing is another helpful coping skill. Because fear and excitement generate similar body sensations, strive to reframe your thoughts from "This is scary!" to "This is exciting!" Anytime you hear your mind saying, "I can't do this," change its volume or tone of voice; make it softer, sexier. By repeatedly choosing exhilaration over panic, you will be naturally inclined to interpret your body's response to fear in an empowering way.

UNCLOAKING FEAR

C

E

N

T

E

R

Collect the energy of fear. Acknowledge and accept that you are afraid. As specifically as possible, name the fear.

Extend outward from your innermost self. See yourself getting through it.

Notice and follow your breath. Come back to the present with slow, deep breathing.

Tell the truth. What helps you reduce your fear? What doesn't?

Explore. What are you most afraid of, and how can you move through it? What is the next obvious step to take?

Reframe. Tell yourself: "This isn't scary—it's exciting! Wow, am I learning from my mistakes!"

What to Do When Others Are Fearful. Helping other people move through fear is a four-step process. First, help them name the fear. Identifying the source of the problem is the best way to move from a generalized sense that something is wrong, to a clear understanding of *what* is wrong. Second, offer reassurance. Explain that fear is universal and that it continues to surface as long as we are growing and evolving. Point out that all people experience fear when they are in unfamiliar territory. Third, using yourself as an example, illustrate that the only way to get rid of the fear of doing something is by going out and *doing* it. Emphasize that moving through a feeling of helplessness is less frightening than living with it. Finally, remind them of their past success in moving through fear.

Whether seeing others through their fears or grappling with your own, remember that fears are allies guiding us to uncharted areas of ourselves. The places we are most afraid to enter are those we most need to explore. Fears stretch us, goad us into moving beyond them, all the while marshaling resources we never knew we had. They remind us to stay awake and alert.

While embarking on the way of acceptance, develop a curiosity about your fears. Walk their edge. Have a conversation with them. What you don't speak to, you won't understand. What you don't understand, you can't learn from. When you don't learn, you stay stuck in destructive patterns.

Having familiarized yourself with your fears, cultivate courage— the willingness to be afraid and act anyway. Sometimes courage will override your instinct to flee; other times it will galvanate you to run away *in full consciousness*. Have the courage to accept the unacceptable, those images of disaster that flood the mind; then create a vision of what you want instead, and see it as already accomplished. Expect the best, and trust that although you may not be given everything under the sun, you will be provided with everything you truly need.

Additional Resources

Jampolsky, Gerald G., MD. *Love Is Letting Go of Fear.* New York: Bantam Books, 1981.

Jeffers, Susan. *Feel the Fear and Do It Anyway.* San Diego, CA: Harcourt Brace, 1987.

Prather, Hugh. *Notes on Love and Courage.* Garden City, NY: Doubleday, 1977.

Explore the Essence of Joy

I'm not often aware that I am happy. But I often remember that I have been happy. Especially when I sit in my kitchen wrapped in an invisible patchwork quilt made of the best moments of yesterdays. These precious things—these leftovers from living on—remain to serve as survival rations for the heart and soul. You can't entirely live off them. But life is not worth living without them. . . . There is no ultimate destination—no finish line to cross, no final conclusion to be reached. It's the way I feel about dancing—you move around a lot, not to get somewhere, but to be somewhere in time.

—Robert Fulghum

Joy is a gift you give yourself, and then scatter all around you. Just as one candle lights another and in that moment of contact sparks a brighter glow, so joy multiplies as it spreads. In the giving is a receiving.

Joy insists on celebration, dissolving boundaries, opening wide the gates of passion and enthusiasm, and enhancing our connectedness to all of life. It invites intensity, asks us to be excessive, nurtures our natural expansiveness. It arises from delight in the world, from the beauty and bounty of our senses, and from the great dance in which simplicity joins with infinite diversity.

True Happiness Lies Within. Conditioned by role models of the past, we spend much of our adult life seeking joy outside ourselves, unaware that it germinates within the body. Joy lives *inside* us, nurtured through our senses. There it blossoms, particularly when we are relaxed in mind, body, and spirit. When stressed by heat, cold, hunger, fatigue, or physical pain, we are least likely to feel its leaves, much less its blooms.

To continually access the unfolding of joy within us, we must learn to instantaneously change our mental state, to take charge of the pictures we rely on to represent our potential. One way to get the best out of yourself is by establishing an internal ecstasy wave—an association of thoughts, ideas, and feelings of happiness. Begin shaping your wave by selecting, while in a state of joy, a combination of auditory, visual, and kinesthetic cues to link you to this state. Later, while in a neutral state, focus on these cues. Feel the joyous energy moving within you, throughout your body. With practice, the state of joy will fill you the moment you evoke it by concentrating on your ecstasy wave. Ride this wave any time you wish to center yourself amid the rough seas of changing moods. Smiling—sometimes known as "mouth yoga"— is another way to alter your attitude at will.

The Essence of Joy. To discover the core of joy within you, simply be yourself, be present, appreciate, and simplify. Look more to who you are than to what you do. Then, after giving yourself permission to be loving, release the magic within you.

Happiness entails the capacity to endure pain, disappointment, and sorrow, and to get on with life, rather than wallow in misery. It asks us to affirm our essential being in spite of unfulfilled desires and nagging anxieties. Joy reflects the courage to say yes to our true being, to declare, "No matter what you say or do to me, I am a worthwhile person." Give yes a try. And while you're at it, practice taking everything people say about you as a compliment.

Wealth is enjoying what we have, feeling appreciation and gratitude for all that is in our lives. When we fail to enjoy life, we take a more scatalogical approach, continuously noticing the missing elements—the many wants that have not been fulfilled. In this state of deprivation consciousness, we tend to forget that our wants are potentially infinite, and that our yearning for abundance is gratified the moment we realize how fulfilled we in fact are. Joy is hard to find in fantasies of the future, for it flourishes in what *is:* the nontoothache that is, the clouds that are, the love that is. Life is here now . . . and so is joy.

Are you forever getting ready to get ready for happiness? Do you chase after joy? Do you look forward to the satisfaction that will come upon finishing a project or accomplishing a goal? If so, stop. The rehearsal is over, and the show is on. Welcome reality as it is; go with the flow; and realize that pleasure comes in *being* rather than *doing.*

How much happiness can you withstand? As a young child, you had to let others decide how you would live your life. In time, you began making choices yourself, based on ideas and information from the outer world. Now you can base your choices on *inner* longings and values. Although it is impossible to control external circumstances, you can choose how to *respond* to them. And you can always invite happiness to play a part in your life.

When Joy Gets Stuck. Our emotions, like other forces in nature, abhor a vacuum. When the flow of joy is obstructed, the feelings that come to the fore are resentments, regrets, and worries. In response, we brood, fret, and agonize.

Are you an approval junkie? Do you feel a sense of belonging only when everyone present notices you? Do you keep a "what if" or "yes, but" journal that shuts out all pleasures? Do you spend five days of each week looking forward to the other two? Are you prone to fatigue, scatteredness, inflexibility, constant desiring, or stagnation? If so, you may be joy-stuck. Letting loose the flow of joy will generate energy, concentration, spontaneity, freedom, gratitude, and wonder.

Healthy Ways to Increase Joy. Angels fly because they take themselves lightly. To lighten up, you need only look for the humor in stressful situations and smile to your heart's content.

Here are some other joy enhancers:

* ✮ Find a teddy bear, love bear, or other stuffed animal to cuddle with when you're feeling down.
* ✮ Keep a gratitude diary.
* ✮ Put yourself in charge of celebrations.
* ✮ Paint the canvas of your mind with beautiful images.
* ✮ Think of all the people you cherish.
* ✮ Start your day by focusing on a happy event.
* ✮ Delight in the gifts of your senses.
* ✮ If you are not getting what you desire, ask for it. Ask until . . .
* ✮ Give in to love, doing what you love, and loving it even more.
* ✮ Allow past joys to radiate into each present moment.
* ✮ Spend a day appreciating everyone and everything you encounter.
* ✮ When friends or loved ones are joyous, allow their energy to flow into your being. Sing, whistle, hum, skip, dance, and laugh along with them.

It is possible to greet each waking moment with astonishment and to love everything as it is. Lavishly acknowledge someone's goodness or a job well done. Set your ecstasy to music, keeping in mind the gypsies' belief that if one does not sing or dance, the sun will not rise. Become an emotional alchemist, turning the simplest tasks into occasions for celebration, radiance, and lightness. Above all, enjoy the ecstasy of being who you are, lighting up your little corner of the world.

Additional Resources

Baylor, Byrd. *I'm in Charge of Celebrations.* Illustrated by Peter Parnall. New York: Charles Scribner's Sons, 1986.

Fulghum, Robert. *It Was on Fire When I Lay Down on It.* New York: Random House, 1989.

Fulghum, Robert. *Uh Oh: Some Observations from Both Sides of the Refrigerator Door.* New York: Random House, 1991.

PRODUCE LESS STRESS

Sometimes, in a summer morning, having taken my accustomed bath, I sat in my sunny doorway from sunrise till noon, rapt in a revery, amidst the pines and hickories and sumachs, in undisturbed solitude and stillness, while the birds sang around or flitted noiseless through the house, until by the sun falling in at my west window, or the noise of some traveller's wagon on the distant highway, I was reminded of the lapse of time. I grew in those seasons like corn in the night, and they were far better than any work of the hands would have been.

—Henry David Thoreau

The first rule of being human is that we will receive a body. Whether we love it or hate it, accept its many parts or reject them, it is ours for the entire journey this time around. Caring for our physical body enhances our well-being and our participation in life.

At root, we are a treasury of kinetic melodies, endless variations on the complex motor sequences we have mastered. The simplest activities of daily life, such as walking and eating, are wondrous orchestrations. While submerged in our senses, we enter into this rich trove—this majestic and bountiful private pleasure-palace.

Your body is your teacher. Through it you learn what is necessary for survival and for growth. You have been with this teacher since birth, but how observant a student have you been? Within the circadian twenty-four hours are ninety-minute cycles in which your energy, focus, creativity, physical comfort, and strength wax and wane: have you detected your own rhythms? Have you explored a variety of ways to maximize physical pleasure? Do you sometimes push your limits of physical comfort? Have you ever taken a journey through your body, recording what you don't fully accept, where you hold stress, which parts you haven't been taking care of? Have your grieved your body's pains—the leg that broke, the site of stitches, the chronic knee pain? When did you last get a massage, or give one?

The human body is constantly exposed to stressors—those internal or external stimuli that exert a constraining force, altering our physiological or psychological equilibrium. Ongoing unmediated strain leads to stress. This condition often arises in response to blockage in the flow of intense emotional energy through the body. Common symptoms of stress include physical tension or tightness, restlessness, sleepiness, and eating or sexual disturbances.

When we experience these reactions chronically, our resistance breaks down, and we become physically or emotionally ill. With regular exposure to unmediated psychological stressors, we begin blaming *others* for our feelings of increased frustration and failure. Entering a declining spiral of emotional volatility, we become more irritable, isolated, argumentative, noncommunicative, and hostile.

PERSONAL STRESS INVENTORY

I define stress as _____.

Four common sources of stress for me are _____.

Four common responses to stress for me are _____.

I cope with stress by _____.

New ways to produce less stress include _____.

Healthy Ways to Cope with Stress. Most adults in our culture have been socialized to take on whatever comes their way. We engage in project after project, problem after problem, ignoring early warning signs of stress until we hit overload. Then we try frantically to create a boundary with anger or tears or physical illness. When our internal stress status reaches this danger zone, another person's actions or words will feel invasive.

Any time you approach the point of danger and wish to avert the downward spiral, try this two-part exercise. First, begin decreasing the stressors in your day-to-day tasks, your family and interpersonal relations, and your work and financial matters. Establish priorities, learn to say no, give something up, delegate, and plan your responses in advance of tough situations. Second, in a clear, stress-free moment, sit down and list the things that calm and comfort you, no matter how silly or embarrassing they may seem. Then activate your list, starting at the top.

Both relaxation and active workouts can help release the blocked emotional energy from your body. The prerequisites for relaxation are: a quiet place, a comfortable body position, a passive attitude of letting go, and a point of focus. The quiet place can be either an inner retreat you escape to when the external world seems crazed or an outer site filled with tranquility. The point of focus can be your breathing, a silently repeated mantra, or the word *one, yes,* or *relax.*

Produce Less Stress

R

E

L

A

X

Reclaim your priorities. Start saying no to more of what you don't want, and yes to what feels good.

Exercise regularly. Pick your pleasure: yoga, tai chi, running, walking, dancing, swimming, Jazzercise, cycling, roller blading, ice skating, or martial arts.

Learn simple, stressless exercises. Try a relaxation response, a regular practice of sighing, quick stretches, or retreats to your inner personal sanctuary.

Allow more touch into your life. Let in hugs, massages, healthy sexual expression, tickling, play wrestling, or slow dancing.

eXpertly shape the day's events. Seize the opportunity to shift stress into a smile.

Another quick stress reliever is sighing: take a slow, deep breath in, and release a sound as you exhale. Stretching your body—especially your neck, shoulders, back, and calves—can dissipate stress in minutes. Frequent short, quiet time-outs will also work wonders. Or create a private sanctuary within that you can easily access by closing your eyes and breathing deeply. For ongoing stress reduction, develop a network of friends or colleagues with whom you can talk openly and honestly whenever you need to.

Physical workouts require a bit more time, yet serve a twofold purpose: they relieve pent-up stress while preventing the build-up of additional pressure. Try walking, running, swimming, gardening, yoga, dancing, tai chi, or any other activity you love, and make it a regular part of your week.

Touching and being touched are among the most effective antidotes to the buildup of stress. The reason is that human touch is a direct conduit to the emotions. We speak of "being touched," meaning our emotions have been stirred. We keep "in touch" with others to remain emotionally connected to them. When we are in a "touchy" mood, we feel extreme emotional sensitivity. We remark on a loved one's "special touch," meaning his responsiveness or distinct manner of relating.

In many ways, touch is our most immediate experience of the world: our skin is said to be our largest sense organ, our eyes touch incoming light, our ears hold the sounds in our midst, our noses and mouths welcome aromas and tastes. When we are well touched and in touch, hostility dissolves.

Notice: The Surgeon General has determined that hugging is good for your health.

Hugging is practically perfect. The only maintenance required is frequent use, which inflicts no wear or tear on moving parts.

There are no batteries to replace, no periodic performance checkups, no insurance premiums, and no monthly payments of any kind. Energy consumption is low, while energy yield is high. Plus it is inflationproof, theftproof, nonfattening, nontaxable, nonpolluting, and, of course, fully returnable.

And . . . hugging is all natural. It is organic, intrinsically sweet, and 100% wholesome. It contains no pesticides, preservatives, or artificial ingredients.

The best person to hug is anyone.

The best place to hug is anywhere.

The best time to hug is anytime.

Letting go in the moment by reframing a tense situation also reduces stress accumulation. Bless the slow driver in front of you; she is reminding you to stop hurrying. Enjoy the long line at the supermarket; it gives you time to share a moment with a stranger. Recite poetry or sing a song while on "hold" during a phone call. Do whatever you can to convert stress into a smile.

We are like otters of the universe, playfully exploring our sensuality. Fully attuned to our senses, paying attention to everything they are registering, successfully reducing stressors, and coping effectively with stress, we are able to transform reality into a wondrous paradise.

Additional Resources

Ardell, Donald. *High Level Wellness*. Emmaus, PA: Rodale Press, 1977.
Epstein, Michael, and Sue Hosking. *Falling Apart*. Sebastopol, CA: CRC Publications, 1992.
Montagu, Ashley. *Touching: The Human Significance of the Skin*. New York: Columbia University Press, 1971.
Moyers, Bill. *Healing and the Mind*. New York: Doubleday, 1993.
Silva, José. *Silva Mind Control*. New York: Simon & Schuster, 1977.

TAME THE WILD HORSE OF MIND

Everything which man creates begins in the form of a thought impulse. . . . Whatever the mind of man can conceive and believe it can achieve.

—Napoleon Hill

We become what we think about. This assertion has been stated many times in various ways: "Argue for your limitations, and they become yours," "You are not what you think you are; but what you think, you are," "Your life is what your thoughts make it," "You currently act as you currently believe," "The way you define reality shapes it, which in turn shapes and defines you," "You behave in accordance with what you imagine to be true about yourself and your environment," "You become who you are as a result of your dominant thoughts and desires."

All these sayings imply that we converse with ourselves continually. And it is true—our wild horse of mind gallops from one thought to another, judging, questioning, interpreting, analyzing, and deciding. What do you say to yourself? While speaking inwardly, do you evoke misery or joy? Are you creating your own hell or your own heaven?

Inner Dialogues. The quality of our lives is dependent on the quality of our inner dialogues. Negative mind-talk takes many forms: "I can't ———," "If only ———," "I don't have enough (energy, time, luck, skill)," "Someday I'll ———," "I wish I had ———," "Yes, but ———," and "I really don't care; it's not important ———." Over time, these negative self-images begin to dominate our sense of who we are. Defeating or shaming conversations with ourselves constitute an invasion of hostile forces from within.

Positive self-talk, on the other hand, awakens inner resources. In these affirmative frames of mind, we become all that we can be.

Developing a Fit Mind. A fit mind, like a conditioned body, possesses strength, flexibility, endurance, and coordination. Its strength comes from *awareness*. Aware of your inner dialogues, you will learn from them and begin responding intelligently to new situations. Oblivious to your self-talk, you will allow the wild horse of mind to kick inner turbulence into your external environment.

The flexibility of the fit mind is established through *attention*—a faculty that recalls and anticipates, sashaying through the past, present, and future in a dance that gives perspective and continuity to life. To stay mounted, you will need to focus your attention in an effortless, relaxed way, which is best achieved through relaxation and meditation. Relaxing your body, breath, and mind will clear the lens of awareness. Meditation, an ideal vehicle for quieting the chatter of thoughts, permits inner wisdom to emerge.

Mental endurance develops through composed *thinking*. Workouts include problem solving, brainstorming, gathering information, memorizing, and concentrating. To test your mental endurance skills, try to count in your head the number of capital letters composed of curved lines.

Mental coordination would be impossible without the regular use of *imagination* and *visualization*. These faculties of mind give way to new possibilities, including innovative patterns of behavior. Using imagination, you can edit and direct your own mental movies. Visualization can assist you in seeing the future as you want it to be. By filling your mind with positive images and mentally rehearsing desired outcomes, you will be able to accomplish tasks with ease. And you will be liberated from the old attitudinal prisons of your own making.

Just as correct physical posture aligns the body with gravity, proper attitudes align the mind with truth. While tending to your attitude, replace destructive, inaccurate thoughts with affirming, honest, and constructive ones. Whenever an answer is beyond reach, say, "I don't know"—three empowering words that invite possibility. See with your mind, not merely your eyes. And when trying to remember something that has slipped your mind, say, "It will come to me soon," then let go of the search. The request for stored information will soon be answered.

GET ON THAT WILD HORSE OF MIND!

R emain aware of your inner dialogue.

Invest in focused attention.

Develop powers of imagination, visualization, brainstorming, and problem solving.

Explore mind-sets and mental attitudes. Choose those that empower.

At any given moment, choose an inner conversation that is empowering. From the horse's back, you will soon see life as a journey in forgetting and re-membering, a continual letting go in order to discover who you really are.

Additional Resources

Orage, A. R. *Psychological Exercises and Essays.* New York: Samuel Weiser, 1930.

The Orange Book: The Meditation Techniques of Bhagwan Shree Rajneesh. Rajneeshpuram, OR: Rajneesh Foundation International, 1983.

Trungpa, Chögyam. *The Sacred Path of the Warrior.* Boston, MA: Shambhala Publications, 1984.

Wujec, Tom. *Pumping Ions.* New York: Doubleday, 1988.

ATTEND TO THE SPIRITUAL

Desolate through forests and fearful in jungles, he is seeking an Ox which he does not find. Up and down dark, nameless, wide-flowing rivers, in deep mountain thickets he treads many bypaths. Bone-tired, heart-weary, he carries on his search for this something which he yet cannot find. At evening he hears cicadas chirping in the trees.

—Kakuan Shien

Intuition is "cosmic fishing," said creative futurist R. Buckminster Fuller. "You feel a nibble, then you've got to hook the fish." Intuition is always responsive to your desires, needs, and intentions. It neither examines nor investigates, but rather offers possibilities and new choices, evoking the "Aha!" of an important insight, creation, or discovery. It can bring a warning, an affirmation, or information. It is often vague and hesitating, though it can be clear and compelling. Intuition may appear when least expected, or arise in response to an immediate need. More like a sense of direction than a road map, it will first appear on the fringe of awareness as a barely perceptible shift in feeling. When it does, breathe deeply, center yourself, and take heed of its still, small voice.

You can awaken your intuition by continually acting upon what you hear. As you begin to experience the aftereffects of its guidance, you will feel a corresponding increase in trust.

The messages of intuition, to be patently recognizable, must first incubate, gestate, and have a life of their own. So refrain from judging them at the outset as good or bad, right or wrong. Fears, projections, and interpretations can likewise obscure their valuable counsel. If at first this form of guidance seems cloudy, accept that as you become more receptive, your inner wisdom will become clearer. Know, too, that whenever you ask for guidance, it will be there, though often in an unexpected form, such as an image, a fleeting thought, a momentary feeling, or a dream.

Through intuition we contact a higher power, also known as an inner guide or the higher self. Religions the world over refer to this power as the God within, a being that gives meaning, purpose, and significance to one's life. Whatever name we give it, this energetic force that resides in the expanding core of who we are knows *only love*. It is our personal connection with the great mystery of the universe and our lifeline to spiritual awareness.

How are the vital signs of your spiritual growth? Are you living in misery because you refuse to surrender your ego to a transpersonal process, power, or design? Are you sometimes in touch with a universal sense of belonging? As you continue to discover who you are, does your life seem to evolve more clearly and purposefully?

Letting Your Heart Lead Your Mind. The universe is conspiring to help us. That is why we keep stumbling onto things, finding answers to questions we haven't yet asked. The more often we come upon a vital lesson, the more we realize that the outer world is continually responding to our inner needs. We see that wherever we are on our journey is precisely where we have wanted to be. We are creating our lives each moment by choosing from among several prerogatives as the different parts of the self pull in often opposing directions.

Although there are no right or wrong choices on our journey through life, there are prudent and imprudent actions. Hopes, wishes, longings, and wants form a breeding ground for unfulfilled expectations, particularly those that are inspired by a desire for power, recognition, or prestige. The more committed you are to act on behalf of these yearnings, the less free you will be to nurture your spiritual growth.

Do you believe that when you get what you want, you'll be happy? (Have you considered that instead you may only want something *else?*) Or are your wants congruent with your highest vision of yourself? Do they stretch your horizons and extend into realms *beyond* the self? The spirit within you wants you to spend more time asking, "Who am I?" instead of wondering, "What do I want?"

The heart-led journey proceeds toward spirit, whereas the mind-led journey winds circuitously through a landscape of endless personal wants. Which of these sojourns are you on? Have you spent years waiting and wondering where you are headed, or perhaps intelligently muddling through, never quite sure if you were following your heart? Is your journey dominated by a series of strategies designed to avert despair, but resulting in maddening predictability, or isolation? Does it accord you pleasures, but no direction? If so, you may want to reevaluate the course you are on.

When you are guided by your sense of spirit, you stand in the creative center of your life. Your essence soars and exudes a torrent of energy that will call forth whatever you need. Grounded in your heart, you lift your vision, expand your awareness, and enlarge your life.

It is never too late to shift your attention and open to the spiritual. If this is your desire, go gently. Leave forcefulness behind, and let go of all resistance. *Honor the sacred in each moment.* Ask your intuition to tell you what is needed each day.

At certain times, under particular circumstances, spiritual consciousness becomes evident: we see that we are at one with the universe and that every moment is a gift. Touching the world from this place of spiritual understanding and inner trust, we sow seeds for a flourishing peace.

Additional Resources

Burkan, Tolly, and Peggy Dylan. *Guiding Yourself to a Spiritual Reality.* Twain Harte, CA: Reunion Press, 1983.

Cameron, Julia. *The Artist's Way: A Spiritual Path to Higher Creativity.* Los Angeles: Jeremy Tarcher, 1992.

Goldberg, Natalie. *Writing Down the Bones: Freeing the Writer Within.* New York: Bantam Books, 1990.

Peck, M. Scott. *The Road Less Traveled.* New York: Simon & Schuster, 1980.

NURTURE YOUR HEALING SELF

We are the mirror as well as the face in it. We are tasting the taste this minute of eternity. We are pain and what cures pain, both. We are the sweet, cold water and the jar that pours.

—Rumi

Do you beat yourself up and drive a stake through your heart to make sure the parts of yourself you don't like are really dead? If you do, bury the stake and try loving acceptance instead. Why bother? Because we are here to be healed, beginning with the portions of ourselves we are trying to kill off.

We experience well-being every time we accept that the present moment—including the discomfort it brings—is exactly as it should be. Hence, whatever you are doing, love yourself for doing it.

Addictions, too, are heralds of healing. An addiction, according to recovery specialist John Bradshaw, is "a pathological relationship to any mood-altering experience that has life-damaging consequences." *Process addictions*, in this context, are as revealing as *substance addictions*, though they are often more difficult to discern.

What is your "drug" of choice? Is it workaholism—the self-martyring pain others applaud? The constant fantasizing and acting out of sex addiction? Future-tripping into a pleasant time and space to escape tough situations? Raging? Gambling? Whatever it may be, the desires and impulses you feel unable to resist are pointing the way to emotions you need to experience in order to heal. Healing begins with the acceptance of every inch of ourselves, including our pain, self-hatred, and personal addictions.

Choosing to Heal. At various times, life presents us with marker events, turning points that inspire us to choose a path of healing instead of further self-destruction. Our self-destructive tendencies are often subtle. Blaming others is one of them, for it places us in a disempowering victim role. Each time you blame an outside force for an emotion you are experiencing, you give away your power, build a wall of defense around yourself, and pave the way to pain, paralysis, and depression.

Protective defenses of any sort, if you don't let go of them soon enough, are also injurious, for maintaining them requires a great deal of energy. If your energy is tied up in an emotional debt from the past, you will have fewer resources left for coping with the present. We heal by surrendering, not by controlling.

Repeated acts of self-destruction lead only to insanity—which some psychologists have defined as "doing the same thing over and over again, expecting different results." Sanity, by contrast, comes with the realization that the old ways do not work. Marker events for the shift toward healing take any number of forms. We may become suddenly sick and tired of being sick and tired, or of waking up to who we are *not* instead of who we *are*. An accident, job loss, divorce, serious illness, or destroyed friendship may also cause a wound that opens the door to health. Problems of this sort always carry rewards with them. In a sense, *we seek problems because we need their gifts.*

Feeling Everything. Some of us know we're screwed up; others know it and can explain why. But does explaining our craziness ameliorate it? The problem is that the practice of assessing and evaluating often ensnares us in a vicious cycle of asking how and why, which only serves to keep us there.

We reach the light not by endlessly analyzing the darkness, but by choosing the light, moment by moment. We heal not by rubbing intellectual goo over our pain, but by feeling each emotion as it surfaces. True recovery lies in facing what we do not want to acknowledge.

Even so, healing need not be a struggle. It can be a gentle, friendly process, provided that you allow the feelings within your body to direct the journey.

Facing the Past. We tend to blame friends and loved ones for violations committed by others in the past. Dynamics of this sort indicate that we have not yet reckoned with our feelings about an old adversary. Healing offers us an opportunity to forgive ourselves, to forgive our oppressors, and to accept that we have neither the wisdom nor the knowledge to be judge and executioner of those who have hurt us in the past. We cannot change the past, but we *can* change our *relationship* to it.

In forgiving ourselves, we leave behind the role of victim. In forgiving our adversaries, we relieve ourselves of hurts, anger, pain, and loneliness.

If forgiveness seems out of reach, proceed slowly. At first allow in a tiny beam of forgiveness, and then just a little bit more. Separating the act from the actor, recognize that although the deed may have been heinous, the doer is worthy of your compassion. All the while remember that forgiveness is a distant shore that can be reached only after crossing the rapids of anger and pain.

Transformation. As we heal, we move from blaming and resenting to taking responsibility, from coping to creating. Self-doubt is displaced by self-discovery. Stagnation transforms into playfulness. Shame turns to self-acceptance.

The healing journey is often difficult, yet it is significantly eased by the support and camaraderie of others. Know in your heart that friends, family, and community can lighten the way. And amid any turmoil you encounter, remember that the world is blessed by the presence of healed people. Your own stirring will help you touch the depths in others. Your shining will ignite their glow.

Additional Resources

Bloomfield, Harold. *Making Peace with Your Parents.* New York: Ballantine Books, 1983.

Levine, Stephen. *Healing into Life and Death.* New York: Doubleday, 1987.

Muller, Wayne. *Legacy of the Heart: The Spiritual Advantages of a Painful Childhood.* New York: Simon & Schuster, 1992.

Siegel, Bernie S., MD. *Peace, Love and Healing.* New York: Harper & Row, 1989.

COMMIT TO COMMUNICATE

Listen up because I've got nothing to say, and I'm only going to say it once.

—Yogi Berra

Young people are victimized every day because they lack basic communication skills for working out problems. As adults they may very well succumb to the relationship disorder known as violence. With proper role modeling, however, their futures will be more promising.

More than anything else, we as teachers need to model fair fighting—something we have little experience in. Most often, we engage in disagreements by alternating between talking and rehearsing while the other person speaks. We use a variety of verbal weapons, such as "You always ———" and "You never ———." We stab with sarcasm, attack on many fronts, and fire parting shots.

Fair fighting instead requires us to engage in *conscious* disagreeing, which clears the air for new possibilities. While consciously disagreeing, we articulate the issue in dispute; express our underlying fears; time the discussion so that both parties can give it their all; take responsibility for our part of the problem; actively listen as thoughts and feelings are exchanged; negotiate; and let go of blaming and judging. In the end, being right is less important than arriving at a win-win solution.

This type of exchange demonstrates the essence of *samma vacha,* Sanskrit for right speech. According to the principles of *samma vacha,* every word is considerate and true, silence is respected, and the words that break the silence make the world a better place.

Overcoming Communication Obstacles. Most barriers to effective communication arise from habitual patterns of speaking. Breaking these habits takes time, yet produces immediate results. Doorways to communication open wide the moment we let go of each O B S T A C L E listed below.

Overgeneralizing: "You always——," "You never——," "Every time ——."

Blaming: "It's all your fault," "You made me ——."

Should-ing: Lecturing, preaching, ordering, threatening.

Telepathy: Reading another person's mind, fortune-telling.

Assuming: "I know what is best for you," "Let me tell you about your problem."

Criticizing: Judging, using right-or-wrong thinking.

Labeling: Name-calling.

Exaggerating/Minimizing: Elaborating on or devaluing another person's feelings.

Improving Communication Contact. Giving up obstructive communication styles is not enough. You will also need to develop skills that enhance communication C O N T A C T, such as those that follow.

Communicate feelings clearly. Use "I" messages. Accept and acknowledge all feeling states. Expand the vocabulary you rely on to express emotions.

Observe body language. Pay attention to the messages you are sending nonverbally, via your posture, degree of physical closeness, and facial expressions.

Notice your tone of voice. The way in which something is said is often more important than the words that are used.

Time your conversation carefully. Allow enough time for a good discussion. Avoid bringing up issues when time is limited. Converse when you are both are likely to be receptive.

Actively listen. Stop talking, concentrate on listening, avoid distractions, look at the other person, and notice the effect you are having.

Clarify, reflect, and summarize. Seek first to understand. Toward this end, refuse to argue mentally, recognize your own prejudices, and leave your emotions in the backseat of your mind. Strive to respond rather than react. Using your own words, reiterate the other person's dilemma, and check to make sure you are correct.

Trust in the power of truth. Be patient; validate; and empathize.

COMMUNICATING WITH YOUNG PEOPLE

Acknowledge and accept your feelings. Use "I" messages: "I feel ——— when you ———. I'd like ———."

Seek first to understand. Spend twice as much time listening as talking. Help your children clarify their feelings.

Share your pain, fears, and confusion. In the midst of a conflict, express *these* rather than your anger.

Talk about your mistakes. Regard them as friends that teach you what you need to know.

Forgive and ask forgiveness. Say, "I'm sorry" and "I don't know" when appropriate.

Check in daily. What were the best and worst parts of your children's day? Of your day?

Ask essential questions. The pivotal ones are: Who are you? What are your gifts? How will you make the world better?

Focus on who they are. Acknowledge and appreciate the positive.

Don't take discontent personally. Use humor to diffuse difficult situations. Laugh a lot.

Model the behaviors you'd like to see. Treat your children with dignity and respect.

Use natural consequences. Let your children safely experience the results of their choices, free of rescuing and lecturing.

Additional Resources

Buscaglia, Leo. *Loving Each Other*. Thorofare, NJ: Slack, Inc., 1984.
Hendrix, Harville. *Getting the Love You Want: A Guide for Couples*. New York: Harper & Row, 1988.
Satir, Virginia. *Peoplemaking*. Palo Alto, CA: Science and Behavior Books, 1972.

ESTABLISH A PLACE OF PEACE WITHIN

We may never be strong enough to be entirely nonviolent in thought, word, and deed. But we must keep nonviolence as our goal and make steady progress toward it. The attainment of freedom, whether for a man, a nation, or the world, must be in exact proportion to the attainment of nonviolence by each.
—Mahatma Gandhi

Violence erupts when our personal shadows burst forth to the surface of our lives. Having been banished from consciousness for years, these shadows normally lie fallow in the unintegrated darkness within. There they hide out, unseen and unacknowledged, holding in custody portions of who we are. As they explode into visibility, we shudder at the pain and confusion they bring, and we begin attacking these parts of ourselves. In effect, we go to war with ourselves.

What would life be like if we called a truce to this internal war and began treating our shadows as our best friends? How can we invite them back into our lives, accept them into our hearts?

Making peace with inner enemies begins when we realize there are no inner enemies, but rather different voices attempting to move us toward wholeness. As each voice is embraced and brought to expression, it ceases its battle cry and becomes an ally. Interestingly enough, you can *feel* the dynamic shift. Try this exercise, for example. Picture yourself at your worst—uptight, hurried, nasty, stressed out, perhaps belligerent. Now appreciate yourself for noticing these characteristics, and hug yourself with a hand of forgiveness and a hand of compassion. What happened to those antagonistic voices?

Forgiveness and Compassion. We cannot forgive others if we do not first forgive ourselves. Self-forgiveness softens, dissolves bitterness and illusion, enlarges our perspective, and helps us accept the flaws of others. To forgive is not to forget; it is to *let go of*. It is the realization that the hurt we have been feeling has its origins not in prior pain, but in *our own holding on*.

Try to recall something you have thought, said, or done against your better judgment. Is the incident continuing to wall off a part of you? Is it causing you to suffer? How tenaciously we cling to the memories we long to be released from!

By the same token, we cannot show compassion toward others if we do not practice it on ourselves. Empathizing with our own struggle to attain happiness and avoid suffering, we become aware that we are all members of a great human family. Immediately, we begin to feel compassion for other men and women engaged in similar struggles. We tap into a love that inspires us to do whatever is needed to bring awareness to a situation. Compasssion is not pity or sympathy; it is a way of walking through life as if all creation mattered.

Creating Peace Within. To sustain inner peace we need an inner peacekeeper experienced in self-forgiveness and compassion. The function of this peacekeeper is to help us transcend our habitual responses by converting annoyances, irritations, or disturbances into peace-promoting energy. Our job is simply to be aware of the offending experiences and, inspirited by forgiveness and compassion, to reframe them in the moment.

Moment by moment, your peacekeeper can help you actively choose the path of nonviolence. All it needs is warmth and love.

Violence in any form is resisted on the battlefield of the heart, with open hands of self-forgiveness and compassion. For peacekeeper sustenance, make up your own ways of hugging yourself with kindness. Welcome the purifying heat of inner conversion. Soon you will see that self-hatred has died—if not from disuse, then from its incapacity to withstand the fire of love.

Strengthening the Inner Peacekeeper

When you become aware of:	Take a breath and say silently:
Negative thoughts	"Next, please."
Rushing around	"What a blessed moment this is."
Judging others	"That is within me too."
Worrying about the future	"I choose peace instead."
Putting yourself down	"I am worthy of love and respect."

A Place of Peace Within

An inner place of peace expands the heart. Once violence has been resisted on the battlefield of the heart, respect and caring flow forth not only to oneself but to others. Human coexistence is then marked by gentleness and living, rather than hurting and killing.

According to all indications, more and more people are cultivating these seeds of harmony within themselves, and as a result inner peace has reached epidemic proportions. Many stressed-out, uptight individuals are tuning in, letting go of the need to control what simply isn't controllable, and striving to create a gradual cease-fire. Routine surveillance indicates that hurry sickness, once a common malady, is burning itself out. Census analysts are predicting that conflict-seeking individuals may soon become an endangered species. Negative-attitude prisons are reporting a record number of escapees. The epidemic is worldwide, and spreading rapidly.

Affected individuals can be recognized by any or all of the following symptoms:

✓ An increasing inability to worry.

✓ An irrational, deepening trust that life provides for human needs.

✓ A deep appreciation for what is, rather than a focus on what is not.

✓ A definitive tendency to enjoy each moment, accompanied by diminishing perceptions of time "wasted" in waiting.

✓ A loss of interest in shaming, blaming, or judging others.

✓ Recurrent eruptions of forgiveness.

✓ A prolonged sense of doing less and being more.

✓ Spontaneous attacks of "wondering around" and smiling frequently.

✓ A chronic discharge of resentments and regrets.

✓ A persistent tendency to turn soft and lovely at the slightest opportunity.

✓ An increased receptivity to love from within and without.

✓ A supreme concentration of energy in the present moment, rather than anxiety about the past or fear of the future.

Additional Resources

Gandhi, Mahatma. *All Men Are Brothers*. Edited by Krishna Kripalani. New York: Continuum Publishing Company, 1994.

Nhat Hanh, Thich. *Touching Peace*. Berkeley, CA: Parallax Press, 1992.

King, Martin Luther, Jr. *Strength to Love*. Philadelphia: Fortress Press, 1963.

Kornfield, Jack. *A Path with Heart*. New York: Bantam Books, 1993.

The Fourth Path

THE WAY OF THE PEACEMAKER

TEN STEPS TO FAMILY PEACE

P	**P**ractice positive discipline
E	**E**xpand emotional fluency
A	**A**pproach conflict with a win-win attitude
C	**C**reate connections
E	**E**mphasize essential values
M	**M**inimize media exposure
A	**A**void victimization
K	**K**eep celebrating diversity
E	**E**ngage in bullyproofing
R	**R**einforce resiliency

We do not believe in ourselves until someone reveals that deep inside us something is valuable, worth listening to, worthy of our touch, sacred to our touch. Once we believe in ourselves, we can risk curiosity, wonder, spontaneous delight, or any experience which reveals the human spirit.

—e. e. cummings

I T'S A COLD, RAINY DAY IN A SMALL APARTMENT. I'M A SINGLE PARENT IN THE middle of a long weekend with my daughters, who are bouncing off the walls and each other. My fatigue, conflict, and tension are palpable. We've already had a time-out, and now the girls are using "I" messages to express their feelings, but in insulting ways. Finally, the little one whacks the big one. I grab the offender roughly and push her down on the bed, yelling, *"We are not a hitting family!"* Of course, as I release some of my tension, my actions are undermining my words. Then everyone is crying, and eventually, after a round of "I'm sorry," we get through it.

We are all born into families of one sort or another—big, small, extended, nuclear, with one parent, two parents, or grandparents. In time, we enter new families, either by adoption, marriage, or a desire for mutual support. Each of these families has strengths arising from its individual members as well as from the unit as a whole. This path suggests practical ways of building on these strengths and preparing our children to step into the world as peacemakers.

PRACTICE POSITIVE DISCIPLINE

Children have never been very good at listening to their elders, but they have never failed to imitate them.
—James Baldwin

Rarely do people exclaim: "Stop! I'm suffering from too many compliments. Please, I cannot take even one more." And yet, we assume that the more positive feedback we give our children, the more we'll fill their heads with illusions of grandeur, and the more spoiled they will be. As a former subscriber to a variation on this belief, I used to fear that praising my children endlessly would turn them into people pleasers, approval junkies with no minds of their own. Now I do my best to seize every opportunity to validate them, and *spoiled* is a word I reserve for vegetables.

Children experience themselves through the reflections beamed back to them by the adults in their world. The more attention and positive recognition we give them, the more we enhance their sense of self. In praising and complimenting our children, we fill the well from which they will drink the rest of their lives.

"Ah, but constructive criticism is essential," say childcare "experts" steeped in labor-force psychodynamics. "Constructive criticism is constrictive crudicism!" retort observant parents. And they are right—children do not learn discipline and respect by engaging in power struggles. Instead, regard for others arises naturally when children have learned to *appreciate themselves*.

Nearly all youngsters reared in an atmosphere of unconditional love and reasonable limit-setting strive for self-improvement *on their own*. We as parents need only keep focusing on the positive. Catch your children being good, and let them know how proud of them you are.

From Dictator to Doormat. Shortly after our first child was born, a neighbor told us that raising kids is really about concocting bribes and threats. Actually, being a parent feels more like chutes and ladders; just when I think I've got it right, I take a downward slide.

Most of us swing between being outright controlling to being loosely permissive in our attempts to discipline our children. We can slide from dictator to doormat in one afternoon. And with little wonder, when we consider the inherent ambiguity in what we are attempting to do. The word *discipline* itself—which derives from the Latin *dis* (apart) and *cipere* (to hold or seize)—means to learn, to comprehend what is good for one by taking it apart. When we focus on a particular action and instruct our children in what is needed, we are teaching them discipline.

While in a dictating mode, we direct, demand, lecture, and punish. We say, "Do ——— right now!" or "Don't ———" or "I'm sick and tired of telling you to stop ———. When I was your age ———" or even "You're grounded for forty days and forty nights." We use the five least empowering words of parenting: *no, don't, stop, quit,* and *not.* Slipping into a permissive mode, we begin rescuing, indulging, explaining, and overprotecting. We say, "Go to your room (at your earliest convenience)." In two-parent households, mothers and fathers often position themselves at opposite ends of the discipline spectrum, attempting to keep the system in balance.

What we are really after is a middle way—one that allows our children to feel respected, encouraged, invited to participate and cooperate, and free to experience the natural results of their actions, as long as those outcomes will not endanger anyone's well-being. A few clear expectations are better than many vague or unspoken ones. And when these expectations are not met, follow-through with agreed upon consequences is better than spur-of-the-moment punishments or no follow-through at all.

The middle way requires us to forgo both the urge to micromanage our children's lives and the inclination to spare our children the consequences of their behavior. The guiding principle is, "Don't just do something, stand there."

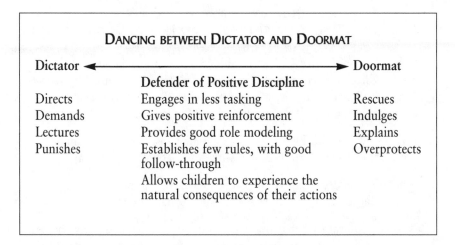

DANCING BETWEEN DICTATOR AND DOORMAT		
Dictator ◄──────────────────────────► Doormat		
	Defender of Positive Discipline	
Directs	Engages in less tasking	Rescues
Demands	Gives positive reinforcement	Indulges
Lectures	Provides good role modeling	Explains
Punishes	Establishes few rules, with good follow-through	Overprotects
	Allows children to experience the natural consequences of their actions	

The least effective method of disciplining children is popularly known as *tasking*—telling them what to do. We say, "Drink your milk" or "Eat your veggies," hoping that our commands are introducing desirable eating patterns. In actuality, they are ensuring that our children will soon become parent-deaf. *Reinforcing desired behavior* is somewhat more productive, yet unable to convey the guiding principles we want our youngsters to have. Discipline ultimately arises from within the child, as an imitative response to loved ones. The most effective form of teaching is therefore *modeling*. Here the underlying message is, "Don't do as I say; do as I do."

Corporal Punishment. Some parents believe that hitting will correct misbehaviors. The truth is that negative acts never foster positive actions. Children do *not* behave better after being made to feel worse. Why? Because punishing children for wrongful actions provides no instruction in right action. Hitting children teaches them one lesson only: that it is okay to use force to get what you want.

If you are accustomed to doling out spankings—or even an "occasional swat"—and if this is not a behavior you would like your children to carry into adulthood, then promise yourself never to hit your children *when you are angry*. Holding to your promise, you'll no doubt be delighted to find yourself never hitting your children at all.

Lashing out with angry words, however, is no better. Young children who feel verbally attacked learn to fear their parents. Older chil-

---

THE SEVEN DEADLY STRESSORS OF CHILDHOOD IN THE FIRST THREE YEARS OF LIFE . . . AND HOW TO COPE WITH THEM

Colic. Remember that 85 percent of babies have some end-of-day fussing around three weeks of age. Assist your baby's transition into sleep with a front carrier and rhythmic, soothing activities. Eliminate overfeeding, and avoid parent fatigue. If you begin feeling abusive, take a time-out.

Awakening at night. Eliminate long daytime naps. Consider a family bed for a while. To feel refreshed, nap with your baby during the day.

Separation anxiety. Clarify the cause. Rehearse separations. Offer reassurance rather than punishment. Use familiar babysitters.

Normal exploratory behavior. Safetyproof your home, and put valuables out of reach. Offer your child alternative objects when necessary.

Normal negativism. Set only a few important safety rules. Don't punish your child for saying no. Offer real choices as often as possible. Allow for transition time in new situations. No-saying is typical for two year olds, so don't take it personally.

Normal poor appetite. Strive for pleasant mealtimes and smaller, more frequent feedings. Offer a variety of foods, and allow your child to self-feed. Give less than 16 ounces a day of cow's milk, and only after a year of age.

Toilet training resistance. Don't push toilet training. When your child is ready to use the potty, take the time to teach her how. Praise cooperation and success. When "accidents" occur, give positive support.

Adapted from Barton Schmitt, MD, *Child Abuse and Neglect* 2 (1987): 421–432

dren become surreptitious about their activities to avoid getting caught. So before reacting to unwanted behavior or broken rules, remember that *what* you say has less impact than *how* you say it. Respect is more important than righteousness. With this in mind, the next time your child misbehaves, try separating the doer from the deed and explain, as calmly as possible, "I get angry when you do ———, and I will always love you."

When we take out our bad moods on our children, yell at them as our stress levels soar out of control, or hit them because we are frustrated, we fail to model the self-control we would like our children to learn. A further point to remember at such times is that most child abuse fatalities arise from parents losing control over normal childhood behavioral difficulties such as those delineated on the previous page.

The moment we realize that we are not behaving as the functional parents we are capable of being, we need to forgive ourselves, strengthen our resolve to use positive discipline, and take better care of ourselves so that we can better care for our children. In the future, we can stop ourselves from acting abusively by taking a refreshing pause *before* harsh words come tumbling out of our mouths or *before* our hand moves out to strike those we love. We are here to be our children's mentors, not their tormentors.

Additional Resources

Brazelton, T. Berry, MD. *Touchpoints*. Redding, MA: Addison-Wesley, 1994.
Johnson, Spencer. *One-Minute Parent*. New York: Random House, 1993.
Nelson, Jane. *Positive Discipline*. New York: Ballantine Books, 1987.
Nelson, Jane, and Lynn Lott. *I'm on Your Side*. Rocklin, CA: Prima Publishing, 1991. For parents of teens.

EXPAND EMOTIONAL FLUENCY

There is nothing wrong with teenagers that reasoning with them won't aggravate.
—Anonymous

To become capable problem solvers, children need to recognize the feelings that live in their bodies, name them, develop an ability to share them with other people, and find appropriate ways of utilizing the energy they generate. They also need to learn skills to help them cope with the strong feelings that live in other people's bodies. Their primary models are, as always, their parents.

But despite our best intentions we parents give our children wounds as well as gifts. I have with sadness watched my older daughter speak to her sister in the same nasty tone of voice I have just used with her. I have felt my father's anger in the finger I've pointed at others while spreading my own anger around the living room. And I will always remember waking from a dream in tears after separating from my wife, and feeling my four year old hugging me as she asked why grown-ups don't cry as much as kids. "I cry when I need to let my feelings out," she said with eloquent simplicity.

Feelings sparked by both the wounds and the gifts form part of the vast keyboard of our children's emotional being. Each feeling has a timbre of its own that begs to come to expression—for unreleased, it will generate extreme confusion and frustration. So it is that children who are sensitized to only a few vibrational variations around middle C must learn to trust that *all* feelings are okay, and then let them flow to expression. As our children's teachers, we need to achieve clarity about our own emotional states. Only then will we be able to *consciously* model the power of emotions and, in the process, pass on the gift of emotional fluency.

Naming the Feelings. Each time we become aware of emotions surfacing in our children, we can reflect back what we see and give it a name. Caught up in the emotional turmoil of these moments, we lose the opportunity for teaching.

The first step in reflecting back this seedbed of activity is to help our children recognize the intense feelings they are holding in their bodies. You might say, "From the tone of your voice, it sounds like you're pretty worried" or "There seems to be tension in your shoulders. Are you afraid?" or "We are not a hitting family. Please find another way to show your sister that you are angry. Use your words!"

The second step is to expand our children's feeling vocabulary. To help accomplish this mission, you might say: "I'm not angry. I'm irritated (annoyed, bugged, peeved, pissed, frustrated)."

Always the goal is to provide direct, high-quality feedback that is free of judgment, shame, and blame. In response, your children will come to understand that feelings are a natural part of life, that they refuse to be ignored, and that it is possible—indeed desirable—to access each one of them.

The Healthy Expression of Emotions.   We can teach children a great deal about healthy emotional release. To begin, we can demonstrate the use of "I" messages: "I feel ——— when you ———. And I'd

MORE WORDS FOR FEELINGS

	Elation	Depression	Anger	Fear
Perceptible Emotions	Relieved	Flat	Peeved	Shy
	Refreshed	Bored	Bugged	Startled
	Glad	Discontented	Annoyed	Uneasy
	Pleased	Resigned	Ruffled	Tense
	Amused	Apathetic	Nettled	Anxious
	Playful	Numb	Harassed	Nervous
	Cheerful	Blah	Irritated	Worried
	Optimistic	Melancholic	Put-upon	Concerned
	Giddy	Blue	Hassled	Timid
	Gay	Rotten	Resentful	Apprehensive
	Calm	Gloomy	Spiteful	Uptight
	Composed	Ignored	Mean	
	Comfortable	Distressed	Irked	
	Cool	Low		
	Secure	Sad		
	Relaxed	Unhappy		
	Confident	Drained		
Moderate Emotions	Delighted	Disappointed	Disgusted	Alarmed
	Jovial	Shot-down	Ticked-off	Jittery
	Merry	Slighted	Mad	Scared
	Bubbly	Bewildered	Angry	Afraid
	Tickled	Disheartened	Smoldering	Frightened
	Glowing	Hurt	Riled	Fearful
	Frisky	Abused	Hot	Threatened
	Festive	Lost	Bitter	Trembly
	Spry	Regretful	Antagonistic	Shaken
	Happy	Ashamed	Contemptuous	
	Proud	Burdened		
	Joyous	Down		
	Excited	Forlorn		
	High	Hopeless		
	Turned-on	Lifeless		
	Great	Dead		
Intense Emotions	Alive	Miserable	Fed up	Cowed
	Blissful	Downcast	Fuming	Dread filled
	Sparkling	Crushed	Furious	Panicky
	Overjoyed	Helpless	Incensed	Terrified
	Vivacious	Humiliated	Infuriated	Terror stricken
	Radiant	Depressed	Destructive	Horrified
	Wonderful	Withdrawn	Hateful	Petrified
	Enthralled	Worthless	Explosive	
	Exhilarated	Abandoned	Raging	

like ———." If speaking in this way seems artificial, try warming up to it by turning it into a game. Make up silly "I" statements. Or have a conversation in which only "I" messages are allowed. Or make up an "I feel" song.

We can also explain that powerful emotions produce energy in the body and that until this energy is released, problem solving tends to be difficult. Tell your children that minimizing, analyzing, or denying the emotions they are feeling will keep the energy locked inside, and may even make them mad. Let them know that the best way to manage any strong feeling is to release in words or actions the energy it has generated.

Preschoolers, especially, need guidance in using their words and their bodies in nondestructive ways. Physical exercise often helps, as does drawing, writing, singing, grunting, dancing, jumping, or walking. Crying, sighing, hugging, and deep breathing will also accelerate the flow of energy.

In addition, we can help our children respond to strong emotions in others. Here are four response tips to pass on to your children:

* When someone you know is angry, let him vent, and keep your distance.
* When someone you know is sad, treat her as you would a crying baby. Offer physical comfort, soothing words, gentle touching, and lots of reassurance. If necessary, change the scene.
* When someone you know is afraid, help him breathe deeply, remain anchored in the present, and begin to take the next step. Encourage him to trust his inner voice. Remind him of his past successes in moving through fear.
* When someone you know is joyous, allow for whatever wildness erupts, and join in the rapture.

The best way to teach emotional support is by being emotionally supportive. A wild, giggling child at bedtime is letting go of the day's stresses with joyous abandon. Learn to welcome it. A child snuggled into bed but not ready for sleep is often carrying emotional residue from the day—a perfect opportunity for you to catch a "snapshot" of the day's events. In anticipation of these leftover emotions, you may want to wind down each evening by asking your children, "What was the best part of your day?" and "What was the worst part?" The answers will both assist in the release of feelings and help you nurture your children's capacity to self-reflect and to sort out and clarify conflicting emotions. A steady diet of hugs and soft touches—the most convincing support of all—will let your children know that whatever strong emotions may be surging through them, you care about them.

ADDITIONAL RESOURCES

Bradshaw, John. *On the Family*. Deerfield Beach, FL: Health Communications, 1988.

Czimbal, Bob, and Maggie Zadikov. *Vitamin T: A Guide to Healthy Touch*. Portland, OR: Open Book Publishing, 1991.

Faber, Adele, and Elaine Mazlish. *How to Talk So Kids Will Listen & Listen So Kids Will Talk*. New York: Avon, 1980.

Schachter, Robert. *When Your Child Is Afraid*. New York: Simon & Schuster, 1988.

APPROACH CONFLICT WITH A WIN-WIN ATTITUDE

We must evolve for all human conflict a method which rejects revenge, aggression, and retaliation. The foundation of such a method is love.
— Martin Luther King Jr.

We grew up witnessing squabbles and fights over housekeeping, sex, money, and children. One parent won, and the other lost—or, more often, both lost and misery ruled the roost. We had no idea that conflict could lead to any other outcome.

To top it off, many of us inherited the notion that conflict is abnormal—that disagreements are synonymous with full-blown battles and that discord can and should be avoided. Consequently, when we have a difference of opinion with our partners, we may refuse to state our point of view for fear of retaliation or of causing hurt feelings. We are terrified of our own anger, scared of starting a conflict that may rage out of control, or horrified at the thought of adding fuel to an already heated situation. When we are at variance with our partners, we either pretend we are not, revert to an familiar conflict style we remember from childhood, or refuse to speak our truth for fear of being disliked, facing the unknown, or finding ourselves ill equipped to resolve the issue.

Families often become mired in ineffective blaming, assertive claiming, fighting over pseudo-issues, emotional withdrawal, or angry venting. What is your conflict style? When you sense a disagreement brewing, do you move into denial, avoidance, confrontation, or problem solving? Denying or avoiding conflict leads to a relationship riddled with conflict. Confronting—through assertive and aggressive behaviors—magnifies practical problems into emotional battles. Acting assertively, you will ward off aggression by protecting your rights and feelings; acting aggressively, you will attack your partner's rights and feelings. Both these styles eclipse the underlying issue and provoke anger.

Couples cannot solve problems while angry. Discussions unfolding in the heat of anger are likely to dead-end with, "My mind is made up. Don't confuse me with the facts!" When confrontation breeds conflagration, sensitive partners will declare a time-out and agree to discuss the matter at a specific time in the near future. Time out is not about punishment; it is about *both* parties seeking the privacy needed to release tension and attempt to feel better before reengaging in resolution. To avoid deadly conflicts in the family, we must clarify our intent: are we looking to cast blame, or are we looking for solutions?

Moving toward Healthy Resolution

Deny >>>>>	Avoid >>>>>	Confront >>>>>	Problem Solve
Unaware	Fearful	Abusive, angry	Time out
Passive	Mistrustful	Blaming	Listen with respect
Submissive	Withdrawn	Assertive	Brainstorm solutions

Creating a Process for Resolving Conflicts. Have you ever experienced a time delay between engaging in an interaction and realizing that something about it wasn't quite right, or that you didn't handle it well? Such delays are common, and emerging from them, you can learn to say, "I don't know what to do about this problem" or "I'm sorry"—two of the most inspiring phrases a parent can utter.

Acknowledging that you don't know how to resolve a situation invites others to come up with ideas. Admitting that you have not handled it well and expressing your regret lets everyone off the hook. What better way is there for children to learn the cleansing power of apology and, ultimately, forgiveness?

To move toward resolution, family conflicts eventually require thoughtful discussion. A wonderful forum for this type of interchange is the family meeting. Regularly scheduled meetings can serve a dual function, helping family members solve immediate problems while preventing the buildup of hostility over unaddressed problems.

General guidelines for a family meeting are as follows:

* ☆ Begin with compliments for one another.
* ☆ Together, decide on the agenda.
* ☆ Take turns describing how you are each affected by the problem;

anyone who is not speaking should be listening actively and respectfully.

⭑ Take turns sharing insights and feedback. This practice teaches children that their opinions count.

⭑ Focus on solutions, rather than blame. All ideas are welcomed, no matter how outrageous or silly they may be. This orientation encourages creative, out-of-box thinking.

⭑ Negotiate patiently, with the understanding that everyone present has a goal in common: to offer support and solutions that are reasonable and respectful of all family members.

⭑ Arrive at clear agreements and follow-through. Acknowledge that mistakes are friends and that it will be possible to do better next time. Also decide on the process that will be used to recognize, reconcile, and resolve the situation should an agreement be broken.

⭑ Conclude by doing something fun together, such as singing songs or taking a family hike.

Building Bridges. If your temperament-based language and mode of perception are dramatically different from those of your partner, problem solving may be especially challenging. One good solution is to build bridges from one person's point of view to the other's. To build strong, sturdy B R I D G E S:

Be open to negotiating a solution. What matters is not who is right and who is wrong, but rather what solution will feel good to both of you.

Reframe. Strive for an attitudinal shift. Say to yourself, "I notice and acknowledge my feelings in reaction to you, and I choose to increase my understanding rather than get hooked into an argument."

Invite creative thinking. As the Talmud says, whenever there are only two choices, always pick the third.

Declare your truth. It is up to you to articulate your point of view to your partner.

Give positive feedback. Building on your individual strengths and on what feels right about the situation will foster the emergence of solutions.

Expect mistakes. Regard mistakes as friends capable of teaching you exactly what you need to know. This perspective will go a long way toward defusing disagreements before they become major battles.

Seek first to understand. Imagine the problem as a blank canvas that little by little fills with brush strokes as you engage in active listening. Ask questions to help complete the painting, and wait till the end before placing yourself in the picture. One person seeking to understand in this way can change the entire nature of a relationship.

Life without conflict is like a flat electrocardiogram: it spells trouble. A relationship without the ups and downs of dissent is surely in a state of critical stagnation. Disagreements, in short, are a sign of vitality—they catalyze our personal growth, deepen our relationships, and, when approached skillfully and sensitively, permit everyone to win.

Additional Resources

Books

Faber, Adele, and Elaine Mazlish. *Siblings without Rivalry*. New York: Avon, 1987.

Ury, William. *Getting Past No*. New York: Bantam Books, 1991.

Organizations

New Mexico Center for Dispute Resolution, 505-242-5966. Offers conflict resolution training manuals for grades K–12.

For more mediation resources, see page 218.

CREATE CONNECTIONS

What the [spiritual] warrior renounces is anything in his experience that is a barrier between himself and others. In other words, renunciation is making yourself more available, more gentle, and more open to others.
—Chögyam Trungpa

If there is a bottom line to the difficulties youth face today, it is that they lack connection. The large majority of teens, in particular, feel estranged from the world around them and from themselves. The good news is that binding forces introduced early in life can forge links that will last a lifetime.

Making Compost. By conditioning the "soil" of our children's lives, we can over time help our offspring establish connections in seven vital areas. The password here is C O M P O S T.

The arenas that need composting in our children's lives are:

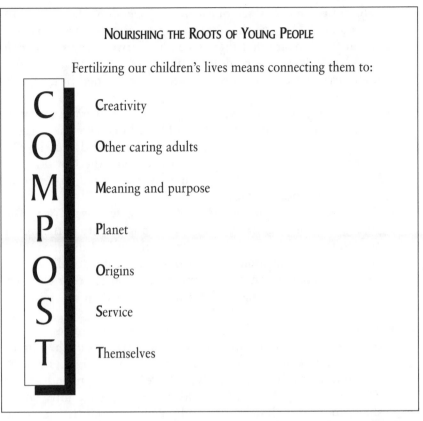

NOURISHING THE ROOTS OF YOUNG PEOPLE

Fertilizing our children's lives means connecting them to:

C Creativity

O Other caring adults

M Meaning and purpose

P Planet

O Origins

S Service

T Themselves

✴ Their own creativity. In addition to being Homo sapiens (intelligent humans), we are Homo ludens (playful humans) by virtue of our instinctual attraction to playing as a way of fostering attachment and bonding. Reading, dancing, playing, singing, and making up stories with your children will stimulate their creative capacities. Allow anything to be part of the action—cardboard boxes, crayons, watercolors, Play-Doh, Tinkertoys, and Legos, as well as real-life items from the kitchen, garden, and wood shop. Yak a lot; talk about what you are both doing. Avoid criticizing or directing your children's efforts, however; let them lead the flow of play. Also let them know that their creations are important. Exhibit them prominently around the house.

✴ Other caring adults. The primary developmental task of adolescents is to metaphorically kill their parents. The parents' job is to not retaliate! When our teenagers seem unable to listen to our counsel because they are trying to separate from us, we can at least ensure that they have one or two other supportive adults to talk to. Our adolescents are seeking, perhaps more than anything else, a sense of intimacy grounded in unconditional acceptance.

* The meaning and purpose of their lives. Teenagers often catch glimpses of their intentions after older adults have asked them such questions as "What are you up to?" "What do you love?" "What are your gifts?" "How will you make the world a better place?" and "What are you most interested in learning about at this point in your life?"

* The planet. Spending time in nature is a wonderful way for youngsters to recognize that the beauty and bounty of the world around them is always there to nurture them. So leave the malls, and head for the mountains. Go for a healing walk in the woods, or take a moment to appreciate a sunset. Your children will remember camping in a storm far better than any toy they are given.

* Their origins. Storytelling evenings can give children a sense of their personal history and of their roots. Drag out the family photo albums or cherished mementos from relatives. Tell stories about family members who have passed on and about what was going on in the world when they were alive. Also share anecdotes about your children's births and their earliest years of life.

* Community service. Participating in community and neighborhood service projects nourishes the roots of cooperation and compassion. It also illuminates the role that giving plays in the circle of receiving. Children who serve in these ways come to understand that they are part of a larger group working to make the world more beautiful.

* Themselves. Adolescence is a peak time in our children's lives for exploring the physical, mental, emotional, and spiritual aspects of their being and for finding out who they really are. To help stimulate your children's quests, let them know of your own—of the personal growth you are currently experiencing and of your sense that each of us finds a home within the great mystery of life.

Strengthening Connections through Ceremony. Ceremonies have been used throughout history to invoke change, mark transitions, celebrate, heal, commemorate, initiate, transform, and facilitate grieving. They help us accept support, alter, or confirm our beliefs, and cement our bonding with a group. Ceremonies have also been used to strengthen ties formed in each of the C O M P O S T arenas listed above, from creativity to selfhood.

Teens, even preteens, enjoy ceremonies. To demystify the essential elements involved in creating one, think back to a birthday party you have arranged for your child. Then prepare for a new kind of celebration:

* Define the purpose of the event, and set a time and place for it.
* Invite supportive witnesses, including family members, friends, angels, guides, anyone whose presence would add to the occasion.
* Open the ceremony by awakening the senses with incense, music, food, or special objects or body movements.
* Incorporate into the proceedings objects or activities that symbolize the bonding that is being honored. Bread sharing signifies the offering of basic nurturance; candle lighting suggests love overcoming darkness; flowers represent growth and beauty.
* Welcome the newly formed bond with sounds, readings, songs, prayers, hugs, holding hands in a circle, or other ceremonial gestures.
* End with appreciations, gratitude, the sharing of food, poetry, movements, prayers, or whatever will bring a memorable closure to the event.

The Role of Gangs. Parents have perennially felt disconnected from their children as they began pushing the comfort zone of the adults around them. The alienating force in the 1960s was rock 'n' roll, in the 1970s sex, and in the 1980s drugs. The major comfort-buster in the 1990s is gangs. Many parents are worried that their children may be participating in gang activity. Some youngsters are, yet more are not. The telltale signs of gang involvement appear in the following charts.

INDICATORS OF GANG INVOLVEMENT

Although many of the following indicators are innocent by themselves, together they may point to gang involvement. If your children are exhibiting several of these behaviors and if you think they may be involved with a street gang, it is a good idea to search their rooms and vehicles for illegal drugs, weapons, or other items that would confirm or deny your suspicions. Such a search is not a violation of your children's privacy; *it is your right as a parent.* You must know what is happening in the lives of your children so that you can protect them as well as the rest of the family.

Change in hair or dress style.

Not associating with longtime friends; having a new group of friends with similar hair and dress styles.

Change in places frequented with new friends, such as public parks or different clubs.

Going out with unusually large groups of people.

Increase in material possessions such as clothes, jewelry, money, or a car.

Discipline problems at school, church, or elsewhere.

A new fear of police.

Increase in confrontational behavior, such as talking back, verbal abuse, or name-calling, as well as disrespect for parental authority.

Phone threats to the family from unknown people (rival gang members).

Overly secretive about new friends—who they are, how old they are, and what they like to do.

Change in normal routines, such as not coming home after school, or staying out late at night with no explanation.

Wanting to just "cruise" in vehicles with friends, not going anywhere specific.

Suspected use of alcohol, inhalants, or narcotics.

Change in attitude about school, sports, or other age-appropriate activities.

Lower grades at school, or skipping school or certain classes.

Graffiti in your children's rooms, or on notebooks or sneakers.

Physical signs of having been in a fight, such as cuts or bruises. A new-found sense of bravado—bragging that they and their friends are too tough to "mess" with, that no one will harm them, or that they can go anywhere and do anything.

Adapted from The New Mexico Street Gang Task Force

LEVELS OF GANG INVOLVEMENT

Fantasy. The young person knows about gangs from TV, newspapers, and movies; or sees gang members "living out a fantasy." He may admire a real gang member, or the gang lifestyle.

At risk. The young person has personal knowledge of gangs and gang members, and associates casually with them; or lives in or near a gang area. He likes the gang lifestyle.

Wannabe. The young person regularly associates with gang members, and considers gangs and related activities normal or admirable. He is mentally prepared to join a gang.

Gang member in training. The young person is officially a gang member and associates almost exclusively with gangs. He participates in gang crimes and other related activities, and rejects the value systems of family and society, but is not considered hard core by the gang. He may be difficult to get out of the gang.

Hard-core member. The young person is totally committed to the gang and gang lifestyle, and rejects all other value systems. He has fully sublimated personal goals in favor of the gang's goals. He is hard core to the core.

Adapted from the Los Angeles Community Youth and Gang Services

A gang is essentially a group of people who gather together for a common purpose. Many adults, too, are in gangs—we call them Kiwanis, Rotary, or support groups of various sorts. Most of us like to have our names on the walls, more often in the form of diplomas and business signs than in scrawls of graffiti. Adult gangs further distinguish themselves from teen gangs by attempting to channel the energy of their connectedness into creative, constructive projects in lieu of criminal activity.

Gangs perform several roles in our culture. Just as the family scapegoat is blamed for problems arising in poorly functioning family units, gangs bear the blame for community and neighborhood woes. They also act out the unexpressed rage, helplessness, and hopelessness experienced by a significant segment of our population. In addition, gangs meet a variety of needs that remain otherwise unfulfilled for many adolescents, providing a sense of acceptance, belonging, companionship, stimulation and excitement, power, respect, rules and limits, security, and status, as well as leadership and older role models. In this sense, gang participation can be viewed as an adaptive response to adverse social conditions.

Gangs—more so than music, sex, and drugs—do succumb to intervention. Already, communities are redirecting the misguided energy of gangs through mediation, service projects, and business opportunities other than drug dealing. Gang *prevention* is best accomplished by ensuring that young people are well connected, inwardly and outwardly, to a series of matrices beyond mom and dad.

Additional Resources
Books
> Creighton, Allan, and Paul Kivel. *Helping Teens Stop Violence*. Alameda, CA: Hunter House, 1990.
>
> Kornhaber, Arthur. *Grandparent Power*. New York: Crown Publications, 1994.
>
> Lawson, Ann. *Kids and Gangs: What Parents and Educators Need to Know*. Minneapolis, MN: Johnson Institute, 1994.
>
> Moore, Robin. *Awakening the Hidden Storyteller*. Boston, MA: Shambhala Publications, 1991.

Magazines and Newsletters
> *Talking Talons*. A youth-leadership newsletter that uses animal stories to teach young people about caring and service. Available by calling 505-294-5188.
>
> *The Tracking Project*. A newsletter addressing a variety of outdoor experiential activities for young people. Available from John Stokes, 505-898-6967.
>
> *Under 21 Magazine*. A youth-produced publication available by calling 505-523-5664.
>
> *Youth Today: The Newspaper on Youth Work*. A bimonthly publication available from the publisher, at 1200 17th Street NW, Fourth Floor, Washington, DC 20036; 202-785-0764.

Organizations
> Academy for Educational Development, Center for Youth Development and Policy Research, 202-884-8267. Offers a variety of useful materials.

EMPHASIZE ESSENTIAL VALUES

The great malady of the twentieth century, implicated in all of our troubles and affecting us individually and socially, is loss of soul.
—Thomas Moore

What were the last words you said to your children? Were they congruent with the values you hold about life?

We often lament the loss of values in our society. Many young people, we say, are developing in a character vacuum dominated by the words *instant, now, me,* and *money.* They are floundering about, unanchored by a set of principles upon which to build their lives. Why? Because we have not taught them well.

Losing and Finding Our Values. Bitter clashes over sexual and religious issues, in particular, have relegated values to a "no man's land" far from the everyday concerns of neighborhoods, schools, and businesses. Unable to agree on *all* values, we avoid discussing *any* values. The phenomenon known as "family values," an increasingly visible exception to this trend, is only adding fuel to the fire, further polarizing us rather than bringing clarity. Values in this context appear as puritanical, punitive principles established to save us from ourselves. The premise underlying family values advocacy is that our young people need old-fashioned hardship and pain to whip them into shape. But is this really what we want for our children?

Values are actually the voices of our hearts, cultivating attitudes of mind that in turn inspire standards of action. Following our hearts, we act in ways that benefit everyone. As we walk our talk, we achieve stability in a changing world, gain a sense of balance in life, and experience inner peace. Allowing our core values to guide our interactions, we soon discover others treating *us* with the kindness and respect we show *them.*

Awakening your children to the importance of values becomes an opportunity to clarify your own. A good way to do this is to concentrate on one value at a time, all the while deepening your understanding of it and enhancing your practice of it.

Values Are Caught More Than Taught. Your children, like sponges, will absorb far more from how you conduct yourself than from what you say. To heighten their awareness of values, strive to lead a value-based life. To deepen their understanding of values, try the following activities:

    ✴ Make a list of the values you would like your children to develop. Possibilities might include compassion, cooperation, creativity, discipline, appreciation, integrity, forgiveness, respect, kindness, justice, and love. Each week introduce one of these values to them.

    ✴ Devise a "values vocabulary" to help your children grasp the meaning of each word. Rely on synonyms and antonyms for clarification. "Honesty," you might say, "has everything to do with honor, integrity, sincerity, and veracity, and nothing to do with lying, deceiving, flattery, cheating, swindling, or robbing."

★ Discuss everyday ways of applying each value. Point out examples of the value in action; praise your children each time they demonstrate it; grant weekly recognition awards; mail your children notes of appreciation; make up a song or story incorporating your children's names and the value; or post a Great Job banner by their beds.

★ Tell stories about your own adventures with each value, or tales about others who have practiced it.

★ Read your children books about famous people who embodied the value under consideration.

★ Ask questions to deepen your children's understanding of each value, and listen closely for areas of confusion. Do some acts require more courage than others? Is there a difference between lying to protect oneself and lying to protect another person?

★ Be creative. Draw, sing, dance, pantomime, sculpt, or write about each value.

★ Role-play. Ask your children how it feels when someone does, or does not, practice a particular value with them. Let them be the dog or plant that no one is respecting, the parent who has been lied to, or the person who benefits from another's courage.

★ Talk about your own core-value dilemmas. Describe difficult situations in which appropriate action was not immediately apparent. Invite your children to your workplace for a day, or spend a morning observing them at school. Let them know how important it is for them to pay attention to the details of their experience.

Values reside at the core of who we are. They shape and influence our responses to choices and challenges that come our way. Unaware of our values, we cannot proceed along the journey to wholeness. Cognizant of them, however, we become both enriched and acutely conscious of what we are really after. What better gift could there be for a child?

Additional Resources
Books

Covey, Stephen, and Roger Merrill. *First Things First: A Principle-Centered Approach to Time and Life.* New York: Simon & Schuster, 1994.

Eyre, Linda and Richard. *Teaching Your Children Values.* New York: Simon & Schuster, 1993.

Heller, David. *Talking to Your Child about God.* New York: Bantam Books, 1990.

Rozman, Deborah. *Meditation for Children.* Millbrae, CA: Celestial Arts, 1976.

Organizations
    Character Counts Coalition, 310-306-1868. Offers material on community
    and school-based approaches to teaching values.

MINIMIZE MEDIA EXPOSURE

Minds are not vessels to be filled, but fires to be set alight.
                                                    —Anonymous

Each year, children average more hours in front of TVs and videos
than they do in front of blackboards. According to current rates of media
viewing, by the time today's children finish high school, they will have
been exposed to not only 16,000 murders but hundreds of thousands of
violent acts—none of which occurred in their immediate environment.

Based on a floor-to-ceiling collection of research papers, the American Academy of Pediatrics announced in a 1985 policy statement:
"Repeated exposure to televised violence promotes a proclivity to violence and a passive response to its practice." Indeed, the large majority
of evidence indicates that, contrary to popular opinion, media violence
does not spark the cathartic release of aggressive energies, but rather
promotes *similarly violent attitudes, sentiments, and actions.*

If family peace is what we are after, we need to be highly vigilant of
the media images our children are internalizing. Just as we would think
twice about feeding their growing bodies a diet of Twinkies and Cokes,
so must we guard their psyches against a steady diet of violent cartoon
programming, R-rated knock-'em-dead videos, shoot-'em-up movies,
and beat-'em-up video games. Even without these, our children are
inundated with media messages that are incongruent with the values we
seek to nurture in them.

Sources and Effects of the Bad News. The agencies of mass communication that we refer to as "the media" include newspapers, magazines, catalogs, junk mail, product packaging, radio, 900 telephone
numbers, telemarketing, recorded music, billboards, bumper stickers,
message T-shirts, movies, television, cable, movie videos, music videos,
MTV, computer games, the Internet, virtual reality experiences, and
CD-ROM games. The list is growing by the year.

The damaging effects are too. Media viewing, with respect to our
nation's youth, has been shown to:

   ✭ Increase feelings of isolation. While absorbed in the media, chil-
      dren are unable to strengthen their personal relationships

through reading, playing, helping neighbors and friends, engaging in intergenerational contact, or simply *be*ing.

✶ Encourage ism-type thinking (as in racism and so forth) as well as abusive humor.

✶ Foster dissatisfaction by reminding children of all that is "missing" from their lives, informing them that they are not good enough, and modeling a consume-the-world perspective.

✶ Reinforce a rapacious "power over" approach to human interactions.

✶ Promote quick solutions to complex problems.

✶ Intensify perceptions of what is wrong in the world rather than what is right, and discourage children from believing they can make a difference in the world *or* in their lives.

✶ Facilitate identification with violent heroes and heroines, to the exclusion of the pain and suffering they cause. By all accounts, more media attention is given to perpetrators than to their victims.

✶ Limit the imagination and serve as an ongoing source of "brain drain."

✶ Increase the fear of stranger violence, without portraying the more prevalent reality of family violence.

✶ Give the impression that seeing images on screen is as good as experiencing them in real life. This is especially true of animal and nature shows.

Sensible Guidelines. On the bright side, the media offer entertainment and educational opportunities. In addition, the "electronic babysitter" serves as part of a parental support system, providing busy mothers and fathers with windows of free time.

Given the media's adverse effects and potential benefits, what constitutes a responsible approach to viewing? Here are some guidelines that may prove helpful:

✶ Minimize your children's involvement with media-related activities, and spend the recovered hours doing other things with them. Remember, the learning potential in real-life experience far exceeds that available through edutainment's simulations.

✶ Inaugurate media-free nights reserved for turning off everything connected to a screen and tuning in to your children. These nights are guaranteed to inspire astounding interactions.

✶ Discourage channel surfing. Tell your children to stick with a TV program if it holds their interest, and then turn it off. Be clear about the whats and whys of off-limit programs. Better yet, choose each program *with* your children, after agreeing on the number and quality of shows they may watch each week.

★ Veto double-dipping. Rule out all requests to play a game (draw, do homework) and watch TV at the same time.

★ Invite your children to talk about any TV, film, or video content that is upsetting. Emphasize the differences between make-believe and real life, how violence hurts, and other ways of solving problems.

★ Discuss advertising and promotional manipulation with your children. Help them see that marketed toys are never as sturdy, exciting, or large as they are when portrayed on screen. Look at catalogs and magazine ads together, and talk about how items are sold. Get in the habit of pressing "remote mute" during TV commercials.

★ Go beyond mainstream media mush. Stock up on high-quality videos, documentaries, games, and CD-ROMs the entire family can enjoy. Choose wisely.

★ Store the TV and computer out of the main family room, or keep them on stands that can be wheeled out of the room. Don't let an electronic device become the centerpiece of family entertainment.

★ Voice your opinions to local cable, TV, and radio stations. Let the program directors know the material you like and the areas in need of improvement.

TREAT TELEVISION AND VIDEO WITH TLC

Talk about TV shows and videos with your children, particularly those that upset them; emphasize the differences between make-believe and real life, how violence hurts, and the other ways there are of solving problems.

Look at TV and videos with your children, noting different ethnic groups, positive male and female role models, and characters who care about others.

Choose TV programs and videos with your children, including the number and quality of shows and movies they may watch.

Adapted from Action for Children's Television

War Toys and Barbie Dolls. Up until the late 1970s, children who played "good guys–bad guys" delighted in the noisy sound effects, explosions, fast action, and other dramatic elements of the game. Their enjoyment bred neither glorification of this type of play nor a desire to magnify it into a real-world preoccupation. Similarly, children playing house dabbled in the intricacies of caring for dolls, cooking elaborate "pretend meals," and other nurturing endeavors. The warm, happy feelings these activities aroused did not translate into a need to look like or act like the play objects. Nor did the aggressive play or doll play reinforce limited sex roles and stereotypes unless parents allowed it to. So why are the dynamics different now?

For one thing, children of the nineties have less time to play, more media exposure, and hence a stronger tendency to imitate what they see on screen. For another, most of the consumer toys and dolls heavily promoted through children's programming are unlike the playthings used decades ago. The nature and purpose of these items have changed: they are now designed to mimic the characters and props featured on TV shows, in movies, and in videos. Marketing strategies have also changed, placing a strong emphasis on having the *right* toys and having *lots* of them. Children, in turn, have shifted from wondering, "How creative can I be with this toy?" to asking "Can I get another, slightly different one?"

Psychologically, there is a significant difference between using a banana as a gun and firing a plastic AK-47 look-alike. The banana can become a healing wand or a disappearing rod, whereas the imitation automatic rifle can do only one thing. Entire product lines have been developed to elicit an unending lust for yet another weapon, character, or prop to enhance our children's play. Wearing character pajamas, sleeping on character-imprinted sheets, and toting notebooks and a lunch box similarly bedecked promotes an ongoing sense of being part of the action. Whether a toy is inspired by G. I Joe, Power Rangers, My Little Pony, or Barbie, its raison d'être is to get children to want to buy more. Such toys tend to be highly sex specific, reinforcing stereotypes of the male as aggressive and the female as passive, cheery, and looking pretty.

Toward a Peaceable Imagination. Play is a vital aspect of development. It invites children to exercise their creativity, combining old forms of expression in new ways; find solutions to real or imagined difficulties; and try on new roles, envision unforeseen outcomes, and adopt fresh points of view. This back-and-forth exchange between fantasy and reality helps children make sense of their experiences and begin to comprehend their capacities. War play, however, introduces a self-limiting and destruction-oriented understanding of who a child is and what he or she can do. Interestingly, the children most likely to engage in such play are those who feel threatened in some way, either by divorce, parental illness, or a stay in the hospital.

To keep play positive and help your children develop a peaceable imagination, try these tips:

★ Avoid buying single-use toys, giving them as gifts, or allowing them in your home. Tell other parents why you see these toys as destructive. To step up your protest, place warning labels on toys in department stores. Ready-made stickers are available with inscriptions that read: "Think before you buy. This is a war toy. Playing with it increases anger and violence in children. Is this what you *really* want for your child?" or "Pretty-girl toys tend to promote looking pretty and being passive as the only ends in life. Is this what you *really* want for your child?" (These stickers are available from Heartsongs Publications.)

★ If prohibition is not your style, try limitation. Negotiate a mutually acceptable number of characters to add to your children's toy collection. Encourage them to purchase these items with their own earnings. After each new product enters the household, be sure to point out how much better it looked on TV. To guard against impulse buying, establish clear expectations about when a toy will be purchased. Always be willing to talk about the values behind your decisions.

★ Cross traditional gender-role lines by buying dolls for boys and tools for girls.

★ Prioritize toys with creative potential, such as art supplies, large and small building blocks, Legos, Tinkertoys, cardboard boxes and tubes, egg cartons, clay, kitchen utensils, gardening implements, and woodworking tools.

★ Minimize war play by reducing the number of toys and situations that lead to out-of-control behavior. Respond to the warning signs of escalation, and honor your own tolerance levels for loudness, roughness, pace, and toys flying through the air. When intervening, forgo shame and blame tactics in lieu of teaching your children to distinguish between play and aggression. Let your children know that play turns to aggression the moment *any*one has stopped having fun. And be sure everyone present respects calls of "No!" "Stop!" or "Don't!"

✶ Observe your children at play. Notice the questions they seem to be tackling and the difficulties they are experiencing. Better yet, *without directing the action,* join in the fun, ask questions, and offer nonjudgmental comments.

✶ When play turns to war or detached passivity, step gently into the scene in progress and redirect your children's energy. Tell them, "Wow! So many people are injured. We need a hospital to care for them." Or "All that action must make an army hungry. Let's cook them a meal and figure out how to get supplies in here." Or "Your doll needs new furniture. Let's build her something."

The day-to-day choices we make regarding media exposure are vitally important. Part of our job as parents is to prevent as much negative fallout as possible. Another part is to let our children know *why* we are shaping their worlds in this way. As we set our sights on creating a more peaceful future, we have no better place to begin than with the imagination and intelligence of our young.

Additional Resources

Literature

Carlsson-Paige, Nancy, and Diane Levin. *Who's Calling the Shots? How to Respond Effectively to Children's Fascination with War Play and War Toys.* Philadelphia: New Society Publishers, 1993.

Children and TV: A Primer for Parents. A booklet published in 1994, available from Boys Town Books, Boys Town, NE; 800-282-6657.

Horton, Joan, and Jenni Zimmer. *Media Violence and Children: A Guide for Parents.* Washington, DC: National Association for the Education of Young Children, 1990. Available from NAEYC Information Service, 1509 16th Street, Washington, DC 20036-1426.

Kid's First! Directory. Contains reviews by adults and children of the best in children's videos. Available from the Coalition for Quality Children's Videos, 505-989-8076.

Videos

Road Construction Ahead, Fire and Rescue, and *Cleared for Takeoff.* Live-action videos for children, available from Fred Levine Productions, Department NY3C, PO Box 2284, South Burlington, VT 05407; 800-843-3686.

Organizations

Children's TV Resource and Education Center, 415-243-9943.

Surfwatch Software, 415-948-9500. Offers software designed to block objectional material on the Internet.

For more media-related resources, see page 208.

AVOID VICTIMIZATION

The root of the problem lies in a social system in which the power of the Blade is idealized, in which both men and women are taught to equate true masculinity with violence and dominance.
—Riane Eisler

The skills needed to help our children live in a more peaceful world include self-protective measures against everyday violence. Increasing numbers of children carry weapons to school to protect themselves, but this is far from a peaceful solution to rampant violence. What is needed is instruction in how to avoid being victimized—training that most adults have never received. We can provide the needed lessons by honing in on areas of personal S A F E T Y.

ANTIVICTIMIZATION SKILLS

S Sexual security

A Abduction protection

F Family chemical use awareness

E Everyday vigilance

T Theft protection

Y Youth suicide prevention

Sexual Security. The first line of sexual defense begins with the realization that children are most likely to be sexually abused by someone they know—either a relative, neighbor, friend, or babysitter. If you notice any one of these people spending time alone with your child, check out how the visit went, and observe your child's response.

To help young children defend themselves against *sexual abuse,* teach them that their bodies are theirs alone and that no one has the right to touch them if they don't want to be touched. By the same token, respect their "No!" or "Stop!" while kissing or tickling them. Don't force your children to hug or kiss people they don't want to be physical with. And help them distinguish between good touch (hugging, massaging, wrestling), bad touch (rough play that hurts, hitting, kicking, biting), and secret touch (contact that occurs in private, often accompanied by an admonition not to tell). Let your children know that if anyone tries to touch them in an area that would be covered by a bathing suit, they should say no forcefully, leave if possible, and tell an adult as soon as they can.

Sexual exploration is common and sometimes upsetting, more often to parents than to children. It is distinguished from abuse by three elements: the absence of coercion, comparable developmental or physiological ages of the children involved, and behaviors that are not usually repeated. Allow your children to talk to you about such experiences, and assure them that this type of behavior is normal. If you stumble upon them engaged in sexual play, avoid shaming them and instead try to understand what they are curious about. Always emphasize the importance of treating their bodies with respect.

Older youngsters need to know that the most common form of sexual assault is *acquaintance rape.* Of all age groups, teens are the most susceptible to this form of abuse. Acquaintance rape occurs both as an isolated incident and as part of the larger dynamic known as teen dating violence, which affects about 12 percent of all high school students. The best protective directive you can give your children is that it is *never okay for a partner or friend to hit them.*

WARNING SIGNS OF TEEN BATTERING BEHAVIOR

Jealousy	Verbal abuse
Controlling behavior	Cruelty to animals or children
Quick involvement	Dr. Jekyll and Mr. Hyde personality
Unrealistic expectations	Threats of violence
Isolation	Use of force during arguments
Blaming	Breaking or striking objects
Hypersensitivity	Always wanting to know where you are

DATING BILL OF RIGHTS

I have the right to:
- ✓ Ask for a date
- ✓ Refuse a date
- ✓ Suggest activities
- ✓ Refuse any activity
- ✓ Have my own feelings and express them
- ✓ Have my values and rights respected
- ✓ Have friends and space aside from my partner

I have the responsibility to:
- ✓ Determine my limits and values
- ✓ Respect the limits of others
- ✓ Communicate clearly and honestly
- ✓ Not violate the limits of others
- ✓ Ask for help when I need it
- ✓ Be considerate
- ✓ Tell my partner when I need affection
- ✓ Refuse attention

Adapted from the Dating Violence Anti-Victimization Program of the Texas Council of Family Violence

Because of the immense confusion about sexuality in our culture, you may find it difficult to establish an open dialogue on the subject with your youngsters. Nevertheless, it is worth every bit of the challenge. Step one is to be honest and responsive, as opposed to reactive. Do you use real terms like "penis" and "vagina" for body parts? What is your response the first time you hear them say the F word? Do you have a conversation about where they heard the word and what they think it means? Do you explain why you don't want them to use it? Or do you punish them outright and create more confusion?

Step two is to believe what your children tell you, and to make it safe for them to tell you anything that may happen. When they do, praise them for not keeping secrets, regardless of their fears. And assure them that another person's violence is never their fault, even if they did something thoughtless, such as getting drunk and accepting a ride with a stranger, or breaking a curfew or safety rule. Castigations such as "You should have (would have, could have) done it differently" serve only to revictimize the victim.

Abduction Protection. Despite the preponderance of milk-carton campaigns designed to step up the search for "missing children," the chances of a stranger-initiated child abduction occurring are about one in a million. Most abductions are carried out by noncustodial parents. And many children reported as missing have in fact run away of their own accord.

Even so, abduction precautions may prove helpful. Here are some guidelines to share with your children:

* Never get in a car driven by someone you don't know.
* Never allow yourself to be picked up from school by someone you don't know or someone your parents didn't tell you to look for. Stay with a teacher until your expected ride arrives.
* If you are ever lost in a store or other public place, ask a clerk or cashier for help. Stay with this person until the adult you were with comes to get you. (*Note:* For easy identification, print your child's name and phone number inside a belt that is worn every day.)
* If someone grabs you and tries to lead you away, do whatever you can to attract attention. Yell, call for help, or scream as loud as possible, "Let me go. You're not my parent!" or "Leave me alone. I don't live with you anymore!"
* Never hitchhike; always arrange for rides.

Family Chemical Use Awareness. Alcohol, especially beer, is often implicated in the tragedies that affect our youth. Consequently, it has become imperative for parents to share with their children information about chemical use of *all* sorts, including over-the-counter remedies, prescription medicines, legal drugs (caffeine, tobacco, and alcohol), and illegal substances (marijuana, LSD, inhalants, crack, cocaine, and heroin).

What your children will hear more than anything else in these discussions is your personal point of view. If you are unsure of your position on alcohol and drug use, or uncomfortable about your own use of chemicals, ask yourself some preliminary heart-to-heart questions: When is it acceptable to offer alcohol to a young person? What will it take to ensure that my teen *never* gets in a car with drunk driver? Why do I use drugs? Is it okay for my children to use them for the same reasons? Is alcohol essential for a party or a "good time"? If the parents of my children's friends have an approach to alcohol and drugs that differs from my own, what can I say to them?

Talk about these matters with friends and family members. Let them help you arrive at a coherent and articulate point of view. Then, in teachable moments, share your perspective on chemical use with your children. Clearly state your expectations of them.

Everyday Vigilance. Begin establishing a basic sense of watchfulness by monitoring the whereabouts of your children. Did they get home from school safely? Who is picking them up from that birthday party later in the day? Where are they going now, and with whom?

Long before your children are likely to be at home without an adult, introduce them to these *Home-Alone Rules:*

* Dial 911 if an emergency arises.
* Don't give out information over the phone unless you know who the caller is.
* If someone calls and asks for "your mother" or "your father," state, without mentioning names, "My parent is outside at the moment. Can I take a message, or would you like to call back later?" (For some children, the best guideline is: Don't answer the phone at all, or answer it only at the time you'll be calling to check on them.)
* Don't, under any circumstances, let a stranger into the house.

In addition, encourage your children to pretend they are detectives observing their surroundings. How well lit is the area? Is it run-down and filled with debris? If your neighborhood is starting to look dilapidated, get the community to clean it up. Areas that look as if no one cares are those most likely to attract crime.

Theft Protection. Teach your children theft prevention by reminding them never to leave valuables untended in public and, if possible, to avoid bringing them to school. Also show them how to center themselves in the event of a possible robbery. A good approach is to breathe deeply, relax their bodies, expand their sensory awareness, and pay attention to what is happening; the key is to expect nothing and be ready for anything. With practice in this technique, your children will be able to muster some degree of calm and confidence in a variety of threatening circumstances.

In addition, encourage your children to trust their instincts. If they feel uncomfortable in a gas station, they need to get out of it; if they feel ill at ease going into an apartment building, they need to stay out of it. Be sure they know of safe neighborhood places they can retreat to if they ever feel scared.

Finally, let your children know how to behave if an encounter should occur. *Pointer number one:* If someone wants your valuables, *do not resist.* Give up the jacket or the sneakers or the lunch money. Escalating an already threatening situation in the presence of a weapon is particularly dangerous. *Pointer number two:* If the attacker has a gun and, unsatisfied with the objects appropriated, forces you to go with him, *turn and run erratically.*

Fifty percent of all attackers do not shoot people who have given up their possessions. Of those who do, 50 percent miss their mark. Of those who shoot down their victims, 50 percent fail to hit a vital organ. Of all victims who are shot in a vital organ, 50 percent survive. In short, running erratically results in only a 5 percent chance of being killed—far better odds than getting shot at point-blank range!

Youth Suicide Prevention. To prevent the most tragic form of victimization, familiarize yourself with the symptoms of depression in young people, the warning signs of suicide, and what to do if a child is harboring a death wish. The first order of business, however, is to realize that the current method of choice for both male and female victims of youth sui-

---

WARNING SIGNS OF SUICIDE

Academic
Loss of interest in classwork, or decline in academic performance
Decrease in the amount of effort expended, or too tired to finish assignments
Giving up easily when attempting homework, or turning in unfinished or messy work

Social and Behavioral
Disruptive, risk-taking, or antisocial (lying, stealing) behavior
Withdrawing from social contact
Extreme fearfulness
Appearing tired or falling asleep
Alienating peers, or becoming unpopular

Cognitive
Inability to concentrate, or forgetfulness
Suicidal thoughts or intentions, or preoccupation with death
Indecisiveness, or lack of confidence

Emotional
Poor self-esteem
Irritability, or excessive complaining
General mood of unhappiness, or feeling guilty

Physical
Changes in sleep patterns
Ongoing pain or illness
Changes in appetite, with sudden weight gains or losses
Acting slowed down or speeded up

cide is shooting. So if your teen is depressed, get the guns out of the house until the crisis has subsided. This advice is doubly important for depressed teens who have a drug or alcohol problem.

The signs of depression are often more apparent to observant family members than to the person experiencing them. The presence of four or more of the following D E P R E S S E D symptoms, persisting for more than two weeks, is an indication that additional help or counseling is needed:

Down mood most of the time.
Energy decrease, fatigue, and a slowed-down feeling.
Pleasurable activities are no longer enjoyed.
Remembering, concentrating, and decision making are more difficult.
Eating problems.
Sleep problems.
Sense of hopelessness, helplessness, worthlessness, and guilt.
Ever recurrent aches and pains that do not respond to treatment.
Death thoughts, or a suicide plan.

Parents who talk about suicide issues with their children often help "immunize" them against it. The greatest protection we can offer is to allow the young people in our lives to voice the sadness they feel and to see that bad feelings *do* go away. We can also encourage them to reframe the experience by saying, "I feel really sad and hopeless, and I'll get through it" instead of "I want to die. I hate my life." To stave off any likelihood of tragedy, remain alert to the warning signs of suicide and the preventive measures summarized in the charts on the preceding and following pages.

These S A F E T Y strategies are a form of victimization immunization. They will prepare your children to encounter potentially dangerous situations with increased awareness and self-protective know-how. Booster doses will most likely be needed.

Additional Resources
Books
Aaron, Jane. *No More Secrets for Me.* Waltham, MA: Little Brown & Company, 1983.
Bishop, Bob, and Matt Thomas. *Protecting Children from Danger.* Berkeley, CA: North Atlantic Books, 1993.
Pipher, Mary. *Reviving Ophelia: Saving the Selves of Adolescent Girls.* New York: Ballantine Books, 1994.
Organizations and Hotlines
American Association of Suicidology, 202-237-2280.
National Adolescent Runaway Hotline, 800-621-4000. Assists young people and their families in a crisis, including potential suicide.

Basic Youth Suicide Prevention

Listen. Listening is critical, for the first person contacted may be the only one the depressed youngster will reach out to.

Accept. Take statements seriously. Don't try to convince the youngster that his or her problems are trivial.

Evaluate. If you sense a definite plan, do not leave the person alone. Youngsters who have developed a plan for suicide, and who have access to the implement of self-destruction, are at critical risk for self-harm.

Ask. If you have been given a suicidal message and are unsure of its meaning, ask the young person directly, "Have you been thinking about harming yourself?" Let the youngster know you care and are concerned enough to step in.

Support. Encourage the youngster to think back on positive events and meaningful people. Remind the young person that death is final.

Consult. Reach out for help. Contact a school guidance counselor, the local school district's suicide prevention team, a community mental health center, or the National Adolescent Runaway Hotline (see Additional Resources on page 133). Don't try to handle this alone.

Act. Avoid reacting with horror or panic to intimations of suicide. Also avoid downplaying the young person's concerns. Instead, the moment you know there is someone at risk for self-harm, call a professional or a crisis prevention team, and remain accessible and supportive.

KEEP CELEBRATING DIVERSITY

You've got to be taught
To hate and fear.
You've got to be taught
From year to year.
It's got to be drummed
Into your dear little ear.
You've got to be carefully taught.

You've got to be taught
To be afraid
Of people whose eyes are oddly made
And people whose skin is a different shade.
You've got to be carefully taught.

You've got to be taught
Before it's too late,
Before you are six or seven or eight,
To hate all the people your relatives hate.
You've got to be carefully taught.
You've got to be carefully taught.

—"Carefully Taught"
from *South Pacific*

In the midst of the 1992 riots in Los Angeles, victim Rodney King asked an essential question: "Can we all get along?" The answer is, "Not quite yet," although the United States has for 200 years prided itself on its ability to welcome diverse people from around the globe to be part of the American Dream.

Our ability to accept human differences spans a vast continuum. At one end is *bigotry*, which causes us to hate individuals who are different from ourselves, express our hatred openly and at times violently, and teach our children to hate. A bit further along the continuum is *prejudice*, which fosters a sense that groups other than our own are inferior and are to be avoided; contact with people in these groups is minimized and often fear based, and actions are usually discriminatory.

MOVING TOWARD THE CELEBRATION OF DIVERSITY

Bigotry >>>> Prejudice >>>> Tolerance >>>> Cultural >>>> Celebration
of Differences   Awareness   of Diversity

Tolerance promotes an ability to accept others as they are; although individual differences are acknowledged and unfamiliar people are less rigidly stereotyped, not much effort is given to increased awareness and contact. *Cultural awareness,* the next niche along the continuum, motivates us to actively seek out knowledge about people who are different from us and to honor their customs and worldviews. *Celebration of diversity*—the most complete expression of "welcome"—fosters both the perception of ongoing contact as a gift and the knowledge that a variety of perspectives and traditions leads us back to our essential similarities as humans.

The more we practice the principles of G E T A L O N G , the closer our children will come to celebrating diversity in their lives. Here are the principles that may well create a new reality in the next generation.

HOW TO BE TOGETHER

G Get in touch with your stereotypes.

E Explore different cultures.

T Talk about isms.

A Acquire allies.

L Look at people in new ways.

O Offer your children real-life experiences in diversity.

N Notice the cultural milieu in schools.

G Grab every opportunity to expand multicultural awareness.

Get in Touch with Your Stereotypes. Only by tapping into them will you be able to cast them out of your life, and out of your child's as well. To locate your stereotypes, try the following activities:

* ✶ Complete this sentence as honestly as possible: "Black (White, Asian, Hispanic, Gay, Lesbian, Jewish, American Indian) people are ———."
* ✶ Make a list of your preconceptions about people. Tell your children how you have tried to move beyond these senseless, fearful ways of seeing other people. Explain, too, that mind-sets of this sort hurt other people, foster prejudice, and spark gender and racial discrimination.
* ✶ Think back on your childhood environment. Were pejorative terms such as *nigger, spick, honky, whop,* and *chink* used casually, or spoken in anger? Was the rule of thumb to stick with your own kind to be safe?

Seeing the effects of judgments we were exposed to in our formative years helps us understand how others were similarly affected. Early television, for example, routinely reinforced stereotypical thinking and taught us to fear or make fun of people who were different. In today's popular media, "bad guys" still wear dark colors or have accents or dark skin. In states around the nation, women still make less money than men in the same lines of work, and gays and lesbians are still persecuted. Compared with earlier generations of TV viewers, we are more aware of cultural bias, yet we remain trapped in many of the same discriminatory behaviors.

Explore Different Cultures. Bring the ways of the world's people—their holidays, foods, and artistic expressions—into your home. Read books and children's stories by authors from a wide range of ethnic groups; listen to their voices live or on audiocassette. Buy ethnically diverse toys, dolls, musical instruments, games, and art supplies. As you incorporate cultural diversity into family life, your children will learn to appreciate passions and mysteries they may have never imagined. And they will discover that "differences" are enriching, or at the very least something to be curious about.

Talk about Isms. Anytime your children are at the receiving end of a discriminatory remark or practice, encourage them to express their feelings aboout the incident. Tell them that they are good people, that anyone who judges them without knowing them is showing ignorance, and that bias of any sort is a sure sign of an undeveloped mind and a wounded spirit. Also remind them that they are not the only victims of hatred.

Conclude by saying, "Never play out a role scripted by someone else. What you make of your life is up to you."

In addition, speak out against racist and sexist jokes or remarks whenever you hear them from your children or anyone else. Children become aware of differences at a very young age and often comment on them at the supermarket, in the street, and at home. These remarks can open the door to discussion. "That girl sure has slanty eyes" is an accurate observation that can be used to heighten wonder and curiosity. "Ketema sure has funny hair" or "Mario brings weird food for lunch" reveals a trace of judgment, offering an opportunity to further explore the meaning of differences. Comments such as "All blacks (whites, Indians, Germans, kids, grown-ups, teachers, cops) are sneaky (lazy, bad, stuck up, cheap, rip-off artists, mean, liars)" call for an explanation about the fact that insults hurt and are rooted in inaccurate impressions.

After hearing slurs of any sort, do not opt for silence, imagining that your children don't understand what they are saying or that they are "just going through a passing phase." A nonresponse from you will only imply acceptance. Conversely, do not blast your children for speaking in this way. Your job is to inquire, not to prosecute. You might say, simply: "I'm concerned about what you just said. What do you mean?"

Your children will be quick to pick up ism-type thinking from the adults they meet. When you hear visitors or house guests utter inflammatory remarks, you can say, "Would you mind repeating that?" or "That's a hurtful statement, and I don't like such talk in my house." If bigoted or prejudiced relatives are coming to visit, discuss their attitudes ahead of time to prepare your children for the encounter.

Acquire Allies. The major reason children grow up fearing people unlike themselves is simply lack of prior contact. Having no familiarity with such people, they are left to form judgments based on inaccurate media portrayals as well as anxiety-provoking gossip. Today's shifting economy and demographics, however, are forcing people of all backgrounds to rub up against one another. As a result, we are in a unique position to expand our circle of friends and enlarge our notion of extended family.

To broaden our circle of contacts, we must be willing to get beyond the false pictures we have of other cultures. Not all Asian people, after all, are from Japan or China. Not all white people have roots in England or Germany. Many black people identify more with Caribbean customs than with African ones. American Indian tribes each have their own customs, beliefs, and languages or dialects. Breaking through our assumptions and getting to know people with skin coloring or facial features different from our own, we begin building bridges of trust. At the same time, our stereotyped perceptions of *groups* become replaced by real perceptions of *individuals*.

Does your life reflect contact with diverse people? Who comes to your house for dinner, plays with your children in the park, smiles back at you from your refrigerator door?

As more time passes we become not only friends but *allies*, fully acknowledging the oppression others have known and working together to overcome it. At this point, we begin to see the interconnectedness between the attitudinal cages we *each* live in, the pain embedded not only in racism but also in sexism, classism (rich is good), elitism (rich with a degree is better), adultism (young people are nothing but trouble), heterosexism, ableism (avoid contact with the differently abled), anti-Semitism and other forms of religious intolerance, nationalism, even anthropocentrism (the human species is the crowning jewel of evolution).

Being an ally entails taking a stand, agreeing to be occasionally misunderstood or unpopular, and supporting changes that nourish relationships defined by "power with," as opposed to "power over." Being in alliance with another means sharing information, organizational resources, financial assets, and leadership roles with—and for—each other.

Look at People in New Ways. *Every* encounter is really a cross-cultural meeting, for no two people have similar histories and perceptions. Any two people may, however, share many other attributes, such as physical characteristics, a love of family, or an affinity for certain foods or modes of artistic expression. To reinforce this perspective in your children, notice the people you pass together on the street, in airports and bus terminals, and on the playground. Then spend time talking about the qualities, traits, or characteristics these people have in common. People-watching is fun, and a wonderful way to increase the acceptance of differences.

Human populations are in many ways homogeneous, but we are easily diverted from acknowledging our commonality. Have you ever attempted to muddle through difficult times by convincing yourself that other people are inferior to you? If so, you are not alone. We all have a tendency to project our anger and frustration onto others. We are also accustomed to seeing others as either successful or unsuccessful, inherently well equipped to live in a postindustrial society or sorely lacking in basic qualities.

To break out of these routines and into the common ground we share with others is quite simple. All it takes is a willingness to look at another person and say to ourselves, "Just like me, this person wants happiness and hopes to avoid suffering." Feelings of compassion and connectedness are sure to follow.

Offer Your Children Real-Life Experiences in Diversity. Take your children into the world, and bring the world into your home. Go to a museum show on African art. Listen to Caribbean music, then eat at a local Asian restaurant. If your children have been curious about a neighbor who is blind, invite her for tea. Get them pen pals from other countries. Host a foreign exchange student. Attend a variety of spiritual or religious celebrations. Gather together in the kitchen, and cook gourmet dishes from around the world. Include older and younger friends in family events. Help boys and girls have fun doing all sorts of things together—beading, playing ball, reading stories, planting seeds, painting, dancing, cooking, and building, Encourage your children to "adopt" a schoolmate as a brother or sister, so that they can share each other's histories and customs.

Notice the Cultural Milieu in Local Schools. From daycare through high school, there is much to examine. How does the ethnic composition of the faculty compare with that of the student body? Do classrooms have culturally diverse books, posters, art materials, and toys? Are the dress-up and dramatic play props representative of different cultures? What's on the bulletin boards? Are the textbooks free of racial and sexual stereotypes? How about the social studies curriculum? Is the music program culturally diverse? What songs are taught? How do teachers respond to name-calling?

Grab Every Opportunity to Expand Multicultural Awareness. Use the teachable moments in each day to discuss human differences and augment intercultural contact. Permeated with a multitude of exposures, your children will no doubt overcome any xenophobic tendencies they may have, and will stop disliking or fearing that which is different simply *because* it is different.

Bigotry has set us miles apart from one another. Many of us have painful memories of being ignored or made fun of because of some unacceptable "difference." Consequently, the notion of viewing differences as *positive* attributes seems to require a big leap in understanding.

And yet, it beckons. In fact, it is our sole means of releasing the baggage of bias we have been carrying for decades. Healing comes with the knowledge that the fabric of a celebrated diversity is woven over time by the little actions we take each day.

Additional Resources

Copage, Eric. *Black Pearls for Parents.* New York: William Morrow, 1995.

Hockenberry, John. *Moving Violations, War Zones, Wheelchairs, and Declarations of Independence.* New York: Hyperion, 1995.

Hopson, Dr. Darlene Powell, and Dr. Derek S. Hopson. *Raising the Rainbow Generation.* New York: Simon & Schuster, 1993.

Martin, April. *The Lesbian and Gay Parenting Handbook.* New York: Harper & Row, 1993.

Matiella, Ana Consuelo. *Positively Different: Creating a Bias-Free Environment for Young Children.* Santa Cruz, CA: Network Publications, 1991.

Teaching Tolerance Magazine. Published by The Southern Poverty Law Center, 400 Washington Avenue, Montgomery, AL 36104.

ENGAGE IN BULLYPROOFING

If we could read the secret history of our enemies, we should find in each man's life sorrow and suffering enough to disarm all hostility.
                                          —Henry Wadsworth Longfellow

About 10 percent of students in the United States are victims of bullying. Approximately 50 percent of school-yard bullies become criminals, 25 percent of whom are charged with serious offenses. A large percentage of these ex-school-yard bullies exhibit patterns of abusive parenting, giving rise to a new generation of bullies.

Bullying is not a niggling "boys will be boys" activity. It is a highly destructive behavior that demands intervention. The playground bully, in an enlightened setting, summons a wide range of helping responses, none of which are punitive and all of which impart pro-social values and a call for immediate reform.

Bullying is commonplace not only in schools, but in families, neighborhoods, and international relations. Indeed, by definition, bullying is *any behavior by a person, group, or nation that physically or emotionally intimidates and violates another person, group, or nation.*

Despite the soaring number of individuals determined to push others around to get what they want when they want it, *no one is born a bully;* bullying is a learned behavior. Children learn how to bully from adults, and grow up to become adult bullies bent on asserting their power over others through words, gestures, or actions.

All these modes of expression appear along the continuum of bullying visible in school and neighborhood environments. This continuum extends from put-downs, name-calling, taunts, ethnic slurs, rumors or slander, and shunning or ostracizing, to aggressive body language and threats, to petty theft, extortion of lunch money, territorial bans, harsh pranks, jostling in corridors and alleyways, assault, and sexual molestation.

Here a Victim, There a Victim. A child who has encountered bullying at the "physical aggression" end of the continuum may come home with cuts, bruises, torn clothing, or missing clothes—new garments that "got lost." Children who run up against bullying in any form invariably feel some combination of anger, shame, humiliation, anxiety, powerlessness, and fear. Over time they may show evidence of low-self-esteem, withdrawal, a conception of the world as threatening and unfair, declining study habits or grades, or increasing timidity, fearfulness, and sadness.

Bystanders can also be affected and, to protect themselves, may steer clear of "danger" zones, such as school bathrooms, school-yard corners, locker areas, and certain hallways. Some become physically ill from the stress, skip school, or feign sickness to avoid going to school. Bystanders as well as children who are picked on are victims in need of support. They are not, however, the only ones who are suffering.

A bully is a victim in disguise, who often feels hurt, angry, afraid, and frustrated. Most bullies are abused by caretakers who apply rules inconsistently, relish in extensive physical punishment, have negative attitudes toward their charges, neglect to monitor their whereabouts, and fail to teach them social skills. Although typically large for their age, bullies lack a sense of personal power, and will therefore create situations in which they can feel strong and superior. When they are afraid, upset, or desperately needing to prove themselves in some way, they act tough. This habitual approach to stress tends to momentarily satisfy their needs.

Sometimes bullies think they are being bullied, and will attack their perceived foe to save face. At other times they act menacing, in an attempt to unload their shame and humiliation onto another person. Like any misbehaving child, they crave attention—which eventually does come their way. The problem is that they seek to fulfill their desires for recognition at the expense of others. Until children and adults alike succeed in giving them the *positive* attention they need, they will continue to act out.

Bullyproofing. Helping our children deal effectively with bullies is a two-part process. First we need to teach them to differentiate between the behavior and the person, the bullying and the bully. Prepared to pay close attention to the bully, our children will be able to see these encounters from a new viewpoint. The salient concern will be, *What does this person really need in this situation?*

Our next task is to give our children a toolbox of effective responses—namely, flee, fight, or flow. Tools for fleeing, also referred to as *flight strategies,* consist of avoiding the bully, ignoring the taunts (but not the person), turning one's back and walking away, or letting out a loud, sharp yell such as "No!" "Help!" "Yikes!" or "Kiai!"—a martial arts word that is said to produce a powerful energy force capable of momentarily distracting an assailant and thereby allowing the defender to get away.

The most helpful *fight strategies* are assertive moves. One approach is to defy the mutually understood keep-it-secret rule by asking for adult help. Seeking assistance acknowledges that bullying is a violation of the community, and not just the individual. An alternative approach is to take a stand by making it clear physically and verbally that one is not going to let the bully do damage. A third option is to adopt a martial stance; leaving a way for the bully to save face in front of onlookers, one can say, "I know you'll win if you fight me, so why bother?"

Losing one's temper, name-calling, or resorting to aggressive strikes will only escalate the action. Standing up for one's rights and holding one's ground will not. Because most bullies expect to arouse fear and anger, the lack of hostility is apt to defuse the situation.

Flow strategies accentuate a continuous transfer of energy. One possibility is to make friends with the bully by being kind and showing respect, while refusing to give in to demands. Telling a joke or being funny can likewise break the tension and change the outcome. Negotiating sometimes works, as in "I won't give you my homework, but I'll help you with yours, and then you can show me how to do that basketball stuff you're so good at." The object is to appeal to the person's inner strength and goodness, and to let it be known that, because you have higher expectations of the bully, the behavior must stop. At times, this may mean agreeing with the insults. Children who have learned to protect themselves from angry energy directed their way (see pages 62–64) won't get hooked, and will be able to take insults as easily as a deeply rooted tree bends in a strong wind.

Creative conning is another flow tool. Duping strategies consist of pretending to have a contagious illness, acting as if a parent is about to arrive on the scene, or casually mentioning an older cousin who lives in town and has a black belt in karate.

Are Your Children Being Bullied? If so, encourage them to tell you about their experiences. Create a safe place in which they can share the many feelings associated with victimization. Be careful, however, of your responses. If you are secretly glad when your children get in physical fights, you may inadvertently reinforce combative behaviors and undermine your goals. Fighting is, after all, a sign of weakness, a measure to be resorted to only when all other strategies have been exhausted; the goal in such a situation is to protect oneself without inflicting harm.

To keep your responses helpful, give your children each of the tools described above. Also try role-playing games in which they take on the parts of both bully and victim. If put-downs are an issue, record the most upsetting remarks and reframe each one in positive terminology. That way, if the verbal blows are delivered again, your children will be able to summon up the new, empowering versions of them.

The playground bully need not keep us awake at night. With patience and practice, we can help defuse the agitation on both sides of these confrontations. As for our children, they can be bullyproofed. Armed with flight, fight, and flow tools, they can learn to see themselves no longer as victims but as warrior peacemakers.

Additional Resources

Books
> *Aikido and the New Warrior*. Edited by Richard Strozzi. Berkeley, CA: North Atlantic Books, 1985.
>
> Doyle, Terrence Webster. *Why Is Everybody Always Picking on Me? A Guide to Handling Bullies*. Middlebury, VT: Atrium Society Publications, 1991.

Scripts
> *The Legend of the Bullyproof Shield* by Arthur Kanegis. A rock opera score available for school or community performances from Future Wave, 505-982-8882.

REINFORCE RESILIENCY

In the midst of winter
I find in myself at last
Invincible summer.
                                        —Zen Master Soen

Why do some children who grow up under the most adverse conditions possible turn out to be healthy, valuable contributing members of society? What factors have enabled them not only to survive but to thrive? Answers to these questions are beginning to pour in from many fields of child development research. Pooling together findings based on belief systems, environmental supports, personal capacities, and developmental attributes, we can access an all-encompassing picture of the characteristics of resiliency. More importantly, we can reinforce these traits in our own children and others we know so that they, too, will be equipped to overcome adversity.

Psychological Hardiness. This concept, developed by psychologist Suzanne Kobasa, clarifies why some children remain healthy in the face of significant stress. The factors of resiliency that contribute to psychological hardiness are commitment, control, and challenge—each of which emerges from an acquired belief system and, with practice and reinforcement, becomes a personalized mind-set. *Commitment,* the capacity to be fully involved in whatever is happening, arises from the belief that there is purpose and meaning behind life's occurrences. It fosters an attitude of no-resistance to unfolding events; curiosity and acceptance will get one through whatever highs and lows may be encountered in manifesting a goal, dream, or vision. Committed people approach rather than avoid, and are engaged in their surroundings rather than alienated from them.

Control emerges from the belief that one has influence over the changing aspects of life. In the event that circumstances cannot be controlled, say adherents, one can always choose how to react to them. People in control see their intentions as being continually shaped and strengthened by their imagination, knowledge, choices, and creative abilities.

Challenge is rooted in the belief that change is more prevalent than stability, and that change can be a stimulating incentive to growth, rather than a threat to security. Challenge prompts one to find the gift hidden in any hardship, and to use it for self-improvement.

The net effect of psychological hardiness is a reversal of the power-lessness and helplessness felt in response to unpredictable and unex-pected events. For psychologically hardy people, these become growth experiences.

Protective Factors. According to a multitude of research, safeguards against risky behaviors occur at the individual, family, school, and com-munity levels. *Individual protective factors* include a sense of humor and the ability to have fun; a healthy sense of detachment ("Oh, yes, my mom is drunk again . . . but it's *her* problem and has nothing to do with *me*"); and the presence of at least one healthy significant adult, not necessarily a parent, who provides a strong sense of bonding, nurtur-ance, and a mirror reflecting other realities. Buffered by these elements, a resilient child works well, plays well, loves well, and expects well.

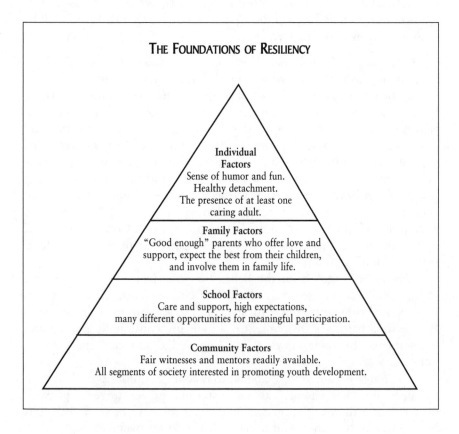

THE FOUNDATIONS OF RESILIENCY

Individual
Factors
Sense of humor and fun.
Healthy detachment.
The presence of at least one
caring adult.

Family Factors
"Good enough" parents who offer love and
support, expect the best from their children,
and involve them in family life.

School Factors
Care and support, high expectations,
many different opportunities for meaningful participation.

Community Factors
Fair witnesses and mentors readily available.
All segments of society interested in promoting youth development.

Family protective factors are provided by "good enough" parents who more than half the time furnish a healthy environment by practicing the *Seven Ls of Childrearing*, which are as follows:

* ✶ Love your children unconditionally. You may not like what they do, but always love them and let them know it. Express affection often, both physically and verbally.
* ✶ Listen to them. They will tell you when they are not getting their needs met, when they are carrying a secret, and what the best and worst parts of their day have been like. Listening with respect to their ideas and problems is a way of inviting their active participation in family life.
* ✶ Limit them. Boundaries are for "bouncing up against" in the process of discovering who they are. Proceed by first setting limits in your own life.
* ✶ Laugh *with* them, not *at* them.
* ✶ Let them live. Let go of inappropriate expectations, remembering that two year olds act like two year olds, not five year olds.
* ✶ Learn from your mistakes. Feedback is the breakfast of champions, and mistakes are friendly invitations to try again. Provide a mirror to reality so that your children will know they are growing and learning.
* ✶ Lead them to increasing independence. A parent's job is to give over a little power every year and to show how to take on the responsibility that comes with it. Expect the best.

School protective factors consist of a caring and supportive environment with high expectations as well as numerous opportunities for participation. Among them is an extensive after-school program in keeping with the interests of a diverse group of students.

Chief among the *community level factors* are fair witnesses—people who inform mistreated children that what is happening to them is not right, not fair, not customary, not their fault, and not the way their lives will always be. Seeing reality through this lens, children realize they are not crazy and come to understand they are living in a difficult family system that they will someday leave. An understanding of this sort becomes a psychic life-raft to hold on to in hard times.

One of America's greatest myths is that we each make it on our own. In reality, we have each "made it" with the assistance of older, caring adults who have reached out a hand to us when we were in need. And now it is *our* turn to reach out a hand to the next generation.

The Significant Seven Characteristics. Young people who succeed in avoiding risky behaviors and accomplishing their goals, according to author Stephen Glenn, have seven characteristics in common; these include perceptions as well as skills. The perceptions, or inner strengths, are illuminated in such statements as "I am capable of doing things well," "I contribute in meaningful ways," "People need me," and "I can influence what happens in my life." Skills encompass a variety of abilities, including self-discipline, emotional understanding, emotional expression, making friends, taking responsibility, and anticipating the consequences of personal actions. Together, these perceptions and skills form a solid bedrock for the growth of self-esteem.

THE SIGNIFICANT SEVEN: THE ESSENCE OF SELF-ESTEEM

Strong perceptions of personal capabilities. The ability to say, "I am capable."

Strong perceptions of significance in primary relationships. The ability to say, "I contribute in meaningful ways, and I am genuinely needed."

Strong perceptions of personal power of influence over life. The ability to say, "I can influence what happens to me."

Strong intrapersonal skills. The ability to understand personal emotions, develop self-discipline and control, and learn from experiences.

Strong interpersonal skills. The ability to work with others and develop friendships through communication, cooperation, sharing, empathizing, and listening.

The ability to respond to everyday life with responsibility, adaptability, and flexibility.

Strong judgmental skills. The ability to use wisdom and to evaluate situations according to appropriate values.

Adapted from the work of Stephen Glenn and Jane Nelson

Every day, in small ways, we can foster these characteristics in the young people we encounter. We can ask for their assistance, praise a job well done, offer choices that will help them develop judgment, and encourage them to reflect on their emotions and communicate their feelings.

Developmental Assets. Peter Benson of the Search Institute uncovered a series of protective factors after studying risky behaviors in more than a quarter of a million students in grades six through twelve. The more of these factors the children had, the less likely they were to veer off into alcohol and tobacco use, suicide, aggressive behaviors, sexual diseases, pregnancy, and drunken driving.

He classified these prototective factors into external and internal assets, explicitly acknowledging the contributing role played by family and community. The *external assets* are support (parental involvement in the young person's life), boundaries (parental monitoring and expectations), and structured time use (extracurricular and community activities). The *internal assets* reflect attitudes and values the children themselves developed, such as educational commitment (school performance and desire to achieve), positive values (concern for others), and social competence (ability to make friends, plan, and be assertive).

The resiliency perspective focuses on strengths and seeks to expand on the positive potential that already exists within our children, that is part and parcel of who they really are. We reinforce this potential each time we create structure for them and give them our support and encouragement, each time we walk the way of the peacemaker.

Additional Resources

Books

Benard, Bonnie. *Fostering Resiliency in Kids: Protective Factors in the Family, School, and Community.* San Francisco: Western Regional Center for Drug-Free Schools and Communities, 1990.

Burns, E. Timothy. *From Risk to Resiliency.* Dallas, TX: Marco Polo Publications, 1994.

Glenn, Stephen, and Jane Nelson. *Raising Children for Success.* Fair Oaks, CA: Sunrise Press, 1987. Available from the Center for Youth Development and Research Policy, 202-884-8267.

Wolin, Steve and Sybil. *The Resilient Self: How Survivors of Troubled Families Rise above Adversity.* New York: Villard Books, 1993.

Organizations

Center for Youth Development and Policy Research, 202-884-8267.

Search Institute, 800-888-7828. Offers a variety of books and videos about empowering youth and understanding assets.

Western Regional Center for Drug-Free Schools and Communities, 800-547-6339 or 503-275-9500.

THIRTY DEVELOPMENTAL ASSETS

Asset Type	Asset Name	Asset Definition
EXTERNAL ASSETS		
Support	1. Family support	Family life provides high levels of love and support
	2. Parents as social resources	Student views parents as accessible resources for advice and support
	3. Parent communication	Student has frequent, in-depth conversations with parents
	4. Other adult resources	Student has access to nonparent adults for advice and support
	5. Other adult communication	Student has frequent, in-depth conversations with nonparent adults
	6. Parent involvement in schooling	Parents are involved in helping student succeed in school
	7. Positive school climate	School provides a caring, encouraging environment
Boundaries	8. Parental standards	Parents have standards for appropriate conduct
	9. Parental discipline	Parents discipline student when a rule is violated
	10. Parental monitoring	Parents monitor "where I am going and with whom I will be"
	11. Time at home	Student goes out for "fun and recreation" three or fewer nights per week
	12. Positive peer influence	Student's best friends model responsible behavior
Structured Time Use	13. Involved in music	Student spends one hour or more per week in music training or practice
	14. Involved in extra-curricular activities	Students spends one hour or more per week in school sports, clubs, or organizations
	15. Involved in community organizations or activities	Student spends one hour or more per week in organizations or clubs outside of school
	16. Involved in church or synagogue	Student spends one our or more per week attending programs or services
INTERNAL ASSETS		
Educational Commitment	17. Achievement motivation	Student is motivated to do well in school
	18. Educational aspiration	Student aspires to pursue post-high school education (trade school, college)
	19. School performance	Student reports school performance is above average
	20. Homework	Student reports six hours or more of homework per week
Positive Values	21. Values helping people	Student places high personal value on helping other people
	22. Is concerned about world hunger	Student reports interest in helping to reduce world hunger
	23. Cares about people's feelings	Student cares about other people's feelings
	24. Values sexual restraint	Student values postponing sexual activity
Social Competence	25. Assertiveness	Student stands up for what she or he believes in
	26. Decision-making skills	Student is good at making decisions
	27. Friendship-making skills	Student is good at making friends
	28. Planning skills	Student is good at planning ahead
	29. Self-esteem	Student has high self-esteem
	30. Positive view of personal future	Student is optimistic about his or her personal future

Reprinted with permission from Peter L. Benson, *The Troubled Journey: A Portrait of 6th–12th Grade Youth* (Minneapolis, MN: Search Institute, 1993)

The Fifth Path

THE WAY OF CREATIVITY

TEN STEPS TO COMMUNITY INVOLVEMENT

Create more Kodak moments in the community commons

Reach out and mentor someone

Envision schools as caring communities

Act on the assumption that schools deserve to be safe

Transcend traditional beliefs

Invent new forms of compassionate service

Value people in the workplace

Invite collaborative business "ventures"

Team up for crisis intervention

Yield to the need for arks of peace

*Community means strength that joins our strength to do the work
that needs to be done. Arms to hold us when we falter. A circle of
healing, a circle of friends. Someplace where we can be free.*

—Starhawk

I WATCH A YOUNG MAN'S FACE LIGHT UP DURING A CHANCE ENCOUNTER IN THE woods, simply because he remembers me from a high school support group I facilitated the previous year. He is doing better now, still in school and surviving difficult family dynamics. Awed by the task and grateful for the opportunity, I take on a room full of priests and ministers. We focus on their role in preventing violence. Feeling a bit like a salesman, I make the rounds of local businesses, seeking support for a communitywide Week of Peace. The generous outpouring of gift certificates is heartening to see. Each of these exchanges heightens my appreciation for the creative involvement people have with one another.

Living in the same area or having interests in common is the glue that binds people together in community. The more points of contact any constellation of people has, the more cohesive its bonds will be—and the more the community will flourish.

Most of us participate in an array of associations, such as school committees, businesses, service organizations, spiritual groups, and the "commons." Each one that is vital and healthy exudes a boundless willingness to make a difference, to engage in socially responsible actions. This path offers possibilities for creative interactions within whatever domain we call our community.

CREATE MORE KODAK MOMENTS IN THE COMMUNITY COMMONS

How shall I achieve a living balance between the mundane and the holy? Between humor and grief? Between what is and what might be? Between self-concern and concern for the common good? Between the worst that I often am and the best I might well become? And is it really possible to do unto others as I'd have them do unto me, and why is it so damn hard?
—Robert Fulghum

The golden rule of treating others as we would like to be treated has become difficult to abide by because we have become increasingly isolated from the "others" in our world. The centers of our towns and cities are either teeming with agitation or deserted because people are too busy to be neighborly. Lacking contact with elders and young people, we fail to respect them both. Trapped in a pattern of working too much, we fail to respect ourselves. We feel, in short, empty and lonely.

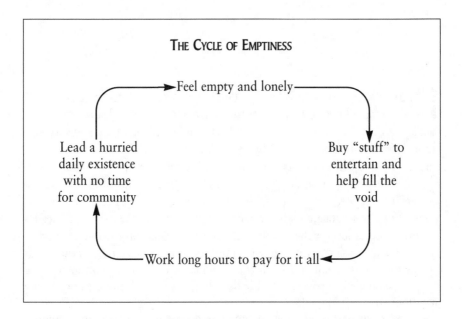

Aware of the separation crisis, many Americans are finding innovative ways of breaking through the barriers. Millions of people have begun donating an hour or more of their time each week to causes they consider worthy. They are assisting in activities at their local library, homeless shelter, hospital, food kitchen, nursing home, senior citizen center, police department, or social service agency. They are contributing in these ways because it enlarges their sense of meaning and purpose, because they enjoy being with people, because it helps them feel connected to the community, and because they are well aware that in the giving is receiving.

In response to this wave of volunteerism, a new phenomenon is cropping up: around the depersonalized zone in the center of many towns and cities are a number of community commons. These peaceful gathering places are filled with the joy and satisfaction of people getting to know one another.

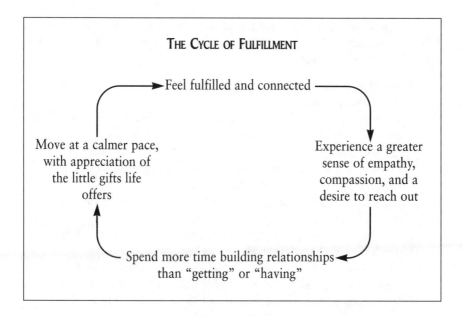

THE CYCLE OF FULFILLMENT

Feel fulfilled and connected

Move at a calmer pace, with appreciation of the little gifts life offers

Experience a greater sense of empathy, compassion, and a desire to reach out

Spend more time building relationships than "getting" or "having"

Enhancing the quality of our daily interactions in little ways can collectively make a big difference. To nurture the community commons, activate the principles of H E L P—wherever help is needed, whenever you can.

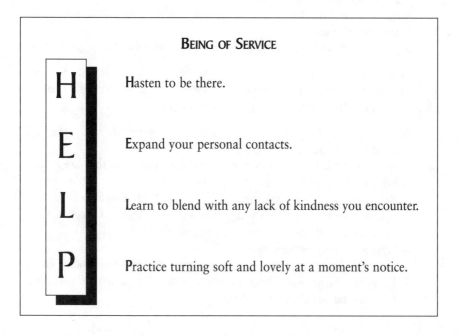

BEING OF SERVICE

H

Hasten to be there.

E

Expand your personal contacts.

L

Learn to blend with any lack of kindness you encounter.

P

Practice turning soft and lovely at a moment's notice.

Hasten to Be There. Small gestures of caring form the web of the commons. Fibers of connectedness are woven each time a hand is extended to someone in need. To be there for others:

★ Adopt a family.

★ Be a foster parent.

★ Offer to spend time with the children of a single parent you know through your office, place of worship, or social networks.

★ Offer to watch a stressed-out neighbor's kids for an hour.

★ Cook a meal for a neighbor grappling with the aftereffects of childbirth, illness, divorce, or a death in the family.

★ Regularly assist an elderly neighbor by washing the car, taking out the trash, or helping with grocery shopping.

★ Give blankets to the homeless, or bring them a meal and talk with them; give a toy to a homeless child.

★ Clean out the closets and donate clothes your family will never wear again to a local rummage sale, the Salvation Army, or Open Hands.

★ Spend time with someone who has AIDS or another chronic illness.

★ Visit people in prison or in the hospital.

★ Pick up trash that isn't yours.

★ Organize a neighborhood cleanup.

★ If you notice a driver having car trouble, stop and ask, "Would you like me to call someone for you?"

★ Write to the local paper or radio station about a community issue you're concerned about.

★ Join a community policing effort or a neighborhood watch group.

Expand Your Personal Contacts. The commons is strengthened by people knowing people. Reaching out in little ways allows trust to form and relationships to deepen. To enlarge your circle of acquaintances:

★ Get to know the people on your block or in your apartment building, condo complex, or trailer park.

★ Borrow and lend with your neighbors. Give eggs when they are needed; ask for honey when your honey pot runs dry.

★ Bring your neighbors little gifts, such as veggies from your garden, newly ripened fruit from a tree in your yard, or cuttings from your plants. Cook extra food for dinner, and surprise a neighbor with a meal.

★ Start a monthly potluck club.

★ Share festivities with someone who is home alone over the holiday season.

★ Exchange names and phone numbers with your immediate neighbors; learn the names of their children.

★ Ask about a neighbor's culture.

★ Pick one elderly resident near you, and check in daily by phone.

★ Smile and say hello to all the neighbors you encounter; stop and chat for a moment.

★ Be a "welcome wagon" for new folks in your neighborhood.

★ Regularly thank your local service providers: the police, garbage collectors, mail carriers, and school traffic crossing guards.

★ Host a neighborhood gathering in your front yard.

★ Organize a block party.

★ Start a tool-sharing, babysitting, or bulk-food purchasing co-op.

★ Create a community garden.

★ Set up a centrally located community bulletin board, or an electronic one.

★ Meet friends in the neighborhood park. If it is overrun by gangs or drugs, launch a Take Back the Park initiative.

Learn to Blend with Any Lack of Kindness You Encounter. When people are inconsiderate, rude, nasty, or unkind, think of how *you* feel when overwhelmed by stress or pressure. Attempt to see their lack of kindness as an expression of their suffering. Then, rather than adding to it, try altering the nature of your interaction.

★ Practice taking all remarks you hear as compliments.

★ Treat with compassion anyone using harsh words. Be extra kind to people who are rude; they are most likely under a great deal of stress.

★ See obnoxious drivers as hurt children, and soften your response.

★ Disarm a conflict with humor.

★ Visit your local dojo and learn about the martial arts.

★ When you see a child being mistreated by an adult, approach with kindness, empathize with the difficulty of the situation, and offer to hold or talk with the child while the adult calms down.

★ When you see young people fighting on the playground, step in and offer to mediate.

Practice Turning Soft and Lovely at a Moment's Notice. Seek out opportunities to exercise kindness on a daily basis. Extending beyond yourself through a simple act of giving will soften your heart.

★ Let someone ahead of you in line or in traffic.

★ Give up the last parking space in the lot to someone else.

★ Do somebody a favor each day.

★ Soften the harshness in your face with a smile.

★ Leave nickels in the park for kids to find.

★ Tuck flowers under the windshield wipers of a stranger's car.

★ Cut or buy a bunch of flowers, and give them out randomly as you walk down the street.

★ Carry around a Polaroid camera, take pictures of happy couples and children, then give them the photos.

★ Buy coffee, doughnuts, or cold drinks for five strangers you see in a local restaurant.

★ Freely dispense compliments, thank yous, and little notes of appreciation.

Additional Resources

Books

Boice, Judith L. *The Art of Daily Activism.* Oakland, Ca: Wingbow Press, 1992.

Canfield, Jack, and Mark Victor Hansen. *Chicken Soup for the Soul.* Deerfield Beach, FL: Health Communications, 1993.

Herbert, Anne. *Random Kindness and Senseless Acts of Beauty.* Volcano, CA: Volcano Press, 1993.

Peck, M. Scott. *A World Waiting to Be Born: Rediscovering Civility.* New York: Bantam Books, 1994.

Organizations

Points of Light Foundation, 800-677-5515. Offers information on how to make a difference in the community.

REACH OUT AND MENTOR SOMEONE

Concentrate not on the results, but on the value, the rightness, the truth of the work itself. . . . In the end, it is the reality of personal friendships that saves everything.
                                                            —Thomas Merton

A mentor is a wise and trusted counselor or teacher. Mentoring is a one-on-one relationship between such a teacher and a youngster that, continuing over time, fosters the growth and development of the young person. Opportunities for increased contact between older caring members of the community and young individuals include Boy and Girl Scout programs, 4-H clubs, foster parenting, the Police Athletic League, boys' and girls' clubs, athletic coaching, Parks and Recreation summer activities, youth support groups in schools, and a host of other programs and activities designed to assist young people into adulthood.

Many of us can remember one or two individuals who made a great difference in our transition to adulthood. They were there when we needed them. They encouraged us to do our best, and even opened doors to jobs or other opportunities. Now it is our turn to help guide the next generation.

The Essence of Mentoring. *Mentoring* is simply a new name for a process that has long occurred naturally in extended families and in municipalities built around intergenerational contact. In earlier times it was often known as apprenticeship. Today's caring adult-child relationships are in some ways more critical than those of earlier decades, for they are often the only form of protection and nurturance for young people growing up in stress-filled environments. As such, they provide the social capital needed to get on with the business of growing up.

One key ingredient in mentoring is *commitment.* The older person agrees to be available and responsive for a defined period of time. This predictable focus on personal attention is often what motivates the young person to succeed. The words spoken are less important than the explorations that unfold and the emotional bond that develops.

Another essential component of the process is *affirmation.* The mentor's task is to ask the who, what, where, when, and why questions that stimulate self-reflection. Over the course of the relationship, the awareness sparked by these questions blossoms into self-understanding and self-confidence. Prepared at last to face the challenges ahead, the young person is able to fling open doors to the future.

The mentor relationship is the most intense form of teacher-student interaction. Good instructors honor their students' unique styles and paces of learning while encouraging them to play their edge, to consciously explore beyond all previous limits. Good teachers also acknowledge the negative, accentuate the positive, and, serving as both parent and friend, inspire students to follow their dreams by reminding them of who they truly are. In addition, mentors model life skills. They know how to wend their way through the administrative complexities of high schools, trade schools, colleges, workplaces, and other sources of employment, demonstrating that with a little know-how, anything is possible.

The Best Mentoring Relationships Are Mutually Transforming. In mentoring, there are no experts—only learners walking the path of mastery, one behind the other. The older person's life is enriched and deepened through this form of contact. And the young person—after hours of joint problem solving, cooperative decision making, and collaboration on numerous projects—comes to see that he or she has something of value to contribute. Not only is the student's advice requested; it is *listened to* and *acted upon.* For young people who have been denied the opportunity to participate in school settings, this type of interaction can serve as a lifeline to the future.

Ideally, the mentor personifies familiarity with facts and ideas, reflection, insight, and cleverness, as well as goodwill and readiness to help—in short, knowledge tempered by experience and guided by values. Such a mentor is the embodiment of wisdom.

Because the recognition of vulnerability lies at the heart of wisdom, aspiring mentors must first become aware of their own destructiveness, live through their own weaknesses, and explore their own shadows. Only then can empathy, compassion, and understanding of suffering emerge. Having learned from these experiences, aspirants are equipped to acknowledge, listen to, and act upon their inner wisdom.

Organized mentoring opportunities are available throughout the country. In addition to the conventional Big Brothers-Big Sisters program are initiatives that match young people with older professionals in their areas of interest such as science, medicine, the visual arts, music, dance, writing, and so on. Other organizations incorporate heritage, traditional dress, and rites of passage into the mentoring process. Whatever form the interaction takes, it usually requires a commitment of an hour or more a week for at least a year.

If mentoring is an option that appeals to you, check out the programs in your community. If need be, start one of your own. Mentoring is an investment that can't go wrong. It pays immediate dividends to one party and yields long-term gains for the other.

Additional Resources

Literature

Bingham, Mindy, Judy Edmondson, and Sandy Stryker. *Challenges: A Young Man's Journal for Self-Awareness and Personal Planning.* Santa Barbara, CA: Advocacy Press, 1984.

Some, Malidoma. *Of Water and the Spirit.* New York: St Martin's Press, 1994.

Organizations

Celebrate Youth, 505-277-5883. A statewide mentoring program with emphasis on the arts and science.

Center for the Study of Sport in Society, 617-373-4025. Sponsors a Mentors in Violence Prevention (MVP) project for male student athletes.

Integritas, Inc., 406-542-2383. Offers structured networking opportunities for mentors.

West Dallas Community Center Rites of Passage Project, 214-630-0006.

Wise Men Wise Women Mentoring, 505-277-5644.

ENVISION SCHOOLS AS CARING COMMUNITIES

A life worth living and work worth doing . . . that is what I want for children (and all people), not just, or not even, something called "a better education."

—John Holt

Some critics have proposed that mass schooling is a form of violence that damages children and frustrates teachers. It separates children from the real world, from their parents, and from older people, thereby thwarting their natural curiosity and evolving interactions with family and community. It focuses on competition, intimidation, and shame for not "making the grade," and introduces learning as a series of compartmentalized exercises interrupted arbitrarily by bells signaling that it is "time" to move on to another subject. Teachers, for their part, are faced with the daunting task of addressing a multitude of psychosocial problems while furnished with too few resources and too many students to be truly effective.

Given that the majority of Americans are struggling to make the best of the mass schooling currently available, how can we eliminate these damaging effects? What do we need to be working toward?

A Resilient School Setting. An atmosphere of concern and caring is a critical protective factor in the lives of children, not only at home but at school. All the resiliency data to date indicate a significant need for school systems to develop a climate of this sort.

The concept of resilient schools is more inclusive than that of the "safe schools" called for in the Year 2000 National Educational Objectives. The safe schools initiative aims to have school populations—including teachers, administrators, support staff, students, parents, and community members—establish weapon-free, fight-free, and gang-free learning environments. By adding to this notion the loftier vision proposed by resiliency studies, we can begin thinking of schools as caring and supportive environments in which children are encouraged to explore, discover meaning, and derive a satisfying sense of purpose.

The Power Model. A resilient school environment has all the components of P O W E R:

★ **Positive expectations.** The governing belief is that every child can learn and achieve. Self-esteem-building activities are seen as more important than competitive workouts. Teachers and parents instill confidence, inspiring students to feel capable of performing tasks. They also help students define goals and progress toward them. Every child is regarded as basically good and worthy of attention and assistance.

A RESILIENT SCHOOL SETTING

P   Positive expectations

O   Opportunities for involvement

W   Work and play

E   Experiencing youth as resources

R   Relationships that are caring and supportive

★ **Opportunities for involvement.** Student participation is encouraged at many levels. Preschoolers who have attended the school's daycare program help incoming students. Peer counseling is offered, as is peer tutoring, buddy systems, and schoolwide cooperative learning. A strong after-school program fulfills the needs not only for supervision but for engagement. Community service projects bring children into the larger world while imparting the value of service. In addition, student art, science projects, music, and drama filter out into the community. The message is that *everyone has something to contribute.*

★ **Work and play.** These elements complement each other. School personnel are aware that learning is fun when children are permitted to follow their sense of wonder and curiosity, that activities allowing for self-expression foster academic success, and that students assimilate knowledge best when given plenty of free time for reflection, interaction, and physical recreation. Several play breaks are built into the day-to-day structure to empower both self-esteem and academic performance.

★ **Experiencing youth as resources.** Young people are viewed as resources, rather than as problems to be fixed—a challenging mind-set to maintain when faced with the large classes and seemingly limited supplies typical of today's schools. Because students are valued for who they are, their input is welcome in solving schoolwide problems, running teen centers, and airing community issues. At the same time, their freedom is respected, and in the interest of balance, they are encouraged to immerse themselves in play.

★ **Relationships that are caring and supportive.** These are the norm. Everyone in the school community belongs to the KID Club, which practices Kindness, Imagination, and Determination on a daily basis. Mutual respect is the hallmark of interactions, and diversity is encouraged. Students and teachers talk regularly about the random kindness and senseless acts of beauty they perform. Administrators and board members meet monthly to continue developing the will and the know-how needed to reach all the students. Adults engaged in every aspect of school life let it be known that they care, that they won't give up on the children, and that they know the youngsters can flourish.

Additional Resources

Literature

Gatto, John Taylor. *Dumbing Us Down: The Hidden Curriculum of Compulsory Schooling.* Philadelphia: New Society Publishing, 1992.

Growing Without Schooling. A bimonthly journal of homeschooling information and resources, including books by John Holt. Available by calling 617-864-3100.

Holt, John. *Escaping from Childhood.* Cambridge, MA: Pinch Penny Press, 1984.

Holt, John. *Instead of Education.* Cambridge, MA: Pinch Penny Press, 1988.

Organizations

Educators for Social Responsibility, 800-370-2515.

Learn and Serve America, 800-808-SERVE. Furnishes information on service-based education projects.

National Parent Teacher Association, 312-549-3253.

National School Safety Center, 805-373-9977.

Parents As Teachers, 314-432-4330. Provides tips on involving parents more effectively in schools.

Tribes, 415-935-7090. Offers materials on cooperative learning from the Center for Human Development.

ACT ON THE ASSUMPTION THAT SCHOOLS DESERVE TO BE SAFE

Deep down we must have real affection for each other, a clear realization of our shared human status. . . . Peace must come through human understanding, not by weapons, not by fear.

—Tenzin Gyatso
His Holiness the Dalai Lama

While conducting groups with young people, I am continually struck by their acceptance of violence as an ordinary part of what happens at school. Most of those I have spoken with feel incapable of doing anything about it. The majority of high school students know what to do if there is a fire at school. Many know how to respond if a schoolmate threatens suicide. Yet hardly anyone knows what to do about violence.

When I ask students how they would deal with a classmate who carries a gun to school, most agree that they would avoid the person. When I ask about fights in the school yard or, as is often the case, just beyond the school grounds, I am apprised of the "Coliseum approach": students gather round and encourage the fight to begin, or to continue. Student awareness has not yet grasped the notion of *telling a trusted adult* about such situations or of *acting differently* when they arise.

Evidently, we have given our children neither the means nor the skills to say, "Stop!" Calling for an end to violence in our schools hinges on a deep-down understanding that they *deserve* to be safe and that we as adults will ensure that they are.

Creating Peaceful Schools. School safety is best approached as an integral part of a comprehensive school health plan, rather than as a stand-alone program competing with others for attention and funds.

Functioning as part of a larger health plan, school safety is likely to take root quickly. One fertilizing element is a mind-set of knowledge, attitudes, and behaviors that permeates the many interactions occurring within the school setting. Another is the perception that safety advocacy is not only for the students; it works best when *everyone* is involved and participating.

The guidelines below can be adapted to your community's efforts to lay the groundwork for safe schools. Following these suggestions is a chart delineating the disciplinary policies needed to maintain a climate of safety.

☆ Train all school personnel in violence prevention, conflict resolution, anger management, mediation, the principles of resiliency, and identification of high-risk youth.

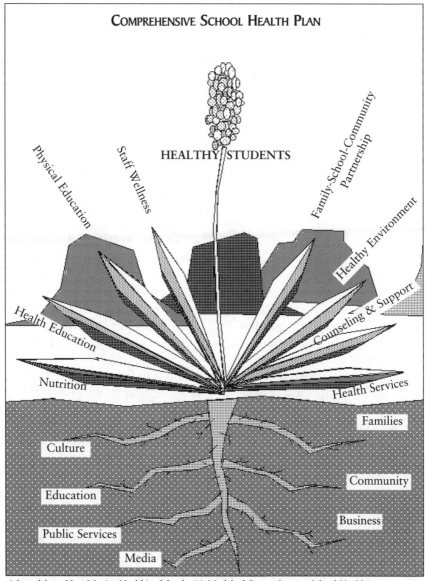

COMPREHENSIVE SCHOOL HEALTH PLAN

HEALTHY STUDENTS

Physical Education

Staff Wellness

Family-School-Community Partnership

Healthy Environment

Health Education

Counseling & Support

Nutrition

Health Services

Families

Culture

Community

Education

Business

Public Services

Media

Adapted from New Mexico Healthier Schools, "A Model of Comprehensive School Health"

★ Implement student-led initiatives such as peer counseling, peer mediation, and student courts.

★ Establish after-school and summer programs that offer cultural, recreational, educational, and instructional activities, as well as mentoring and community service programs.

* Integrate violence prevention into the curriculum. Incorporate insights and techniques into routine lesson plans, community service projects, and field trips to prisons, martial arts dojos, and emergency rooms. Host classroom presentations by guest speakers, including survivors of violence who can inform students about the long-term ramifications of assault and experts on gun safety who can educate students in what to do if they encounter a gun.

* Form a core team to case manage school violence as well as drug and discipline problems. This team should also be responsible for coordinating needs and assessment activities with education, law enforcement, judicial, health, social service, juvenile justice, gang prevention, and other community agencies.

* Conduct a yearly schoolwide safety review of programs, policies, practices, and facilities to determine any changes needed for reducing or preventing violence and for promoting safety and discipline. Consider installing metal detectors and hiring security personnel if needed.

* Hold regularly scheduled parent forums to help foster resiliency, promote school safety, and prevent school violence. Topics for discussion might include practical advice on child and adolescent parenting. To increase attendance at these meetings, provide food and childcare.

* Sponsor community education programs to help strengthen school links with local businesses, faith communities, and service providers. Coordinate community-based gang prevention strategies.

* Create safe zones of passage to protect students traveling between home and school. Consider such measures as drug-free and weapon-free areas, enhanced law enforcement, and neighborhood patrols.

* Develop counseling programs for victims and witnesses of school violence and crime. Implementation may require significant outreach to community mental health centers and the use of federal Early Periodic Screening Diagnosis and Treatment (EPSDT) funds.

* Offer disciplinary alternatives to out-of-school suspensions or expulsions when students exhibit violent or antisocial behavior.

* Compile data—in the form of surveys, nursing logs, records of disciplinary actions, and tallies of victims identified and counseled—to ascertain program effectiveness.

TEN ESSENTIAL COMPONENTS OF SCHOOL DISCIPLINE POLICIES

1. The rules are clearly understood by everyone in the school community, including students, teachers, parents, administration, and support staff. There is agreement on leadership, promptness of response to unacceptable behavior, consistency, firmness, and primacy of the interests of the nondisruptive student. The school principal verbally presents to the entire student body the rules, expectations, and consequences for disciplinary offenses.

2. Before a child is admitted to campus, a nonviolence contract is discussed, agreed to, and signed by both the students and their parents. The contract stipulates that no violent act will be free of consequences.

3. Consequences are commensurate with the magnitude of the offense, which may range from violating the dress code to ditching, gang association, threats, violent acting out, or dangerous weapon carrying. In-house suspension, including Saturday detention with a parent present, is the primary deterrent. Suspension time is allotted to instruction in communication skills, education in violence prevention, and service projects.

4. Teachers are given the right to guarantee their own safety and that of their students by insisting on the removal or suspension of any young person they consider a threat. The benefit of the doubt is always given to the teacher.

5. Any student with a history of threatening or violent behavior must provide the school with a complete discipline history.

6. Substitute teachers are advised of any student in the classroom who may pose a threat to their safety or anyone else's.

7. Mandatory monthly reports are made of incidents involving bringing a gun or knife onto school property, stabbing, discharging a firearm, assault, or battery.

8. All public schools have closed campuses. Safety features include two-way communication systems (phone, beeper, walkie-talkie) between classrooms and the main office, the presence of additional security officers, and extensive interchange among teachers, administration, local police, and juvenile justice providers.

9. A counseling referral network is in place to address problems before they become intractable.

10. Neither corporal punishment nor emotional abuse of students is tolerated. Mediation is available at all grade levels. Positive values are stressed, and the student body as a whole is rewarded for nonviolent behavior.

Additional Resources

Coping with Violence in the Schools: A Report of the 1993 Summer Conference of the Centers for School Counseling Practitioners. Cambridge, MA: Harvard University Graduate School of Education, 1993.

Hodges, Robert. *Becoming a Peaceful Warrior: A Guide to Experiential Activities for Teens.* Albuquerque, NM: Rites of Passage Institute, 1992.

Prothrow-Stith, Deborah, MD. *Violence Prevention Curriculum for Adolescents.* Newton, MA: Educational Development Center, 1987. Available from the publisher, at 617-969-7100.

School Safe Culture Project: Making the School Environment Safe. A variety of trainings and materials, available from Dennis Brown, 802 North Lincoln, Creston, LA 50801; 800-399-7996 or 515-782-5487.

School Safety: Promising Initiatives for Addressing School Violence. US General Accounting Office Report to US Senate, 1995. To order, call 202-512-6000 and request publication #GAO/HEHS 95-106.

Second Step: A Violence Prevention Curriculum, Grades 6–8. Seattle, WA: Committee for Children, 1990. Available by calling the publisher, at 206-322-5050.

TRANSCEND TRADITIONAL BELIEFS

The wondrous voice, the voice of the one who attends to the cries of the world. The noble voice, the voice of the rising tide surpassing all the sounds of the world. Let our mind be attuned to that voice.
— Buddhist Sutra

In the midst of difficult circumstances, particularly family violence, communities of faith can be a primary source of refuge and support. Indeed, there can be no true healing without a spiritual transformation leading to kindness, compassion, and forgiveness.

To be of assistance, spiritual communities must first examine their own teachings, policies, and methods of counseling to see how they relate to the modern-day epidemic of violence. Such questioning is apt to elicit intense debate among pastors, priests, rabbis, ministers, abbots, monks, nuns, mullahs, and other spiritual leaders active in the community, for clearly, such counsel as "Turn the other cheek" is not substantial enough to help.

Having deeply questioned the traditional principles guiding religious discourse and counsel, spiritual leaders will be able to build bridges into their congregations, rather than barriers of separation. The way is simple: A S K and you shall receive.

Accumulate Knowledge and Understanding. Learn everything you can about family violence, including the dynamics of abuse and why it is often difficult to break the cycle. Also get to know the local resources that are equipped

---

THE TASK OF SPIRITUAL LEADERS

A Accumulate the knowledge and understanding needed to effectively deal with family violence.

S Share the information and insights whenever you counsel.

K Keep bringing up issues of abuse with members of your community—through formal teachings, informal discussions, and newsletters.

---

to deal with this problem in more depth. In short, attempt to understand why "Trust in God" *must be augmented with advice about shelter, safety, intervention, and treatment.*

And plan to keep learning. New knowledge is constantly coming to light, not only about effective coping methods but also about preventive approaches. Hence, studies in family violence need to be an ongoing endeavor.

Share What You Have Learned. Ask about abuse in premarriage counseling sessions, raising the subject with the prospective bride and groom both separately and together. Mention the topic while addressing marriage encounter groups. Be on the lookout for families at risk, remembering that many youngsters who act out are simultaneously serving as scapegoats in violent family settings.

Here are some points to keep in mind while counseling members of your community:

* ✶ "Pray harder" is only part of the solution.
* ✶ Suffering, according to theologians worldwide, is not in God's plan for us and does not serve as redemption for past deeds.
* ✶ Minimizing a person's suffering, or painting it in a positive glow while it is occurring, is not experienced as helpful.
* ✶ Couples counseling is not appropriate in instances of domestic violence. The reason is that couples counseling presumes that both partners share power and control, and are equally free to bring up sensitive issues.
* ✶ If advice received from outside the faith community is at odds with your own, attempt to augment rather than negate the counsel; the more har-

monious the approach is, the less torn and betrayed your client will feel. Meantime, communicate and cooperate with other advisors, keeping in mind the point of reference you share: you both *care about the victim.*

Many members of the faith community tend to jump immediately to forgiveness, suggesting that years of tears should be forgotten by both parties the moment the abuser apologizes—a practice best avoided. When counseling abusers, it is important to remember that repentance entails admission of wrongdoing, asking for forgiveness, and changing the abusive behavior, which may be impossible without outside help. When counseling victims, remain aware that true forgiveness is possible only after a wide range of emotions has come to expression and the abuser's behavior has changed. Forgiving is not forgetting, or pretending that nothing happened; it is *consciously and unconditionally surrendering.* Survivors forgive at their own pace, and only after they are ready to face each day without letting the trauma dominate their lives.

Keep Discussing Abuse. When addressing your congregation, remember the power of your words. "Wives, be submissive to your husband in all things" and "Spare the rod and spoil the child" can have serious ramifications when preached by a person invested with spiritual authority.

Misinterpretation and misuse of traditional beliefs frequently contribute to the guilt and suffering experienced by victims of violence. "If you are suffering, God must be displeased with you" doubly victimizes many individuals, causing them to believe the trauma was their fault. Such a statement can also contradict the internal experience of survivors, causing them to feel abandoned by their faith.

"The Bible says . . ." is often used by perpetrators and victims alike to rationalize, excuse, or justify abusive behavior. To discourage this practice, sermons, lectures, and discussions need to emphasize that the Bible *never condones family abuse.* Jewish congregants can be reminded of the custom known as *shalom bayit* (peace in the home). Christians can be referred to the New Testament passage "Be subject to one another, out of reverence to Christ" (Ephesians 5:21) as confirmation that both parties are expected to treat each other with respect and love.

References to divorce are widely misused. Many victims of domestic violence who are contemplating divorce are accused of wishing to "break the marriage contract," when in fact the preexisting violence has already broken the covenant of trust. What destroys the family is the violence; divorce, in such instances, is merely a painful public admission that the marriage has been broken by abuse. The point to remember when counseling prospective divorcees is that *no one should be expected to remain in an abusive relationship.*

Similarly, the commandment "Honor thy father and thy mother" is often mis-used, particularly in authoritarian and hierarchical households engaging in incest or in physically abusive punishment for disobedience. To counteract this tendency, you may want to redirect congregants to biblical passages that emphasize the need for parental guidance and positive discipline.

"Abuse is never justifiable" and "Abuse must stop now" are among the pri-mary messages that need to be conveyed by spiritual teachers of every denomina-tion. These decrees refer not only to family dynamics but to acquaintance rape, elder abuse, anger, and the use of alcohol or other drugs. The pulpit, counseling sessions, newsletters, bulletin boards, and informal discussion groups can all be used to get the word out, and to reinterpret the old biblical "tales of terror" in peace-enhancing ways.

Additional Resources

Books

Fortune, Marie. *Violence in the Family: A Workshop Curriculum for Clergy and Other Helpers.* Cleveland, OH: Cleveland Pilgrim Press, 1991.

Presbyterian Peacemaker Series. Extensive resources on peacemaking from a Christian perspective, available by calling Presbyterian Publications, at 800-524-2612.

Videos

When You Preach, Remember Me: A Pastoral Response to Domestic Violence against Women. A video for homilists, available by calling 800-235-8722.

Organizations

Center for the Prevention of Sexual and Domestic Violence, 206-634-1903. Offers a variety of faith-oriented materials.

National Council of Churches, 212-870-3112. Sponsors a Things That Make for Peace initiative.

The Prayer Network, 505-473-0095. Individuals involved in violent situations will be included regularly in this group's prayers.

INVENT NEW FORMS OF COMPASSIONATE SERVICE

Better to light one candle than to curse the darkness.   —Anonymous

Faith communities that are knowledgeable in the needs of our times are in a unique position to respond to membership needs through new forms of compas-sionate service. At the same time, they can inspire members to form links with the larger community and the diverse cultures within it.

Both initiatives can lead to innovative spiritual approaches. The following areas of focus can help G U I D E the way to a more peaceful future.

THE SERVICE OF SPIRITUAL COMMUNITIES

G
U
I
D
E

Groups of all kinds are formed to provide support and safe spaces in which to talk about congregants' issues of concern.

Use of resources is expanded to benefit more community members.

Initiations and other healing ceremonies are performed in response to, and as a deterrent to, outbreaks of violence.

Daycare, after-care, and summer programs are provided.

Events that are safe and drug-free are sponsored on a regular basis for teens.

Groups. Support groups are needed in every community, especially those in which mental health services are hard to access. The function of a support group is to provide a safe space in which members can talk about what is really going on in their lives. Groups usually consist of between six and twelve members who meet on a regular basis and maintain a specific focus; some include a trained facilitator.

Spiritual communities are well equipped to organize groups of this sort, nurture them, or provide meeting space and publicity to get them started. The focus of choice depends on the needs of the congregation. You may want to initiate a traditional twelve-step group or parenting groups or support groups for survivors of abuse. Or you may decide to host multicultural gatherings in which people of diverse backgrounds can begin to understand the dynamics and beliefs that keep them separate. Consider launching groups for teens, singles, single parents, blended families, children of divorce, grandparents, elders, or bereaved parents. The possibilities are endless, and the number of groups you form depends only on the start-up energy that is available.

Use of Resources. Establish a lending library of parenting resource materials. Allow community groups to use your space for their social service meetings or healthcare forums. Or combine forces with other faith congregations, and *together* provide needed services or create community events.

Initiations and Other Healing Ceremonies. Form a parish response team to honor victims and survivors of violence. The members can enact a purification ceremony for someone who has been abused, celebrate a renewal of commitment for a relationship that has begun to heal, invite the community to grieve the loss of one of its young people to gun violence, or mark the latest site of a youth homicide. In addition, designate a committee to plan teen rites of passage into adulthood, a community welcome for newborns, ceremonies that young people help create and participate in, celebrations for any occasion at all.

Daycare. Preschool, after-school, and summer programs rank high on many parents' wish lists. Perhaps the parents in your congregation would like an affordable, nurturing environment for their children—one in which conflict is handled constructively, war toys are not allowed, video and TV exposure is minimized, and cooperative rather than competitive play is emphasized.

Events for Teens (and Sometimes Adults). Sponsor drug-free, violence-free, and fun-filled camping trips, nature discovery tours, service projects, museum field outings, dances, arts and crafts shows, or events designed to increase contact between teens and older caring adults. Or set up a teen hotline for young people in need of a time-out from family life. Ideally, such a service would be activated by either the parent or the child, and would connect the teen with another family for a night, a weekend, or however long it will take for the crisis to resolve.

In the end, today's spiritual communities might strive for an even grander vision of service. Nearly fifty years ago, Mahatma Gandhi said, "God has no religion." Was he perhaps a spiritual mouthpiece for our times? Is it not possible to transcend traditional congregational boundaries and create a unified voice and vision for peace in our society?

Additional Resources

Books

> Anderson, Sherry Ruth, and Patricia Hopkins. *The Feminine Face of God.* New York: Bantam Books, 1991.
>
> Rohr, Richard, and Joseph Martos. *The Wild Man's Journey: Reflections on Male Spirituality.* Cincinnati, OH: St. Anthony Messenger Press, 1992.

Organizations

> Bikur Cholim Directory of Resources, 212-836-1197. A referral service. (*Bikur cholim* is Hebrew for "visiting the sick as a form of service.")
>
> Carter Center Interfaith Health Program, 404-420-5151. Publishes *Faith and Health,* a quarterly newsletter.

The Congress of National Black Churches, Inc., 202-371-1091.
Interfaith Alliance, 202-639-6370.
National Council of Catholic Women, 202-682-0334.
National Observance of Children's Sabbaths, 202-628-8787.

VALUE PEOPLE IN THE WORKPLACE

There are six intrinsic factors that make work satisfying: variety and challenge, elbow room for decision making, feedback and learning, mutual support and respect, wholeness and meaning, and room to grow.
—Fred Emery

Think about your workplace. Does it promote peace? Are policies in place that protect your right to parent your children? Are crayons or small games available for youngsters who visit? Are efforts made to support worthwhile initiatives in the community?

Talking business means addressing the bottom line. And the bottom line as we approach a new millennium is that while making a healthy profit, businesses have a social obligation to contribute significantly to the growth of peace—in the workplace, in the community, and above all, in the lives of their workers.

Why Family-Friendly Policies? Business has a stake in community well-being. The primary reason is that customers and workers alike hail from the community. The cycle of poverty, poor educational achievement, substance use to mask the pain associated with economic failure, and increasing neighborhood violence is generally bad for business.

To break the cycle, firms invest in the community. They create decent-paying jobs. They also pay corporate taxes that help fund social programs. Slowly, businesses are chipping away at the ravages of poverty. In the process, something else is happening. Amid today's emphasis on customer satisfaction and quality circles, in which all echelons of company personnel participate in problem solving, corporations are beginning to realize that investing in *people* pays out huge dividends. One small leap away is the dawning awareness, already occurring in some firms, that it makes good business sense to invest in *staff workers*.

The impetus to create family-friendly policies for workers is rooted in at least four observations. Employees who experience significant family-related stress are less productive. Illnesses that are not tended to immediately often lead to increased employer health insurance premiums. Low morale due to poor working conditions impacts on customer satisfaction. From a personnel perspective, unrelieved stress, poor health, and low spirits all contribute to increased job turnover, resulting in added costs for recruiting and training new people to do the work.

How to Be F R I E N D L Y to Families. Here are eight steps you can take to extend goodwill to parent workers while increasing all-around satisfaction.

FAMILY-ORIENTED BUSINESS POLICIES

F — Favor flexible work schedules.

R — Respond to requests for working at home.

I — Invite workers to learn and grow.

E — Establish employee assistance programs.

N — Normalize job sharing.

D — Develop worker safety measures.

L — Look for opportunities to serve.

Y — Yield, and keep open the channels of communication.

★ Favor flexible work schedules. Most parents of young children do not appreciate the stress imposed by 9-to-5 jobs. Arriving home just in time to make dinner, they are left with few precious hours to spend with their children before tucking them into bed. Businesses that allow for more flexible schedules—such as 8 to 4, or 8 to 11 and 1 to 5, or four long weekdays, or whatever it takes to log in a certain number of hours per year—are reporting excellent performance outcomes.

★ Respond to requests for working at home. As we enter the emerging whirlpool created by the information superhighway, home offices are coming to the fore as an efficient solution to juggling work and family life. Many tasks can be performed at home, not only during daylight hours but in the evenings and on weekends. Relieved of the unending hum of office phone calls, politics, and socializing, the home worker is often able to accomplish more in a shorter period of time.

★ Invite workers to learn and grow. Post notices on a centrally located bulletin board to let employees know about local events of interest, upcoming classes, or communication tips. Sponsor brown-bag lunchtime talks on parenting, stress reduction, conflict resolution, cultural diversity, or emotional fluency. Say yes to anyone who wants to initiate a walking club or organize a yoga or Jazzercise class in the conference room at noon. Celebrate something *other* than a traditional holiday.

★ Establish employee assistance programs. All people need support during stressful times and periods of transition such as marriage, childbirth, divorce, a death in the family, or the illness of a child or partner. A generous leave policy can help provide that needed support. If you are aware of alcohol or other drug use, which can impact significantly on personal productivity and collective safety, provide access to counseling services and emphasize the need to address these behaviors. State the rules, and give your employees a chance to clean up the out-of-control parts of their lives.

★ Normalize job sharing. In most two-parent households, both parents work outside the home. Some prefer part-time work, enabling them to spend more time with their children. Job sharing accommodates any two people seeking this option either together or individually. It also elevates morale, heightens the desire to contribute, and keeps business running smoothly during vacations and sick days.

★ Develop worker safety measures. Workplace violence encompasses physical assault, homicide, near misses, verbal abuse, sexual harassment, and acquaintance rape. Directly affected employees are not the only ones to suffer; serious trauma also results from witnessing violence or being fearful of attack.

Is the parking lot too dark? Do employees work alone, stay late, or handle lots of money? Must customers, clients, or patients spend long periods of time waiting? Most workplace violence, like other forms of violence, is not random and can, with proper precautions and know-how, be prevented. To enhance worker safety, consider providing metal detectors, closed-circuit TV cameras, a restricted facility entrance, mobile phones for field personnel, additional staffing during nonpeak hours, or training in violence prevention or verbal judo techniques. Maintain clear policies for reporting incidents of abuse or attack, and support all employees who become involved.

★ Look for opportunities to serve. Treat your employees as well as you do your customers. Does the lounge area need a facelift? Can you find a more comprehensive, yet still affordable health plan? Do you model conflict resolution skills so that everyone at work has a chance to see them in action? Think of your employees as "internal customers" worthy of a high level of regard and consideration.

★ Yield, and keep open the channels of communication. Allow employees to share their difficulties with you, and attempt to respond to suggestions for improvement. Most concerns—such as "Can you create a space where I can breastfeed in private?" or "I need to help out at my child's school on Tuesday afternoon"—are likely to be reasonable and simple to accommodate.

Businesses that adopt a people-oriented viewpoint garner respect in addition to worker satisfaction and economic gain. Communities respond favorably to companies that serve as involved, caring partners to their employees.

Additional Resources

Literature

Chappell, Tom. *The Soul of a Business: Managing for Profit and the Common Good.* New York: Bantam Books, 1993.

Griffin, William, James Montsinger, and Nancy Carter. *Personal Safety Handbook.* Durham, NC: Brendan Associates, 1995. Available from the publisher, at 919-489-1351.

Hawkin, Paul. *Growing a Business.* New York: Simon & Schuster, 1987.

Peters, Tom. *Thriving on Chaos.* New York: Harper & Row, 1987.

Weisboard, Marvin. *Productive Workplaces: Organizing and Managing for Dignity, Meaning, and Community.* San Francisco: Jossey-Bass, 1981.

Working Mother Magazine, especially its annual feature on 100 best companies for working mothers. Available from Lang Communications, 230 Park Avenue, New York, NY 10169; 212-551-9500.

Organizations

Co-op America, 800-584-7336. Publishes a quarterly newsletter on business and social responsibility.

INVITE COLLABORATIVE BUSINESS "VENTURES"

You see things, and you say, "Why?" But I dream things that never were, and I say, "Why not?"
—George Bernard Shaw

Just as there is a wide range of family-friendly policies for businesses to enact, so, too, is there a menu of possibilities for reaching out to the community. The bottom line can be favorably impacted in this domain as well. Networking with local groups, collaborating with the schools, and helping young people all provide visibility for businesses. In addition, the expanded sense of connection to the big picture further increases worker satisfaction. When businesses prosper, inform, and contribute to their surrounding localities, everyone benefits.

Reach Out to Promote Peace. Businesses are the lifeblood of the community. Hence, communicating with the community is an essential business skill. To do it well, R E A C H out in every way you can.

COMMUNITY-ORIENTED BUSINESS PRACTICES

R Revitalize formal school-business partnerships.

E Educate by sponsoring local events.

A Allow employees time off.

C Create opportunities for youth to learn about the business world.

H Help raise consciousness about solutions specific to your line of work.

✷ Revitalize formal school-business partnerships. By the year 2000, an estimated 80 percent of the labor force will be composed of minorities, women, and immigrants—amounting to a generally undereducated pool of workers. At the same time, jobs will demand more reading, writing, mathematical, and problem-solving skills. The surest way to rectify the impending discrepancy is to form partnerships with schools and tackle problems together as they arise. In combining efforts with local schools, you will come to appreciate their strengths and weaknesses, and you will help students—the next generation of laborers—learn about work-force needs and about the demands and opportunities inherent in entre-preneurial endeavors.

Successful partnerships begin with easy-to-do activities. The school, for example, can provide speakers to address a variety of topics; high-light the business in school publications; offer classes for business employees; share library, audiovisual, and athletic resources and exper-tise; and furnish entertainment for business events. The business can rec-iprocate with student incentives. In the Renaissance Program—a school-business partnership that promotes academic leadership through a busi-ness approach to education—attendance, good grades, and academic improvement are acknowledged by different-colored cards entitling their bearers to a range of school privileges and discounts for T-shirts, movies, clothing, and books from local businesses. Participating schools nationwide have increased their reading and math scores, upped their attendance, and decreased discipline referrals.

Teacher incentive awards are another possibility. The teacher of the month could win a free dinner, a fitness club membership, use of a new car, or some other reward donated by a local business.

✷ Educate by sponsoring local events. Depending on the occasion, contribute time, advice, money, supplies, meeting space, tickets, gift certificates, or other in-kind resources. Or help create a community forum to discuss the area of youth development you are most passionate about—music, per-haps, or sports, science, theater, foreign studies, history, or poetry.

Many business-related clubs such as Kiwanis, Elks, and Rotary help organize fundraisers for local community agencies, participate as a group in community-sponsored events, or take on short-term communi-ty projects. They also provide a network to help promote violence awareness and substance abuse education.

✷ Allow employees time off. A certain number of hours off each month for community service offers many rewards. Let workers spend time help-ing out at their child's school, mentoring, tutoring, or teaching someone to read.

★ Create opportunities for youth to learn about the business world. Participate in career days at schools, arrange student tours of your business, be a classroom presenter, create an experiential business day at a local school, hold youth art or photo exhibits at your workplace, help produce a yellow pages directory or a newsletter for students, create part-time jobs or summer business internships for youth, establish drug-free events for teens, or chaperon field trips or dances.

★ Help raise consciousness about solutions specific to your line of work. If you work in an industry that contributes to the escalation of violence, think of ways to become part of the solution. Some alcohol companies fund designated driver education programs. Many gun clubs present information on gun safety. TV producers have begun portraying less use of alcohol and more pro-social attitudes.

Change will continue to dot our landscape as more people working in these major industries become voices of compassion and concern, and begin exercising their talents in transformative ways. In lieu of more alcohol, more guns, and more media violence, our society needs less advertising directed at youth, better gun safety features, and more media images of people grappling with conflict in healthy ways.

Additional Resources

America 2000, 800-872-5327.
Join-a-School Programs, 505-84-3649.
Renaissance Educational Foundation, 800-624-5534.
Texas Business and Education Coalition, 512-480-TBEC.

TEAM UP FOR CRISIS INTERVENTION

The brains of traumatized children develop as if the entire world is chaotic, unpredictable, violent, frightening, and devoid of nurturance. And unfortunately, the systems that our society has developed to help these children often continue to fill their lives with neglect, unpredictability, fear, chaos, and most disturbing, more violence.
—Dr. Bruce Perry

The eruption of community violence demands a collaborative response. We need red coats (fire and emergency personnel), blue coats (police), white coats (health providers), green coats (parks and recreation specialists), gray coats (volunteers), black coats (judges and juvenile justice workers), and no coats (mental health practitioners, social workers, and other community-based child health workers). Most importantly, we need groups that have been trained in identifying the effects of violence, in crisis intervention, and in team-work skills.

Brain Basics. Mounting evidence reveals that the adverse neurological effects of experiencing or witnessing violence are considerable. The brain is designed to sense, process, store, and then act on information related to survival. The more activated a particular area of the brain becomes, the more stimulated it will be to organize and develop—often at the expense of other areas of the brain. This process is known as "use-dependent learning."

Essentially, we have a three-brain structure, composed of a midbrain (which we share with the reptiles), a limbic system emotional brain (which we share with the other mammals), and a cortex thinking brain (which is distinct-ly human). We store memories and information at each of these sites. The stored material is later activated in several ways. We use *cognitive memory* to recall a phone number or a person's name. *Emotional memory* brings on sad-ness when we hear an oldies song reminiscent of a long lost love. Relying on *spatial memory,* we are able to find our way home without a map. *Kinesthetic memory* helps us ride a bike even when we haven't been on one for years.

A type of memory we don't often think about also exists. It is called *"state" memory,* or *reflexive memory,* and it is associated with the midbrain. Research has shown that a Vietnam vet, after hearing a helicopter overhead, may exhib-it an elevated pulse rate and increased blood pressure as well as general body tension and irritability for a period of time. This constellation of symptoms occurs because his internal alarm system designed to set off a fight-or-flight response has been activated by the "state" memory he experienced in combat. His body, informed by his midbrain, "remembers" the trauma of combat, although he may not consciously associate the helicopter with his battleground experience.

The same phenomenon occurs in children who have been traumatized. The younger a child is, the more likely she is to internalize a state memory of a trau-matic event. The more often her brain's fight-or-flight response is stimulated with repeated exposures to trauma, the more enhanced and "turned on" her midbrain functions will be. A toddler who has been harshly punished or who has watched mom being beaten by dad, for example, will, in a moment remi-niscent of the trauma, very quickly pass from a state of relative calm to one of either vigilance, alarm, fear, or terror. Correspondingly, her body will prepare to either run or do battle, and her pulse rate will increase significantly, indicat-ing precisely where she is on the response-to-threat continuum.

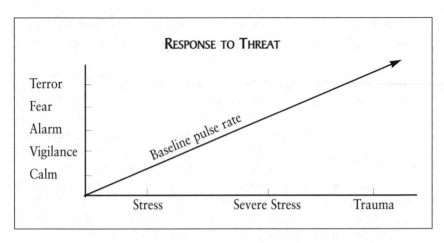

The traumatized toddler has, like the Vietnam vet, internalized a state memory. Her physiology has been altered as a result of her exposure to violence. With repeated exposure, her baseline pulse rate will be reset at increasingly higher levels, and her brain development will be adversely affected.

Post-Traumatic Stress Disorder (PTSD). Infants and young children who repeatedly experience fear-provoking situations eventually begin showing signs of post-traumatic stress disorder. PTSD is, in essence, a persistent triggering of the alarm system by an exaggerated state memory. What was originally a protective bodily response has become detrimental.

PTSD is typically accompanied by three patterns of behavior:

* ✶ Recurrent and intrusive recollections, also called flashbacks, in which a threatening event is relived with all one's senses. These recollections often manifest as nightmares or a repetitive reenactment of the traumatic events during play. Children whose play becomes focused on trauma have fewer opportunities to engage in forms of play that stimulate brain development in areas other than the midbrain.
* ✶ Avoidance of stimuli or numbing of general responsiveness to the environment. In the first instance, children will become extremely withdrawn and cautious in their play. In the second, they may "space out" when asked about a behavior related to the original trauma. Having observed that adults are unable to restrain themselves, the children may believe they cannot learn to control their *own* behavior. They may also blame themselves for post-traumatic events and, out of fear and inadequacy, shut down completely. In addition, they will most likely avoid triggers—key reminders of the trauma that elicit intense distress. An infant may pull away from someone with a beard, for example, or a young child may refuse to go to a park with rope swings.

★ Persistent symptoms of increased arousal. Children may experience night terrors, hypervigilance, frequent startle responses, or sudden, angry outbursts. Unable to concentrate, due to sleep deprivation and the constant search for clues to a threatening situation, children often have difficulty in school.

In summary, infants, toddlers, or older children who experience or witness violence at home or on the street are apt to feel fear, anger, powerlessness, guilt, confusion, despair, sadness, or shame. These feelings are most often expressed through bodily pains and acting-out or withdrawn behaviors.

The Effect of Family Violence on Caretakers. Parents living in violent settings experience increased stress, which further affects their children's development. Many parents, unable to protect their children from the violence, develop a debilitating sense of helplessness during these episodes and become increasingly overprotective in other aspects of child care. Some become so immersed in their own grief that they are unable to meet their children's needs for comfort. Others, wrestling with their own trauma response, become demanding, irritable, and angry because their *children* are unable to help *them*.

Violence in the household can take an even heavier toll on the caretaker-child relationship. Recurrent outbreaks of rage and abuse may bring back painful memories for parents who prefer not to deal with the past, causing them to withdraw further from their children. Living with violence can also produce depression, in which case a parent's TLC turns to "talk less, look sad, and can't control mood swings." Depressive states have devastating consequences, particularly for young infants, who are programmed to interact with lively, talkative, and consistently caring adults.

Making a Difference in this Crisis. When the sociological incubators in which children are evolving become so damaged, service providers must organize effective responses. Current responses, as we know, are pitifully inadequate. Due to the failure of early identification, fragmented intervention, and a dearth of mental health resources, we are left with a large pool of untreated victims of violence, each of whom invariably experiences more neglect, unpredictability, chaos, and violence.

The challenge before us is to begin viewing victims of violence through the lens of social ecology, and to build solid inroads into this previously impenetrable landscape. What is needed is a C R I S I S response composed of the following elements.

RESPONDING TO UNTREATED VICTIMS OF VIOLENCE

C   Crisis support is available.

R   Recognition and immediate referral of abuse is widespread.

I   Improved management of the violent scene is ongoing.

S   Stress debriefing teams assist all service providers.

I   Intervention is specific to the needs of each individual.

S   Security and consistency of close relationships is emphasized.

★ **C**risis support. All families exposed to violence must be given on-the-spot assistance.

★ **R**ecognition and immediate referral. Instances of suspected child abuse and sexual assault need to be acknowledged, and children living in violent households need to be placed in the hands of knowledgeable case-management teams.

★ **I**mproved management of the violent scene. Children should be removed from the scene as quickly as possible. If they must be interviewed, it should take place *once*, in a session conducted collaboratively by law enforcement and health professionals; this is especially important in cases of sexual trauma. Follow-up services must be provided to assist children in processing the event and to minimize the onset of PTSD.

★ **S**tress debriefing for all service providers. On-the-scene teams as well as follow-up teams require assistance in processing the complexity of emotions and high stress levels that accrue from intervening in trauma.

Debriefing will help these individuals deepen their understanding and enhance their readiness to help other victims in the future.

★ Intervention that is tailored to each individual. Personal histories must be taken so that victims can be helped to process the event, comprehend the meaning it has in their lives, learn skills to avoid future maladaptive coping, and, if needed, follow up with therapy to treat anorexia, substance abuse, or other trauma-related behaviors.

★ Security and consistency. For improved chances of recovery, children exposed to violence require close relationships with caring adults, consistent and reliable childcare routines, and safe, familiar environments.

PTSD and compromised brain development can be prevented through early support and intervention—both of which are best provided by a strong community response to violent events. With well-integrated teamwork, we can also reduce the *suffering* of these untreated victims of violence.

Additional Resources

Books

Caring for Infants and Toddlers in Violent Environments. Richmond, VA: Zero to Three, 1994. Available from the publisher, at PO Box 25494, Richmond, VA 23260-5494; 703-528-4300.

Garbarino, James, et al. *Children in Danger: Coping with the Consequence of Community Violence.* San Francisco: Jossey-Bass, 1992.

Isaacs, Mareasa R., PhD. *Violence: The Impact of Community Violence on African American Children and Families.* Arlington, VA: National Center for Education in Maternal and Child Health, 1992.

Perry, Bruce. *Maltreated Children: Experience, Brain Development, and the Next Generation* (in press).

Organizations

Center for Mental Health Services, 301-443-2792. Offers information on PTSD.

Project Loss and Survival Team, 504-525-7525.

YIELD TO THE NEED FOR ARKS OF PEACE

There are two ways of spreading light: to be the candle or the mirror that reflects it.

—Edith Wharton

Most of us have become sensitized to the physical abuse of children. As a result, our social systems are less willing than ever before to tolerate this form of child abuse. Only recently, however, has much attention been paid to *emotional* abuse—a more subtle form of violence that damages self-esteem. We as a society must now become aware of the signposts of emotional abuse and take a stand against these behaviors too.

Can we create a positive environment that is free of physical *and* emotional violence? Is it possible to imagine a world in which children are fully nurtured by their families *and* communities?

Emotional Abuse. Many children in our culture grow up emotionally abused or neglected. Emotional abuse is most often delivered in words that hurt instead of help—in remarks such as "You clumsy fool," "Don't touch that," and "Stop bothering me," in lieu of "You can do it," "Great job," "You're terrific!" and "I'm proud of you." Emotional neglect, part of the spectrum of abuse, occurs when parents or caregivers consistently fail to provide support, attention, and affection.

Our households and communities are sometimes unaware that they are violating children emotionally. Here are the most common signs of this form of A B U S E.

Avoidance. The child's activities are of little interest to the parent, whose primary desire is to restrict them or limit the child's peer relationships.

Blame. The child is scapegoated whenever things go wrong, including events that have little to do with the child.

Use of extreme punishment. The child is hit, or locked in a room or closet, because this is what's "needed" to teach the child a lesson.

Shaming. The child is subjected to a torrent of belittling, criticizing, and invalidating remarks or behaviors.

Excluding. The child is barred from parental love and affection, which is given freely to others in the household.

Healthier Communities Honor Their Children. A healthier community is one in which abuse is replaced by honor. Such a community organizes its resources to support residents attempting to reach their full potential. In the process, it creates physical and social environments that evoke a sense of belonging and a feeling of safety while one is playing, working, and learning. Here, no child is abused physically, sexually, emotionally, or by witnessing violence.

Healthy communities H O N O R their young by continually evolving in these areas:

Human basics. The needs for food, housing, and clean water, air, and soil are all met.

Opportunities for involvement. Meaningful work is available, along with opportunities for recreation, education, and following one's dreams.

Nurturance. Nurturing the young is given highest priority.

Ongoing safety. Protective measures are in place, along with caring support. From time to time the needs for safety and support are reassessed, and improvements are made.

Respect. Residents show reverence for the uniqueness of each individual, the varied family structures present, the diversity of cultures, and all living things.

Building Arks of Peace. Although we are not quite evolved enough to develop sizable communities capable of honoring in these ways, we can certainly begin establishing small arks of peace *within* our communities. Focusing on the development of young people under the tutelage of older caring adults, these lights of possibility would not be concerned with fixing problems or identifying risky individuals. Nor would the youth be viewed as passive recipients of needed services. They would be seen as *creators of their lives.*

These arks of peace—formed collaboratively by the school, faith, business, and service provider sectors—would serve as small "biotopes," preserving the human assets of the region until it becomes possible to incorporate them into the larger "biosphere" of community. In this sense, the youth would be seen as *valuable resources to the greater community.*

In a report entitled "A Matter of Time: Risk and Opportunity in the Non School Hours," the Carnegie Task Force on Youth Development, although not proposing arks of peace per se, states clearly their underlying philosophy: "Families and schools represent two sides of a triangle of human development. The third side is surely those community organizations that provide safe havens and caring role models, especially during the out-of-school hours. Excellent schools combined with actively involved families are necessary, but they are often not the reality. Even when schools are available, they are not sufficient in today's complex world. All major institutions of the society affecting young people must become partners with strong community organizations to bring young adolescents into their mutually protective embrace."

Little preparatory work is needed. The physical space can be provided by schools with empty buildings or rooms that can be utilized sixteen hours a day, seven days a week, 365 days a year. Security can be furnished by trained community volunteers and youth. Entrepreneurial pursuits encouraged and supported by each center, in addition to employment positions offered by the center, can help meet the income-generating needs of the youth.

Activities can include some or all of the following:

- ★ Leadership development, acquired as the young people attend meetings about running the ark, deploying resources, and evaluating success.
- ★ Special community events.
- ★ Community meetings and forums.
- ★ Community service projects.
- ★ Sports and recreation.
- ★ Drama, music, choir, dance, film, and visual arts programs.
- ★ Babysitting and daycare, provided by older teens for younger ones attending community events.
- ★ Parenting education.

⭐ Housing, job, and daycare referrals conducted by social service agency representatives.

⭐ Basic healthcare services.

⭐ Educational assistance such as tutoring, GED preparation, and off-site community college courses.

Once they are up and running, arks of peace will demonstrate many more ways in which older caring adults can help create a healthier "next generation." They will also reveal what can happen when collaboration, cooperation, respect, and problem solving are modeled on a daily basis. In arks of peace, *abuse will be transformed into honor.*

Additional Resources

Books

The American Psychological Association Commission on Violence and Youth. *Violence and Youth: Psychology's Response.* Washington, DC: American Psychological Association, 1993. Available by calling the APA, at 202-336-6046.

McLaughlin, Milbrey, and Merita Irby. *Urban Sanctuaries: Neighborhood Organization in the Lives and Futures of Inner-City Youth.* San Francisco: Jossey-Bass, 1994.

Youth Development Institute Fund for the City of New York, *1993 Beacons Initiative Report.* Available from the Youth Development Institute Fund, 121 Avenue of the Americas, New York, NY 10013.

Organizations

Caring Communities, 314-231-3720. Assists groups wishing to help schools function as round-the-clock community centers.

Carnegie Council on Adolescent Development, 202-429-7979. Provides a variety of resources associated with young people.

Erikson Institute, 420 North Wabash Avenue, Chicago, IL 60611; 312-755-2250. Offers information on children's developmental needs.

The International Healthy Cities Foundation, 510-271-2660. Furnishes models for creating positive communities.

The Sixth Path

THE WAY TO UNDERSTAND

U	
N	**U**nderscore universal support
D	**N**eutralize gun violence
E	**D**emonstrate to educate
R	**E**nlighten the media
S	**R**einvent friendship, restitution, and pilgrimage
T	**S**taff a National Peacekeeping Corps
A	**T**each men to talk
N	**A**pply mediation anytime and everywhere
D	**N**urture a peaceable imagination
	Declare your intentions

Never doubt that a small group of thoughtful, committed citizens can change the world. Indeed, it's the only thing that ever has.

—Margaret Mead

I N OLDEN TIMES, CARTOGRAPHERS WHO HAD MAPPED OUT ALL DETAILS WITHIN the scope of their knowledge and understanding would often inscribe along the edge of the parchment, "Beyond be dragons." Having traversed the territory of ourselves, our families, and our communities, how can we stop short of confronting the "dragons" of cultural change? What steps seem to make sense in this arena?

The task of altering the larger cultural fabric at first seems formidable. Who am I, we wonder, to make a difference in such a complex system? After a while we may decide to focus on getting laws passed. Having participated in the legislative process, I see this as a necessary though insufficient ingredient of social change. Laws, it turns out, alter behavior only half as much as peer persuasion does. The potency of *mass numbers* is the real motivating force behind most cultural reformation. After all, citizens are the ones who continually redefine what is acceptable in their society. This path explores a visionary framework for strengthening the grass-roots movement needed to create a more peaceable America.

Underscore Universal Support

We can, of course, help through all that we do. But at the deepest level we help through who we are. We help, that is, by appreciating the connection between service and our own progress on the journey of awakening into a fuller sense of unity.
                                                                —Ram Dass

A great need will often evoke an identical response in many places at the same time. As the response comes to expression with sufficient frequency, a threshold is reached, beyond which the pace of change quickens and the response intensifies. This process, known as the "hundredth monkey" phenomenon, is as indicative of human societal shifts as it is of the changing dietary habits of monkeys, which gave it its name. Here's what happens in the social realm: as soon as a particular constellation of attitudes has captured the attention of a sufficient number of people, others' lifestyle patterns are suddenly changed.

We are approaching this point in America. A great need for personal well-being has sparked a self-help movement evident from coast to coast. The grandfather of these initiatives, the twelve-step support group process, continues to flourish as new forms and strategies for group support take shape. People meeting for the first time are able to understand each other's plight—so much so that an affirming nod of the head in response to painful stories and tears is often more comforting than a thousand words from someone who lacks this understanding.

The Spread of Self-Help Groups. Without much notoriety or even fanfare, about half a million different self-help groups have sprung into being over the past ten years. These groups provide a reciprocal form of emotional support and assistance to a total of 10 million people, each of whom has chosen to gather with others experiencing similar circumstances.

Social networks of this sort serve a threefold purpose: they help healthy people stay well, speed the recovery of those who are dis-eased, and improve the lives of those for whom full recovery is not yet possible. Whether challenged by physical or mental illness, addictions, "disabilities," or feelings of personal or familial oppression, these people have moved beyond the rhetorical "My dis-ease is worse than yours" to create a system of support that works.

The fierce sense of ownership and self-determination that triggers self-help groups has become a hallmark of their success. Individuals recognize the need for change, share this discovery with others, and form a group. By way of this natural, organic unfolding, advocacy for change is passing from the personal to the societal level.

A group is an effective vehicle for coping with problems, stress, hardship, and pain because it:

- ☆ Welcomes the expression of emotions and, in understanding them, alleviates feelings of isolation, powerlessness, and hopelessness.
- ☆ Demystifies labels for diseases, problems, disabilities, treatments, and services rendered by care providers.
- ☆ Delineates realistic emotional, physical, financial, and social expectations based on firsthand experience.
- ☆ Provides exposure to more effective coping styles.
- ☆ Extends support and information to friends and family members.
- ☆ Has the potential to advocate for social reform.

The Emergence of Co-Counseling. Another self-help modality is co-counseling, a powerful process by which two people share areas of personal concern, reflecting back to each other their insights and observations. This form of counseling, like all others, utilizes elements of the therapeutic process and produces a sort of "Counselor Troy effect." Troy, the counselor on board *Star Trek's Starship Enterprise*, often helps people in crisis. Her approach consists of four components:

* ✸ Emotional processing, or telling the story—which is often painful to hear—in a supportive environment.
* ✸ Cognitive processing, or an attempt to make sense of the experience, including any decisions made in response to it.
* ✸ Identifying the next step as well as potentially helpful resources. The objective is to decrease any tendency toward maladaptive coping through avoidance, self-destructive acts, or the use of alcohol or other drugs, in order to reduce one's chances of being revictimized.
* ✸ Looking to the future, and deciding on the follow-up needed for ongoing healing.

Redefining Mental Health. Already the self-help movement has given rise to a host of new practicalities and perspectives. Currently, more than forty clearinghouses nationwide are responding to calls for information, compiling state directories, publishing newsletters and how-to manuals, assisting in the formation of new groups, presenting self-help approaches at conferences, and using electronic technologies to develop telephone computer conferencing systems as well as new linkages of people, ideas, and concerns. Along with this extensive networking has come an enormous grass-roots response to violence-related needs. Support groups now exist for people who have lost loved ones through homicide or suicide, women and men recovering from the effects of incest or sexual assault, parents attempting to break the chain of abuse while raising their children, and men trying to free themselves from the cycle of domestic violence in their lives. Even children who have *witnessed* violence can find support in their hometowns or nearby.

These and other support groups are redefining mental health in terms we have not yet begun to appreciate. Indeed, we lack a language for articulating this aspect of human need. "Preventive mental health," although an accurate description of it, is hardly suitable for use as a sound bite. Catchier terms might be "awareness discovery," or "limbic holism," or "essence integrity."

What we *can* appreciate is that the stigma associated with admitting to the need for help and asking for it is gradually dissolving. Some days it is even possible to envision 800-SHARE IT phoneputer systems in full operation throughout the country, neighborhood counseling centers, and a pervasive consciousness that will foster a view of people as weak or in denial if they are *not* involved in a support group.

Whatever realities self-help networking ultimately inspires, humanity is certain to provide for its continued evolution. This important social movement is guaranteed a place in our future by the realization that what makes a long-term difference is not what is done to us but rather *what we do for ourselves*. Its future is also ensured by the growing awareness that when we are assisting others, we are also helping ourselves.

THE TWELVE STEPS

We:

Step one. Admitted that we were powerless over the effects of addiction [to violent behaviors] and that our lives had become unmanageable.

Step two. Came to believe that a Power greater than ourselves could restore us to wholeness.

Step three. Made a decision to turn our will and our lives over to the care of God as we understood God.

Step four. Made a searching and fearless moral inventory of ourselves.

Step five. Admitted to God, to ourselves, and to another human being the exact nature of our wrongs.

Step six. Were entirely ready to work in partnership with God to remove our ineffective [violent] behavior.

Step seven. Humbly asked God to help us remove our shortcomings.

Step eight. Made a list of all persons we had harmed, and became willing to make amends to them all.

Step nine. Made direct amends to such people wherever possible, except when to do so would injure them or others.

Step ten. Continued to take personal inventory and, when we were wrong, promptly admitted it.

Step eleven. Sought through prayer and meditation to improve our conscious contact with God as we understood God, praying only for knowledge of God's will for us and for the power to carry that out.

Step twelve. Having had a spiritual awakening as the result of these steps, we tried to carry this message to others, and to practice these principles in all our affairs.

Additional Resources

Books

Dass, Ram, and Paul Gorman. *How Can I Help? Stories and Reflections on Service.* New York: Alfred Knopf, 1985.

Dyer, Wayne, and John Vriend. *Counseling Techniques That Work.* Alexandria, VA: American Counseling Association, 1975.

The Twelve Steps: A Way Out. San Diego, CA: Recovery Publications, 1989. Available from the publisher, at 619-275-1350.

US Department of Health and Human Services. *Surgeon General's Report on Self-Help and Public Health.* Washington, DC: USDHHS, 1990.

Organizations

American Self-Help Clearinghouse, 201-625-7101.

Avance, 512-270-4630. Provides referrals to self-help groups in housing projects.

Re-Evaluation (Cocounseling) Counseling Communities, 206-284-0311. Furnishes information as well as a newsletter.

NEUTRALIZE GUN VIOLENCE

Our culture promotes guns as acceptable toys. Many children play with cap guns, "laser" guns, and water pistols. Our children routinely see unsafe and irresponsible gun handling on television programs and in movies. The difference between "pretend" and "real" actions and consequences is often not clear to a child. Our children need to know: Real guns are not toys.
                                                    —National Rifle Association

The need to eliminate gun violence brings us into murkier territory filled with seemingly irreconcilable interests. On the one hand, a gun is a tool many people enjoy having. Some use it for sport shooting, hunting, and protecting humans, pets, cattle, and crops from animal predators. Others like to have one at home for protecting themselves against potential robbers or intruders, who may—or may not—also be carrying one.

On the other hand, despite our best intentions, a steady stream of guns manages to flow into the hands of those who use them illegally, such as domestic violence criminals who threaten or harm family members. These guns are either obtained legally, stolen, or purchased from licensed dealers who value profit over rules restricting sales to minors or prohibiting their interstate transport. Currently, more than 38,000 gun deaths are reported *each year* in the United States—more than half the total number of Vietnam War fatalities.

Federal discussion about security measures is at a standstill, deadlocked in the opposition between two powerful, uncompromising factions. At one extreme are public health radicals who would like to see every gun in America melted down and the industry banned from ever making another one. At the other are National Rifle Association (NRA) officials bent on blocking any form of gun legislation, whether or not it makes public safety sense. In the middle are the majority of Americans, who either want to have guns or want to allow others to have them, yet also hope to reduce the suffering and carnage they cause. Beneath our political differences is a common theme: *we are all against gun violence.*

Aware of this mutual concern, we can break free of the gridlock and begin moving forward. The following eight areas for F I R E A R M S action can, if implemented, begin to provide some measure of safety. Most of these suggestions all parties can agree on.

ACTION AGENDA

F Focus on eliminating firearm deaths among young people.

I Improve gun safety features, especially trigger locks and storage practices.

R Restrict unsupervised access to guns by young people.

E Ensure that every school is a safe school.

A Abolish guns from the homes of adolescents who are depressed or chemically dependent.

R Remove guns from the hands of criminals involved in domestic violence or other violent misdemeanors.

M Maximize the availability of nonlethal protection devices.

S Systematize the surveillance of firearm injuries and deaths.

Focus on Eliminating Firearm Deaths among Young People. Our society no longer tolerates women dying in childbirth. Every state currently appoints a committee to routinely review birth records showing maternal death, to determine what went wrong and what can be done differently in the future. Nor do we accept, as we once did, that our children may contract polio at the local pool or swimming hole. Whenever a young person comes down with a debilitating infectious disease, a group of healthcare providers meets to evaluate the source of the problem. Some states investigate all infant deaths to ferret out the causes of infant mortality.

We have reached a similar point in our struggle to reduce youth gun casualties. It is time to declare that we will *no longer tolerate the senseless loss of life to firearms* and that we will *do everything in our power to understand why these tragedies occur and what can be done to prevent them.*

What is needed at this juncture, perhaps more than anything else, are "zero tolerance" teams dedicated to ensuring that not one death occurs among individuals under the age of eighteen. Each team, crossing all debate lines, could be composed of a parent of a young person with a firearm, an NRA enthusiast, and representatives from the medical examiner's office, law enforcement, public schools, the juvenile justice system, social services, public health, community youth programs, and the emergency room. Team members could meet three times a year to review the youth firearm deaths reported over the previous four months, ascertain why these tragedies occurred, and shape preventive efforts for the future. The team's findings would need to be made public, and the victims' names withheld to protect the privacy of their families.

Improve Gun Safety Features. The number of negligent childhood poisonings dropped significantly with the introduction of childproof pill bottles. The number of negligent childhood shootings can decline, too, with the widespread installation of gun safety features. Inexpensive trigger locks and storage devices, capable of preventing young children from accidentally shooting off a loaded gun, are already available. To increase their accessibility, we can insist that these devices be included in the cost of buying a gun. We can also advocate for gun safety curricula in the schools so that students can learn what to do if they come in contact with a gun.

The best solution is to insist that gun manufacturers become accountable for the safety of their products, just as toy and doll manufacturers are. Consumer product safety awareness can be easily integrated into gun manufacturing technology. A simple gun stock combination lock, like those used on briefcases, for example, would enable parents to protect their children from misfiring. It is clearly time to promote the manufacture of "smart guns."

Restrict Unsupervised Access to Guns by Young People. Does it really make sense for anyone under age twenty-one to be handling a weapon without adult supervision? Current laws—which prohibit people under the age of twenty-one from purchasing handguns, but not from *possessing* them—seem to imply that it does. Hence, our first move as responsible citizens would be to require parents to assume liability for damages, including pain or suffering, wrought by minors who have gained access to the family gun. In addition, communities can initiate gun buy-back programs, gun exchanges featuring tickets or games, or toy-guns-for-books swaps. Each of these endeavors will let our young people know that *guns do not solve problems.*

Ensure That Every School Is a Safe School. We must do whatever is necessary to keep guns at least 1,000 feet from schools and school events. In addition, we must convert other areas into gun-free zones. Health facilities, public parks, daycare centers, and all public buildings can be as purged of guns as airports are. Many cities do not allow handgun possession without a permit; perhaps yours would like to join their ranks. To help maintain the peace, establish a system for handling reports of illegal weapon carrying or discharge. Following in the footsteps of those who established a toll-free number for reports on drunk drivers, why not operate an 800-WEAPONS line for calls about firearms.

Abolish Guns from the Homes of Adolescents Who Are Depressed or Chemically Dependent. Guns are now the suicide implement of choice for both young men and young women. In many communities across the United States, more young people are lost to suicide gun deaths than to homicide gun deaths. The sanest preventive approach if your teenager is depressed or chemically addicted is to obtain help and to store all guns at a relative's or neighbor's house until you are certain the risk of self-harm has passed. For this, no law is needed—only common sense and a strong media campaign.

Remove Guns from the Hands of Criminals Involved in Domestic Violence or Other Violent Misdemeanors. This suggestion is likely to stir up the most controversy, particularly among NRA members and others who claim: "Guns don't kill people. People kill people." To counter this line of reasoning, you can point out: "Motor vehicles don't kill people. The people driving them do"—a reality that has not stopped our society from enacting driving regulations.

Many such regulations are in effect. A prospective driver must reach a certain age before applying for a license; must demonstrate the capacity to use a car safely before being granted a license; must register the vehicle; must renew the registration yearly; and must officially transfer it upon selling the vehicle. The fees that accompany registration procedures help pay for the motor vehicle registration program and also contribute to the tax base, offsetting some of the public costs entailed in treating injuries sustained from improper vehicular use. Registration further facilitates the recovery of stolen vehicles and the ability to trace drivers involved in a crime.

In addition, several penalties are in place for abusing the privilege of driving. These range from warnings and fines to the revoking of licenses and the impounding of vehicles. Furthermore, because so many people are injured or killed in crashes, all drivers are expected to carry insurance to help pool funds for paying these bills. Automobile insurance companies, in an effort to keep premiums affordable and reduce their payouts, have moved to the helm of auto safety campaigns.

Reasonable equivalent regulations, penalties, and insurance requirements are *not* in place for individuals who operate guns. In most states, domestic violence criminals can buy and possess as many guns as they want, despite their abuse of this tool. Licensing and registration policies, as well as penalties for misuse, would certainly help control the ownership of such firearms. Yet, just as driving-while-intoxicated initiatives do not stop alcoholism but do prevent some of the resulting slaughter, regulating guns will not stop violence but will reduce the number of tragedies that occur each day.

Toward that end, here are some options worth considering. To ensure that all *currently owned* guns are registered, we could enforce laws requiring customers to show proof of registration before buying ammunition or reloading materials, at least for a number of years. To keep guns out of the hands of violent people, we could tighten the enforcement of existing dealer distribution laws. We could also insist that all judges issuing protective orders ask if firearms are currently in the home and, if they are, have them removed for the duration of the order.

Gun insurance is another possibility. For one thing, it would help cover the $33,000 average cost of each hospitalized gunshot wound patient. For another, insurers may be just the agents needed to inspire improved gun safety design and to offer gun owners courses in firearm safety and conflict resolution.

Maximize the Availability of Nonlethal Protection Devices. Many people keep firearms to protect themselves from stranger-inflicted violence. If nonlethal devices were more readily available, this sector of the weapon-bearing population might be willing to trade in their guns for other articles of self-defense. Sticky glue, pepper spray, mace, tranquilizer darts, and tasers do not cause permanent injury or death; firearms often do.

Systematize the Surveillance of Firearm Injuries and Deaths. Progress in preventing highway deaths improved markedly with the establishment of a national reporting system that enabled analysts to unravel patterns of vehicular injury and death. This system helped alert citizens to the epidemic of drunken driving and spurred on the development of many automotive and highway safety features. With a similar system in place to monitor firearm violence, we would achieve advances in home and neighborhood safety comparable to the progress made in highway safety.

Additional Resources

Center to Prevent Handgun Violence, 202-289-7319.

Eddie Eagle Firearm Safety Program of the National Rifle Association, 800-231-0752.

Firearm Injury Prevention Curriculum, 505-272-5062. A New Mexico Emergency Services for Children Project designed for grades K–8.

HELP (Handgun Epidemic Lowering Plan) Network, available through the Children's Memorial Hospital, 2300 Children's Plaza #88, Chicago, IL 60614.

Not Even One (Gun Death in a Young Person), established by the Carter Center, 404-420-3843.

Stop Firearm Injury, sponsored by the American Academy of Pediatrics, 708-228-5005.

DEMONSTRATE TO EDUCATE

I do not want to give the impression that nonviolence will work miracles overnight . . . it first does something to the hearts and souls of those committed to it. It calls up resources of strength and courage they did not know they had. Finally it reaches the opponent and so stirs his conscience that reconciliation becomes a reality.

—Martin Luther King Jr.

I will never forget the power I felt while participating in the September 1994 Silent March against Gun Violence in Washington, DC. Thirty-eight thousand pairs of shoes, one for each of the gun deaths that had occurred in this country the previous year, were laid out before the Capitol. Each pair had a note or photo attached, personalizing the dry, nameless statistics of the event.

Months of preparation in my own state had given me the opportunity to make contact with a large number of families personally affected by gun death. Their openness and willingness to help was profound. What came across again and again was a deep desire to have their loss *mean* something, to in some way contribute to a larger purpose.

The night before the march, I spent hours listening to groups from across the country, most of which were organized by grieving relatives who had lost young people to gun violence. Their stories brimmed over with passion, and with a commitment to keep on keeping on until they had made a difference.

Rallies, Vigils, and Speak-Outs. All across the nation, similar groups are forming, giving rise to a network of people affected by violence and willing to speak their peace. Those willing to listen are forever changed.

On a cold spring day, hundreds of people turn out for the annual Take Back the Night March. At the follow-up rally, women and men take turns speaking out against sexual violence and offering positive alternatives for the future. A woman presents an extraordinary theatrical performance dramatizing camouflage fashion and her need to dress in a way that no one will notice her, or bother her. The district attorney calls for a tough local stand on rape prosecution. A group of young people sings songs of peace. A doctor reminds us of the need to take back more than the night—to take back the day-to-day responsibility of talking with our children about sexuality. When the rally ends, we return to our respective homes, our hearts filled with a sense of promise and renewal.

In the predawn hours of a brisk autumn morning, 100 men gather by candlelight to speak of the violence of war and the devastating effects it has had on them. Between tears, they share stories of young people lost, lives ruined and reclaimed, and the senseless tragedies other men have caused them. As the sky begins to lighten, they discuss ways in which men can reduce the violence in our society.

In a large hotel conference room, a group of health providers silently views T-shirts decorated by participants in The Clothesline Project. The shirts are hanging from a clothesline that stretches from wall to wall. Some shirts depict a woman or child killed by domestic violence. Others illustrate survivors' experiences of battering, rape, sexual assault, incest, or child abuse. The clothesline keeps alive memories of events that must *not* be allowed to continue.

The entrance to a spacious sanctuary sizzles with excitement. People here, as elsewhere across the country on this day, are meeting for the first ever To Tell the Truth national speak-out. The women and men will spend hours sharing their experiences of childhood sexual assault, incest, and betrayal by those they loved. They will laugh, recite poetry, sing songs, and in their own way help shatter the silence surrounding childhood sexual abuse. Their hope is not only to bring the secret out of the closet but to demonstrate that victims who embrace a healing process are able to lead productive lives.

A sunny fall afternoon finds people of all ages gathered in the town plaza. Gang members share the stage with the mayor. She reads a proclamation, then delivers an impassioned plea for unity. They describe how the recent citywide gang truce was constructed. After more speeches and entertainment, participants wander over to a "wailing wall" to draw or write about how their lives were affected by violence. A table is staffed by local social service agency representatives eager to answer questions and provide information. Prizes, donated by local businesses, are awarded to express community support for peace. Throughout the remainder of the week, local schools and faith communities conduct discussions and classroom activities on the theme of violence. Hundreds of people sign personal pledges of peace. Participants agree unanimously to hold a second community event in honor of Peace and Justice Week the following year.

A Personal Pledge of Peace

I, _____, do hereby make a commitment to create peace within myself moment by moment, and to encourage non-violence in my family, my workplace, and my place of worship.

I promise to treat everyone I encounter with kindness and respect, and to attempt to settle as peacefully as possible any conflicts or differences that may arise.

I will not use guns or other weapons to harm or threaten another person.

I will acknowledge any anger I feel, and do my best to express it in a way that is not destructive to others, especially children and young people.

Because I am aware of the intimate connection between violence and alcohol, I will get help for myself and anyone close to me with drinking difficulties or violent acting-out behaviors.

As much as possible I will choose to forgive and be forgiven, and will allow for the healing of personal wounds or resentments.

I welcome love and trust into my life, instead of fear and hate.

The Power of Telling Our Stories. We cannot change what happened to us in the past, but we *can* change our relationship to it. We can move through the shame and secrecy that keep us socially isolated and emotionally insulated. Breaking open the inner prisons that have us convinced the violations of our past were our fault, we move through denial and begin to speak the truth.

At first, a victim of childhood violence simply looks truth in the face. After a while it becomes possible to share it with one or two trusted friends. In taking the risk of sharing our pain with others, we suddenly begin to *feel* more and, perhaps for the first time ever, to *experience safe intimacy*. Emboldened, we join a community of courageous people who are no longer willing to suffer in solitude. Then together we begin breaking the silence in the world outside our respective, now shattered prison walls. The beauty of this journey is that through the simple act of telling our stories, we become strong, whole, and equipped to participate in ending the violence.

Gandhi coined the term *satyagraha,* which means unmasking injustice to bring truth to light, holding on to that truth, and resisting oppression through nonviolent means. Surely, the nonviolent defense of truth through storytelling radiates outward into the minds and hearts of others, whereas the violent assertion of truth produces only temporary wins that leave a ripple of negative consequences in their wake. The reason organized demonstrations by violence survivors have had a dramatic impact on our society is that Gandhi's principle of *satyagraha* has been upheld.

Just as telling the stories is transformative for the individuals who lived them, *hearing* the stories is healing for communities, perhaps even for the nation. People's stories of violence touch policymakers and power brokers, engendering within them a desire to institute change. We can expect to see a great deal of civic healing in our times, for when people with these stories join together to inspire political action or community advocacy, there is no stopping them!

It has often been said that to accomplish anything in America, you must get a bunch of moms mad. Imagine all that could be accomplished if moms, dads, and everyone else affected by violence started to let the world know how they feel. So don't hold back—demonstrate to educate. Organize. Find your common ground of suffering, tell your stories, and state your demands. Be a huge thorn in somebody's side until you get what you know you need. You can rest assured that plenty of others need it too.

Additional Resources

Books

Bass, Ellen, and Laura Davis. *The Courage to Heal.* New York: Harper & Row, 1988.

Herman, Judith. *Trauma and Recovery.* New York: HarperCollins, 1992.

Ratner, Ellen. *The Other Side of the Family: A Book for Recovery from Abuse, Incest, and Neglect.* Deerfield Beach, FL: Health Communications, 1990.

Organizations
Men Overcoming Violence, 415-777-4496.
Mothers against Violence, 609-695-8002.
Mothers against Violence in America, 206-343-0676.
National Association of Victims' Rights, 800-784-2846.
National Clothesline Project, 508-385-7004.
National Coalition against Domestic Violence, 303-383-1582 or 202-638-6300.
National Victims' Resource Center, 800-627-6872.
Silent March, 718-636-9811.
SOSAD (Save Our Sons And Daughters), 313-833-3030.
To Tell the Truth, 800-578-1292 or 505-986-9844.

ENLIGHTEN THE MEDIA

Knowledge is like a garden. If it is not cultivated, it cannot be harvested.
—African proverb from Guinea

How can we build on the strengths of the media and move toward more enlightened industry standards? How can media conglomerates become part of the solution? Progress is possible on both fronts, provided that we T H I N K about the issues in human terms.

A NEW APPROACH TO THE MEDIA

T Teach reporters to reframe stories.

H Help screenwriters depict characters who deal with emotions and conflict.

I Improve broadcast standards.

N Nurture the development of new heroes and heroines.

K Keep expanding public awareness.

Teach Reporters to Reframe Stories. The unwritten rule of reporting seems to be: If it bleeds, it leads. Instead, broadcast and print media can make a concerted effort to reframe their coverage of events. Reporters and anchors alike could start and end their segments with human interest stories that emphasize the good in people. Disasters could be portrayed more affirmatively. Earthquake in progress? Show neighbors helping each other, and document how rescuers are saving lives. Political scandal in a government department? Interview employees who are getting important work done. Airplane crash? Release phone numbers that relatives can call for more information.

In addition, the violence reporting could itself be less one-dimensional. Reporters can be urged to focus on public health realities—the alcohol component of crimes and the fact that violence occurs between people who know each other. Either follow-up stories or statistics cited as part of the initial coverage could convey this information. Emphasis also needs to shift from profiling perpetrators to showing the plight of victims. How are they coping? What resources are available to them?

When communicating with reporters, urge them to affix a solution-based reality lens to the cameras they are using. And when you see evidence of reframing, be sure to say: "Thank you. Good job." Positive feedback on a job well done is food for the soul.

Other ways to reframe the news exist as well. TV 101, out of Albuquerque, New Mexico, has involved young people in the production and direction of its shows. Teens decide on topics, do fieldwork, and conduct interviews, after which their pieces are aired a few times a week on the evening news. Increased diversity in the age and ethnic mix of reporters more accurately reflects the composition of our culture. In-depth stories, as opposed to sound-bite results, help recast news items in a more productive light.

Help Screenwriters Depict Characters Who Deal Effectively with Emotions and Conflict. Publishers and broadcasters have made great progress in realistically portraying the effects of alcohol, especially with regard to driving. Now it is time to do the same for violence.

Both the Washington, DC-based Institute of Mental Health Initiatives and Mediascope, in California, are helping script developers redefine the norms of conflict management as portrayed in screenplays. Their goal is threefold: to show violence as unrewarding and unglamorous, to present the suffering of victims as well as witnesses and perpetrators, and to portray constructive ways of coping with anger that can benefit both the scripted characters and the viewers. Consults with mental health providers can further enrich the screenwriter's grasp of the emotional complexity of human beings and of the developmental stages involved in learning about feelings.

Improve Broadcast Standards. Consumer awareness is just beginning to take hold in the broadcast industry. The channel-blocking V-chip, currently used in some hotel rooms, helps protect children's TV viewing to a certain extent. Overall, however, scenes of senseless violence still predominate. Previews accompanying children's movies, despite an "approved for all audiences" tag, are often needlessly gory and filled with sexual innuendoes. So, too, is much of the Saturday morning children's fare and programs shown during "family" viewing hours. A healthy starting point for change would be a new rating system that directly addresses violent programming.

With respect to children's home videos, the highly creative consumer-based Coalition for Quality Children's Videos (see page 126) has come to the fore. This group enlists a panel of children and adults to review films, and places a Quality Children's Video seal of approval on those that feature pro-social values, creative imagination, entertainment diversity, and an absence of violent images.

Watchdog groups are also needed to monitor advertising directed at children. Currently, toys and programs are jointly marketed to the public, convincing little ones that they must have certain accessories to act out the adventures of their favorite characters. One way to address this problem is by reinstating some of the regulations abandoned during the Reagan years—specifically those that prohibit the sale of toys associated with television shows and those that limit the number of advertising minutes per hour on children's television.

In addition, tobacco, alcohol, and toy weapon advertising is impacting heavily on teen culture. Why not omit these ads from television, and limit them to the print media, *excluding* magazines read by minors?

Nurture the Development of New Heroes and Heroines. A new genre of televised role models is urgently called for. Every society relies on its heroes and heroines to inspire dreams, inform goals, and impart the notion that actions matter. Our society—replete with people acting nonviolently to resolve significant conflicts—desperately needs more of these simple acts of courage dramatized on stage and screen.

Broadcasters can take their cues from *Kung Fu* and *Next Generation Star Trek,* in which violence is de-emphasized, is considered the last resort of the hero, and is applied only when wits and communication skills have not yielded results. These shows depict perpetrators of thoughtless violence as villains and fools. Their use of weapons is often portrayed as a sign of weakness and ineptitude.

Positive input is also available from other quarters. Disney characters can usually be counted on to have pro-social values and a desire to resolve conflict in creative ways. Future Wave, a group that specializes in "working for alternatives to violence in entertainment," will soon release a full-length feature, entitled "Astrocops," about peacekeepers of the future who project holographic images, play soothing music, or transmit energy waves to calm down an aggressor.

The point to remember is this: *any time our children begin cheering for a hero or heroine who routinely kills or hurts people, they are watching the wrong show.* Children and adults alike long for leading characters who use goodness instead of superior violence in their confrontations with evil.

Keep Expanding Public Awareness. Young people want to become enlightened about the world through the media, and knowledgeable about the media through the world. Hence, the first order of business is to insist that the media provide an education in violence prevention. At the very least, "peacekeeping infomercials" could offer a wealth of guidance in harmonious coexistence.

Possible Peacekeeping Infomercial Themes

★ "All feelings are okay; all behaviors are not."

★ The sign of the T. "Time out is not just for sports; it also works at home to defuse anger and tension."

★ "For children to do better, must they first be made to feel worse?"

★ "Give a kid a chance—give a kid a job."

★ How to be a nonhitting family.

★ "War toys provide training in the use of violence to solve problems."

★ The pros and cons of being in a gang.

★ "Friends don't let friends fight." How to break up a fight that has already started.

★ "Domestic violence has never solved a problem."

★ "What do violent families fight about? Money, the children, how they spend time together . . . the same things *any* family fights about, except that the rules are different."

★ "When adults listen, teens talk out their problems instead of acting them out."

★ "If you own a gun, be smart, be safe, keep it locked up."

★ "Violent TV programming causes mind pollution. Turn off the TV, and go for a walk or read a book with your children."

★ "Most children who survive adverse circumstances have bonded with a caring adult who let them know that the hardship was not fair, not right, not their fault, and not something they would always have to live with. Be that someone for a young person."

★ "There's no excuse for hitting your partner."

★ "Getting her drunk isn't the same as getting her permission."

★ "Some rapists use loaded guns; others use loaded victims."

★ "No means no. And 'no answer' means no, as well."

Compiled, in part, from material published by the Acquaintance Rape National Campaign and the Domestic Violence Prevention National Campaign

The second task is to ensure that young people become more media literate. Presently, $130 billion a year is pumped into broadcasting networks to promote envy, anxiety, and insecurity—all of which are presumed to be relieved by buying the right product or service. Preying on human desires for comfort, companionship, status, power, and sex, advertising has only one goal: to persuade viewers to consume. To put the power back in the hands of our children, we need to teach them about target marketing, false promises, and the real message behind the glitz.

Additional Resources

Organizations

Center for Media and Values, 310-559-2944.

FAIR (Fairness and Accuracy in Reporting), 130 West 25th Street, New York, NY 10001; 212-633-6700. A media-watch group that attempts to correct bias and imbalance in the news, pointing out allegiances to official agendas and insensitivities to women and minorities. Publishes *Extra!* magazine.

Future Wave, 505-982-8882.

Institute of Mental Health Initiatives, 202-364-7111. Offers information and *Dialogue,* a quarterly publication.

Mediascope, 818-508-2080.

National Coalition on Television Violence, 217-384-1920.

TV 101, 505-243-2285.

Major Network Contacts

ABC, 2040 Avenue of the Stars, Century City, CA 90067; 310-557-7777.

CBS, 7800 Beverly Boulevard, Los Angeles, CA 90036; 213-852-2345.

NBC, 3000 West Alameda Avenue, Burbank, CA 91523; 818-840-4444.

REINVENT FRIENDSHIP, RESTITUTION, AND PILGRIMAGE

In a real sense all life is inter-related. All men are caught in an inescapable network of mutuality, tied in a single garment of destiny. Whatever affects one directly affects all indirectly. . . . I can never be what I ought to be until you are what you ought to be, and you can never be what you ought to be until I am what I ought to be.

—Martin Luther King Jr.

Some of my most rewarding experiences occurred while helping to start a multicultural men's group. It was made up of five American Indians, five African Americans, five Hispanics, and five of us "others," including a Jew, a Norwegian, an Irishman, an Italian, and a Scot. We met for six hours once a month. We told our stories, shared meals, played music, and in general tried to understand what was keeping us separated from one another. Discussion of Christopher Columbus's "discovery" of America filled an entire day. Gradually it became possible to really hear about each man's past and present oppression.

The Gifts of Friendship. Friendship is a long-term dialogue based on equality. A friend invites you to be insecure, unsafe, and vulnerable. Your connection allows each of you to be present with your emotions without feeling "wrong." You can both be open about your interdependency, sharing areas of concern that are difficult to reveal to others. Lowering your barriers in this way, you become confronted with a new sense of self.

Friendships are never conflict free. But agreement is less important than the honest sharing of feelings, thoughts, and desires. And when differences arise, the process of resolving them deepens the bonds of reliability and trust. If you judge a friend harshly for something, learn to say, "That is within me too." Instead of responding to a friend's actions and words, learn to recognize his intentions.

Friends offer comfort by sitting with you in silence. Their simple words can be touchstones that bring you out of confusion. Like a rock cairn, they help you recall the path you were on so that you can return to it. They remind you that regardless of your imperfections, you are eminently worthy. Friends greet you with "Namaste," a Hindu term meaning "I honor the place in you where, when you are in that place in you and I am in that place in me, there is only one of us."

Listening deeply, I have taken the voices of friends into my heart. I have learned about the magnitude of their oppression and the psychic ambushing their ancestors endured. Now, while examining present-day violence in America, I am constantly reminded of the historical violence that has occurred on these shores. And I can say, "I'm sorry for the past." Someday, perhaps, we will have a process in place for apologizing *as a culture* and addressing our common destiny.

The Bounties of Pilgrimage. The concept of pilgrimage is ancient and widespread. The Koran commands all Muslims who are financially and physically capable of the journey, to conduct a *hajj* to Mecca at least once in their lifetime. Many Buddhists travel to the Place of the Diamond Scepter in India, where Buddha achieved enlightenment more than 100 generations ago. Both Jews and Christians traverse the sacred sites of Jerusalem, reaffirming their spiritual connections. Hindus trek to the source of the Ganges River, or to its sacred junction with the Jumna River. Huichol Indians of Mexico return each year to Wirikuta, a high desert plateau hundreds of miles from their mountain homelands; this highly ritualized journey lasts several weeks as the pilgrims, or *peyoteros*, retrace the steps of the ancient ones.

A physical pilgrimage provides opportunities for exploring inner land-scapes. In the process of surmounting the difficulties inherent in these long journeys, individuals discover inner resources and develop the strength, determination, and courage to face problems. The physical treks quickly become spiritual explorations—a powerful adjunct to every pilgrim's life.

Although journeys of this sort are not customary in our culture, they can be easily adopted as an individual or group activity. They will not help you escape from parts of your life you'd prefer not to encounter, and will not satisfy a desire to run away in denial. To the contrary, they will reconnect you with nature and with yourself. Going out into the world is a way of bringing you closer to the true dwelling place of your inward village. And though you may return from each pilgrimage you embark on with more questions than answers, you are sure to come back with renewed understanding.

Restitution. Each time I travel to the Vietnam Memorial in Washington, DC, I am deeply moved and better for the journey. Often I have wondered what our interactions would be like if a similar monument honored the slaves who gave their lives to the original thirteen colonies that formed the United States, and another monument commemorated the Indians who were killed as America expanded and broke its treaties with the Native peoples. Would memorializing these people inspire us to provide restitution to their descendants? Would it open our hearts and evoke public apologies to those who still suffer as a consequence of damage inflicted in the past?

It is possible to memorialize the people who were eradicated in the building of America. First, we would need to create a fund for this purpose. Citizens could donate to the fund by filling in a check-off box on income tax forms. Or proceeds from the sale of a special postal stamp could be channeled into the fund. Or an "endowment for oppressed peoples" project could be underwritten by major corporations that would be given tax breaks for their contributions.

What if each state individually chose to erect a monument to those who suffered so that its residents could prosper? These would be places worthy of a pilgrimage—places where new friends might enter our lives and expand our understanding.

Additional Resources

Black Elk Speaks, as told through John G. Neihardt. Lincoln, NE: University of Nebraska Press, 1988.

Haley, Alex. *Roots.* New York: Dell Publishing, 1976.

Keen, Sam. *Faces of the Enemy.* New York: HarperCollins, 1986.

Mander, Jerry. *In the Absence of the Sacred: The Failure of Technology and the Survival of the Indian Nations.* Pasadena, CA: Sierra Club Books, 1991.

Peck, M. Scott. *In Search of Stones: A Pilgrimage of Faith, Reason, and Discovery.* New York: Hyperion, 1995.
Wallace, Paul. *The Iroquois Book of Life: White Roots of Peace.* Santa Fe, NM: Clear Light Publishers, 1994.

STAFF A NATIONAL PEACEKEEPING CORPS

Waking up this morning, I smile, twenty-four brand new hours are before me. I vow to live fully in each moment and to look at all beings with eyes of compassion.
—Thich Nhat Hanh

To truly move toward violence prevention and enforce it on every front, we will need a National Peacekeeping Corps. This extensive network of peacekeepers would be composed of state and local representatives, including volunteers, part-time paid helpers, and full-time personnel recruited to work at the community level. Its mission would be to interact with existing systems while continuing to explore channels for increasing the peace.

The National Peacekeeping Corps would consist of four branches. *Guardian Angels* would interface with community policing and juvenile first-offender programs. *Mentors* would bring mediation, meditation, multiculturalism, and martial arts to the schools. *Builders* would partner with housing authorities, parks and recreation agencies, and labor leaders to improve housing, provide youth employment, and help staff the emerging arks of peace (see pages 187–188). *Family Friends* would work in cooperation with social service and health agencies to pay home visits to new families.

Family Friends. This arm of the National Peacekeeping Corps would fill a critical void in our culture, which has long recognized that the earlier in life prevention and intervention activities take place, the better the chances are of raising a significantly less violent generation. All new parents, including those living in isolated regions, deserve to get off to a good start and avail themselves of crisis and support services when necessary. Regularly scheduled home visits would serve both these purposes.

Family Friends would initiate its services prenatally with a home visit to the expectant family. The Family Friends worker would return to welcome the newborn into the world and help the parents learn how to care for their baby. Services would be tailored to meet family needs. Visits to the family would continue at least once a week for three to five years, with an emphasis on parental support, parent-child interaction, and education in child development and school readiness. Much of this contact would highlight "reparenting the parent" to help the new mother and father experience the support and encouragement missing from their own childhoods.

Workers would be recruited primarily for their nonjudgmental, compassionate approaches conducive to the establishment of trust. They would receive an initial period of standardized training and additional in-service training every three months. Each worker would serve between fifteen and twenty-five families, depending on experience, and would be supervised by professionals to ensure quality care and establish links with the local network of health and social service supports.

The success of this initiative would hinge on the development of high-quality, caring, supportive relationships between Family Friends workers and expectant mothers and fathers. With well-nurtured bonds and good parenting practices in place at the start, patterns of abuse will wither before their seeds are able to spread.

The Secretary of Peace. The luminary of the National Peacekeeping Corps would be the secretary of peace, who would ensure that:

* People working in weapons technology are given assistance in finding other work and receiving on-the-job training as the industry is phased out, beginning with a progressive ban on the sale of weapons overseas.
* Land mines are outlawed within five years. Although these mines cause suffering and dismemberment worldwide, most often among innocent people after hostilities have ended, the initial objective would be to ban their manufacture in this country and disallow their use by United States military forces.
* Citizens opposed to war on moral grounds are able to open escrow accounts to hold a portion of their income tax. These dollars would constitute the beginning of a Peace Tax Fund to be channeled into peace research.
* The punitive prison system is gradually converted to a prison ashram system. At root, prison life resembles monastic life in many ways: both provide plenty of time for solitude, reflection, and simple work that contributes to community functioning. The conversion would foster inner transformation.
* The death penalty is abolished on the basis of being a racist policy that does not deter crime.
* The National Guard, in conjunction with DARE programs for school-based drug education, expands its drug demand reduction activities and gives 10 percent of its time to youth-based community projects.
* Corporal punishment is banned, first in school systems and then in homes and public places. Adults who have tantrums and hit their children in public would receive emergency treatment and be given immediate counseling. "No Hitting" signs and billboards would proliferate.

✷ War toys are made illegal, or are gradually taxed out of existence.

✷ Links are preserved among people of different ethnic groups whose fates are intertwined with one another.

Additional Resources

Books

The Gaia Peace Atlas. Edited by Dr. Frank Barnaby. New York: Doubleday, 1988.

Hedemann, Ed. War Tax Resistance: A Guide to Withholding Your Support from the Military. Philadelphia: New Society Publishers, 1992.

Lozoff, Bo. We're All Doing Time. Durham, NC: Human Kindness Foundation, 1985.

Organizations

Healthy Families' America Home Visitation Initiative, US Department of Health and Human Services, MCH Bureau Division of Healthy Start, in Rockville, MD; 301-443-0543.

National Committee for the Prevention of Child Abuse, 312-663-3520.

War Resisters League, 212-228-0450.

TEACH MEN TO TALK

Manhood is what we look forward to when we are powerless boys and what we look back on with pride when we are limping toward the grave. To be known as a good man is the highest compliment for a man. It is what men despair of achieving when depressed—in our careers, our family life, in our sexuality, in our values. Our idea of manhood is our motivation toward self-respect. And most of us could not be more aware that the old images of manhood need revision.

—Stephen Shapiro

Statistics concerning men's health are poignantly revealing. Men, compared with women, experience much higher rates of morbidity and mortality due to heart disease, substance abuse, and violence—all of which have their origins in emotional repression. The release of emotions, on the other hand, is believed to contribute to well-being. Studies in psychoneuroimmunology are beginning to show that positive emotional states increase the number of healing cells circulating in the body. Laughter and improved mental outlooks alone can help reverse the course of some progressive illnesses.

A convergence is presently occurring in our country. Mainstream medicine is slowly acknowledging that body, mind, emotions, and spiritual perspective are interconnected, and that dis-ease in one of these realms produces symptoms in another. The men's movement has arrived at the same conclusion.

The Men's Movement. The endeavor to achieve male health and well-being is nourished by four taproots: mythopoetic artistry, Jungian archetypes, twelve-step wisdom, and body-based emotional release techniques. The life force of the movement emanates from thousands of small support groups around the country. Here, men meet regularly to talk about important matters in their lives. Over time, they experience trust, acceptance, and respect from others males, instead of competition, put-downs, and violence.

RAINBOWS
Hank Blackwell

Wherever you go,
however far away it is,
take my love
on your shoulders, riding
as I did
down those steep trails to our fishing place.
(The only times I remember embracing you as a child.)
Smelling the cigarette smoke, the sweat
the canvas vest
like perfume,
the smell of a father
to a son.

Whenever you go,
cast away your silent desperation
like a dry fly into the current.

I will probably walk those trails
when you
are gone . . .
crying, remembering how you were
during those magical times.
I felt your body move as it carried me
down to the river;
you in search of trout
me, hoping the trail
would never end.

From *Talking from the Heart: An Anthology of Men's Poetry* (Albuquerque, NM: Men's Network Press, 1990). Reprinted by permission of the author and publisher.

Many men are in pain. They live in isolation with few, if any, close friends. To varying degrees, they have bought into destructive cultural beliefs about masculinity and are stuck in the male box that emphasizes "power over" and "control" as the operative behaviors for men. They have become trapped in mind-sets that stifle growth.

Sturdy as oaks that feel no pain and need no help, they endure until their hearts attack them. Or they act out their stress by abusing their children, express control through domestic assault, or power through acquaintance rape. They commit suicide because they can't admit they are hurting, or homicide in response to a remark that bruises their fragile sense of self. Or they get lost in a maze of addictions to subdue the inner turmoil. Most of these men are success objects running a competitive maze, searching for perfection, confused by a material world that does not leave them time for satisfaction.

Losing themselves, men lose the ability to care for the earth and be active, loving family members. Lacking inner peace, they wage war, endlessly draining away the precious resources needed to fight the poverty and disease they are running from.

Talking Is Transformative. Health statistics, together with the ordinary events in the lives of men, indicate that change is urgently needed. More than anything else, men require tools to use in forging ahead to new awareness.

One of the most handy and functional tools available is *articulation*. Talking helps us gain access to ourselves. Telling our stories and listening to those of other men shed new insights into ways to conduct our lives. Talking together, we find that we are sons, fathers, lovers, grandfathers; some of us have sex with women, some with men, some with men and women. And beneath our differences, we discover that we are all *men*. As such, the archetypal king, warrior, magician, and wildman hold secrets for us in their hands. Mentors and elders, too, have the power to resurrect for us ancient aspects of maleness.

We want to know how to become heroes, healers, brothers, and friends. We yearn to awaken and integrate the feminine aspects of ourselves. Bringing these desires to fruition requires a stable, ongoing source of support—a forum that encourages us to express how we are feeling about our life path and how we are grappling with the difficulties before us. Talking about our journeys keeps us on course. It also serves to reduce male violence.

Talking, essential at each juncture of a man's journey, is more critical than ever during the transition to fatherhood. The powerful forces at play on the threshold to fatherhood bring a man face to face with the gifts and the wounds received from his parents. Feelings about how he was parented are sure to arise, and in sharing them he will be able to increase his consciousness about the new role he is undertaking.

Expectant and new fathers alike desperately need a safe space in which to express their hopes and fears. Fortunately, fathering centers are springing up around the country to support men as they connect with this nurturing part of themselves. Older men who have raised children are also stepping forward as trail guides. Still, much more counsel is needed, especially for teen fathers who may be overwhelmed by the difficulties of parenting, or by the extraordinary range of emotions it stirs up.

Every man has inner wisdom: he has encountered pain and survived. Now he must learn the language of feelings. Where he learns to express himself does not matter, provided that it takes place in a *supportive atmosphere* on a *regular basis*. The journey toward wholeness begins with a willingness to enter the darkness within; embrace our shadows; explore the contours of our anger, fear, and joy; and talk out, rather than act out, the emotions we have held hostage since childhood.

Additional Resources

Literature

Full-Time Dads, a periodical available by calling 207-829-5260.

Heinowitz, Jack. *Pregnant Fathers: Entering Parenthood Together.* San Diego, CA: Parents As Partners Press, 1995.

Kauth, Bill. *A Circle of Men: The Original Manual for Men's Support Groups.* New York: St. Martin's Press, 1992.

Keen, Sam. *Fire in the Belly.* New York: Bantam Books, 1991.

Kivel, Paul. *Men's Work: How to Stop the Violence That Tears Our Lives Apart.* Center City, MN: Hazelden Publishing Group, 1992.

Meade, Michael. *Men and the Water of Life.* New York: HarperCollins, 1993.

Sonkin, Daniel, PhD. *Learning to Live without Violence: A Handbook for Men.* Volcano, CA: Volcano Press, 1989.

Zilbergeld, Bernie. *Male Sexuality.* New York: Bantam Books, 1978.

Organizations

Abusive Men Exploring New Directions (AMEND), 303-832-6363.

Domestic Abuse Intervention Project, 218-722-4134.

EMERGE, 617-422-1550.

The Fathering Center, Albuquerque, NM; 505-266-9233.

Apply Mediation Anytime and Everywhere

I have just three things to teach: simplicity, patience, compassion. These three are your greatest treasures. Simple in actions and in thoughts, you return to the source of being. Patient with both friends and enemies, you accord with the way things are. Compassionate toward yourself, you reconcile all beings in the world.

—Tao Te Ching

Mediation alters consciousness, and should be at least as accessible as cash machines. Divorcing spouses need these skills, as do bickering neighbors, squabbling supervisors and employees, juvenile offenders and their parents, kids arguing on the playground, victims and perpetrators, and rival gang members. For most people never exposed to the magic of mediation, verbal or physical abuse is the only strategy known for dealing with stressful, hostile, or problematic situations.

Mediation Skills. Training programs in mediation introduce four basic disciplines: understanding the nature of conflict, expressing feelings, developing good communication skills, and problem solving. *Understanding the nature of conflict* begins with reflection. One thinks back on a conflict, examining what led up to it, what the disagreement was really about, and what happened during it and afterward. It then becomes possible to understand one's *own* conflict style, which may entail avoiding or denying (concluding that conflict does not exist, is bad, or will erupt in a nonproductive fight), engaging in conquest (having to win, needing to be right, or lunging into a hit-and-run confrontation), settling on a Band-Aid or bargain approach (finding a quick fix so as to avoid dealing with the underlying problem, or striving for peace at any price), or actively searching for solutions.

Expressing feelings is introduced by exploring and naming the emotions that arise during conflict. The goal is to learn to identify them and talk about them before they become repressed or diverted into physical expression.

Developing good communication skills takes lots of practice. First, one must become proficient in conveying feelings clearly and honestly. In addition, one must listen actively and reflect messages back to others, in an attempt to understand what *they* are feeling (see pages 91–94).

Problem solving rests on the awareness that actions have consequences and that the parties can choose from among a variety of solutions. A good solution is one that meets the needs of the disputants, is viable, and feels fair to all concerned. Good solutions emerge in a comfortable atmosphere governed by mutually agreed upon ground rules such as "No physical violence," "No put-downs," and "No interrupting."

School-Based Mediation. Conflict resolution skills, the nuts and bolts of mediation, are becoming increasingly popular in schools seeking a more peaceful climate. Everyone in these institutions is taught mediation. Some students and teachers are further trained as mediators. Student mediators—selected from a range of academic proficiency levels—learn the basics through role-playing, group dialogue, and highly interactive sessions. Then they advance to hands-on applications on the playground or in the cafeteria, where they work in pairs during recess and lunchtime. Most programs include sessions in teacher-student mediation, teacher-teacher mediation, and teacher-administrator mediation.

Institutions that provide this type of training report positive results. Those that offer the training in kindergarten through twelfth grade have the most impressive results of all: fewer playground fights, reduced disciplinary actions, improved morale and respect, and an enhanced sense of safety.

Some conflicts in life are minor nuisances, whereas others destroy important relationships. Too often, loving bonds turn toxic simply because we do not know how to settle our differences. Mediation is the perfect remedy, for it teaches us to clarify our desires and satisfy our needs while honoring others who are trying to do the same for themselves.

Additional Resources

Books

Fischer, Roger, and William Ury. *Getting to Yes.* New York: Houghton Mifflin, 1981.

Moore, Chris. *The Mediation Process: Practical Strategies for Resolving Conflict.* San Francisco: Jossey-Bass, 1986.

Weeks, Dudley, PhD. *The Eight Essential Steps to Conflict Resolution.* Los Angeles: Jeremy Tarcher, 1992.

Organizations

Educators for Social Responsibility, 212-870-3318.

New Mexico Center for Dispute Resolution, 505-242-5966. Offers training manuals for K–12, gang-involved youth, and parent-child mediation.

Resolving Conflict Creatively Program, 212-387-0225.

NURTURE A PEACEABLE IMAGINATION

Consciousness precedes being, and not the other way around. For this reason, the salvation of the human world lies nowhere else than in the human heart, in the power to reflect, in human meekness, and in human responsibility.

—Vaclav Havel

Plato, who was deeply interested in the creative process, coined the term *poietai* to describe artists, storytellers, inventors, builders, and other original thinkers. When life travels through creative people, he observed, it comes out in a new way. This occurs because the minds of creative people long to explore, their hands yearn to get in on the act, their demeanor is relaxed, curious, and wondering. There is a willingness to hold on to a question while wandering around, drifting through fantasy. With it comes a desire to look beyond first ideas and to intertwine seemingly different ideas, altering aspects of each of them, one at a time.

To move into this out-of-box state of being, begin by expecting the unexpected. Then launch generative ideas into action, and narrow your focus. Remain open and flexible as you play hunches and go all out for an idea that is initially unclear. Finally, move through trial and error until you arrive at the elegant solution—the yes!

Creative thinking is the mode of reflection we will need in our attempt to establish a more peaceful world. It is the faculty of mind required to develop an ecology of peace. One way of inaugurating this state of mind is by consistently fostering the development of multiple forms of intelligence.

The Seven Forms of Intelligence. More than ten years ago, Howard Gardner, of the Harvard Project on Human Potential, delineated seven forms of intelligence: linguistic, logical/mathematical, spatial, body/kinesthetic, musical, interpersonal, and intrapersonal. To strengthen all seven of these capacities, be sure to immerse yourself in a wide variety of activities.

DEVELOPING THE SEVEN FORMS OF INTELLIGENCE

Mode of Intelligence	Growth-Promoting Activities
Linguistic	Read books; listen to tapes; make time for storytelling.
Logical/Mathematical	Play strategy games; work with science kits.
Spatial	Use cameras; build with Legos; do visualizations.
Body/Kinesthetic	Shape clay; interact with animals; wear costumes; negotiate obstacle courses.
Musical	Play percussion instruments; sing; listen to nature sounds.
Interpersonal	Engage in cooperative learning; play group games.
Intrapersonal	Keep a journal; sit in a tree house; meditate.

Each form of intelligence can also be nurtured in peace-promoting ways. What type of music, for example, do you find most soothing? Which aspects of interacting with animals foster compassion for humans? While journaling, can you detect conflict before it erupts? Can you discover new approaches to feeling physically relaxed and open? What effect do world village stories about overcoming adversity and oppression have on your understanding of peace? What effect might such stories have on the residents of your community, or of our country? How hard would it be to stage community theater puppet or dance shows as teaching tools for nonviolence?

The Technology of New Ideas. Progress in peace may ultimately hinge on a pool of ideas that will spread and germinate into as yet unimagined forms of expression. At the present point in human evolution, ideas have already acquired a "biological" reality. Author Lyall Watson refers to them as "memes"—thought forms that are implanted simultaneously in many individuals, are transmitted rapidly, and gain increasing visibility as they penetrate the larger culture.

In some creative thinkers, these memes are likely to pave the way to material inventions that will help ensure the unfolding of peace in our world. Such technological innovations might include the following:

* Smart guns that will shoot only if the fingerprint of the operator matches that of the legal owner, as encoded on a computer chip sensor embedded in the stock; or smart guns that will fire only if the operator properly sequences a combination lock similar to those on briefcases.
* Better gun detectors to help enforce the establishment of gun-free zones in cities and public places.
* Bracelets that monitor prisoners during periods of probation.
* Devices that automatically signal the police when the wearer—an offender under a domestic violence protection order—comes within 1,000 feet of a transmitter kept in the victim's home or workplace. Eventually, the transmitter might be small enough for the victim to carry in a pocket or purse, or wear like a beeper.
* Coded chips with summaries of laws, including the penalties imposed for breaking them, installed in the pocket-notebooks of law enforcement agents.
* More competent video and audio monitoring of domestic violence scenes to ensure convictions when law enforcement responds to calls.
* A portable V-chip designed for home use and travel, to block reception of irresponsible TV programs.
* Psychoneuroacoustic advances beyond Muzak, to create calmer sound environments.

✷ Improved tasers—gun replacements for individuals wishing to stop an assailant without causing permanent injury.

✷ Immobilizing foam, currently under development in national weapons labs for use in crowd control, available in dispensers for individual use.

✷ On-site recordings of world village stories about people who have overcome adversity and oppression.

✷ CD-ROMs, computer programs, and games to enhance problem-solving skills, introspection, pro-social values, and peacekeeping strategies.

✷ Extensive conversations on the Internet among people working on peace and justice issues.

✷ Virtual reality and other mind-expanding, consciousness-altering products that, unlike addictive chemicals, do not disinhibit aggressive impulses.

✷ Interactive counseling booths. Put your quarter in and get a five-minute support session.

✷ CD-ROMs chock full of references on violence prevention.

Additional Resources

Books

Armstrong, Thomas. *Discovering and Encouraging Your Child's Personal Learning Style.* Los Angeles: Jeremy Tarcher, 1987.

Cassidy, John, and the Exploratorium Staff. *Explorabook: A Kid's Science Museum in a Book.* San Francisco: Klutz Press, 1991. Available from the Exploratorium Store Mail Order Department, at 800-359-9899.

Fluegelman, Andrew. *The New Games Book.* Tiburon, CA: Headlands Press, 1976.

Murdock, Maureen. *Spinning Inward: Using Guided Imagery with Children for Learning Creativity and Relaxation.* Boston: Shambhala Publications, 1987.

Journals

Utne Reader. A bimonthly available by calling 612-338-5040.

Whole Earth Review. A quarterly available by calling 415-332-1716.

Organizations

Institute for Global Communications, 415-442-0220. Offers Internet discussions of peace-related issues on Peacenet, Womensnet, Econet, Conflictnet, and Labornet.

Nonviolence through the Arts: Dances of Universal Peace, 505-982-5802.

DECLARE YOUR INTENTIONS

Until one is committed there is hesitancy, the chance to draw back, always ineffectiveness. Concerning all acts of initiative (and creation), there is one elementary truth, the ignorance of which kills countless ideas and splendid plans: that the moment one definitely commits oneself, then Providence moves, too. . . . I have learned a deep respect for one of Goethe's couplets:

"Whatever you can do, or dream you can, begin it. Boldness has genius, power and magic in it."

—W. H. Murray

Deep personal change, as opposed to major societal shifts, doesn't have to take eons. It can occur in a flash, the moment one takes a no-nonsense stand against any monstrous ingrained behavior. In other words, the legion of heartbreaks resulting from out-of-control behaviors need not wear us down eternally. The pall can lift; the air can lighten; and compassion and safety can become powerful new habits.

If a meme for nonviolence has joined your repertoire of thoughts, and if you wish to contribute to the energy being charged by ideas of peaceful coexistence, then it is time to make a personal commitment to nonviolence. Head to the courtroom to put the skids on abusive activity. Push bills through the legislature. Most importantly, compose a personal declaration of intent, then state your objectives whenever the opportunity arises. What exactly is the picture you envision contributing to?

When speaking your peace, avoid the language of victimization. Steer clear of negative statements such as "I can't" and its corollaries "It will never work," "We've never done it before," "We don't have the time (money, resources, expertise)," "It's a waste of time," "It's not going to get any better," and "Let somebody *else* deal with it." Positions of this sort only invite more helplessness and hopelessness into the world. They commit a form of violence against humanity.

Remember this, too, while drafting your declaration of intent. In fact, before setting pen to paper, consider the purpose of this exercise. Most often, a declaration captures a vision of possibility to strive toward in our daily thoughts and actions. It also serves as a reminder of how we want to be treated.

The most powerful declarations, including those that appear on the following pages, embody universal truths that can apply to any stage on our life journey. Read silently or aloud, privately or in a group, they can connect us with others who share our sentiments. Good declarations publicly affirm beliefs we know to be true in our hearts. They fill the body and mind with hope, and form a wellspring of inspiration for the spirit.

I Am Me

Virginia Satir

I am me. In all the world, there is no one else like me.
There are persons who have some parts like me, but no one adds up
   exactly like me.

Therefore, everything that comes out of me is authentically mine
     because I alone chose it. I own everything about me
my body, including everything it does;
my mind, including all its thoughts and ideas;
my eyes, including the images of all they behold;
my feelings whatever they may be
anger, joy, frustration, love, disappointment, excitement;
my mouth, and all the words that come out of it, polite, sweet or
     rough, correct or incorrect;
my voice loud or soft;
and all my actions, whether they be to others or to myself.

I own my fantasies, my dreams, my hopes, my fears.
I own all my triumphs and successes, all my failures and mistakes.

Because I own all of me, I can become intimately acquainted with me.
By so doing I can love me and be friendly with me in all my parts.
I can then make it possible for all of me to work in my best interests.

I know there are aspects about myself that puzzle me, and other
     aspects that I do not know.
But as long as I am friendly and loving to myself, I can courageously
     and hopefully look for the solutions to the puzzles and for ways
     to find out more about me.
However I look and sound, whatever I say and do, and whatever I
     think and feel at a given moment in time is me.
This is authentic and represents where I am at that moment in time.

When I review later how I looked and sounded, what I said and did, and
     how I thought and felt, some parts may turn out to be unfitting.
I can discard that which is unfitting, and keep that which proved fit-
     ting, and invent something new for that which I discarded.
I can see hear, feel, think, say, and do.
I have the tools to survive, to be close to others, to be productive, and
     to make sense and order out of the world of people and things
     outside of me.
I own me, and therefore I can engineer me. I am me, and I am okay.

From the book *Peoplemaking* by Virginia Satir (Palo Alto, CA: Science and Behavior Books, 1972), p. 67. Used with permission of Avanta, The Virginia Satir Network.

PRINCIPLES OF NONVIOLENCE

Martin Luther King Jr.

Nonviolence is a way of life for courageous people.
Nonviolence seeks to win friendship and understanding.
Nonviolence seeks to defeat injustice, not people.
Nonviolence holds that suffering can educate and transform.
Nonviolence chooses love instead of hate.
Nonviolence believes that the universe is on the side of justice.

PRINCIPLES OF NONVIOLENCE

Mahatma Gandhi

Nonviolence implies as complete self-purification as is humanly possible.

Man for man, the strength of nonviolence is in exact proportion to the ability, not the will, of the nonviolent person to inflict violence.

The power at the disposal of a nonviolent person is always greater than he would have if he were violent.

There is no such thing as defeat in nonviolence.

Nonviolent opposition:

Implies not wishing ill.

Includes total refusal to cooperate or participate in activities of the unjust group, even to eating food that comes from them.

Is of no avail to those living without faith in the God of love and love for all mankind.

Asks that he who practices it must be ready to sacrifice everything except his honor.

Must pervade everything and not be applied merely to isolated acts.

A BLESSING

Helen Weaver

O our Mother the Earth, blessed is your name.

Blessed are your fields and forests, your rocks and mountains, your grasses and trees and flowers, and every green and growing thing.

Blessed are your streams and lakes and rivers, the oceans where our life began, and all your waters that sustain our bodies and refresh our souls.

Blessed is the air we breathe, your atmosphere, that surrounds us and binds us to every living thing.

Blessed are all creatures who walk along your surface or swim in your waters or fly through your air, for they are all our relatives.

Blessed are all the people who share this planet, for we are all one family, and the same spirit moves through us all.

Blessed is the sun, or day star, bringer of morning and the heat of summer, giver of light and life.

Blessed is the moon, our night lamp, ruler of the tides, protector of all women, and guardian of our dreams.

Blessed are the stars and planets, the time-keepers, who fill our nights with beauty and our hearts with awe.

O Great Spirit whose voice we hear in the wind and whose face we see in the morning sun, blessed is your name.

Help us to remember that you are everywhere, and teach us the way of peace.

FOR EVERY WOMAN . . . THERE IS A MAN

Anonymous

For every woman
who is tired of acting weak when she knows she is strong,
There is a man
who is tired of appearing strong when he feels vulnerable.

For every woman
who is tired of being called an "emotional female,"
There is a man
who is denied the right to weep and be gentle.

For every woman
who is tired of being a sex object,
There is a man
who worries about his potency.

For every woman
who is denied meaningful employment of equal pay,
There is a man
who must bear the full financial responsibility for another human being.

For every woman
who is tired of acting dumb,
There is a man
who is burdened with the constant expectation of "knowing everything."

For every woman
who was not taught the intricacies of an automobile,
There is a man
who was not taught the satisfaction of cooking.

For every woman
who takes a step toward her own liberation,
There is a man
who finds the way to freedom has been made a little easier.

EVERY HUMAN'S BILL OF RIGHTS

I have the right to:

Be treated with respect.

Be listened to with respect.

Have my own feelings and opinions.

Express my feelings and opinions.

Make my own decisions and set my own priorities.

Say no without feeling guilty.

Say, "I don't know," "I don't understand," or "I don't care."

Ask for what I want.

Get what I pay for.

Ask for information from professionals.

Make mistakes.

Seek privacy.

Change my mind.

Be illogical in making decisions.

Fail.

Disappoint others.

Refuse to accept responsibility for other people's needs, wants, feelings, and actions.

Choose whether or not I want to find solutions for other people's problems.

Inconvenience others in order to protect myself.

Offer no reasons or excuses to justify my behavior.

Judge my own behavior, thoughts, and emotions, and take responsibility for their initiation and consequences.

Choose not to assert myself.

Adapted from Bloom, Coburn, and Pearlman, *The New Assertive Woman* and M. J. Smith, *When I Say No I Feel Guilty.*

THE NEW MALE MANIFESTO

I. Men are beautiful. Masculinity is life affirming and life supporting. Male sexuality generates life. The male body needs and deserves to be nurtured and protected.

II. A man's value is not measured by what he produces. We are not merely our professions. We need to be loved for who we are. We make money to support life. Our real challenge, and the adventure that makes life full, is making soul.

III. Men are not flawed by nature. We become destructive when our masculinity is damaged. Violence springs from desperation and fear, rather than from authentic manhood.

IV. A man doesn't have to live up to any narrow, societal image of manhood. There are many ancient images of men as healers, protectors, lovers, and partners with women, men, and nature. This is how we are in our depths: celebrators of life, ethical, and strong.

V. Men do not need to become more like women in order to reconnect with soul. Women can help by giving men room to change, grow, and rediscover masculine depth. Women support men's healing by seeking out and affirming the good in them.

VI. Masculinity does not require the denial of deep feeling. Men have the right to express all their feelings. In our society this takes courage and the support of others. We start to die when we are afraid to say or act upon what we feel.

VII. Men are not only competitors. Men are also brothers. It is natural for us to cooperate with and support each other. We find strength and healing through telling the truth to one another—man to man.

VIII. Men deserve the same rights as women for custody of children, economic support, government aid, education, health care, and protection from abuse. Fathers are equal to mothers in their ability to raise children. Fatherhood is honorable.

IX. Men and women can be equal partners. As men learn to treat women more fairly, they also want women to work toward a vision of partnership that does not require men to become less than who they authentically are.

X. Sometimes we have the right to be wrong, irresponsible, unpredictable, silly, inconsistent, afraid, indecisive, experimental, insecure, visionary, lustful, lazy, fat, bald, old, playful, fierce, irreverent, magical, wild, impractical, unconventional, and other things we're not supposed to be in a culture that circumscribes our lives with rigid roles.

From the book *Knights without Armor* by Aaron R. Kipnis, PD (1991). Published by Jeremy P. Tarcher, Inc. Distributed by St. Martin's Press. This may be reprinted without permission. To order, call 800-288-2131.

Ten Recommended Attitudes about Technology

Jerry Mander

Since most of what we are told about new technology comes from its proponents, be deeply skeptical of all claims.

Assume all technology "guilty until proven innocent."

Eschew the idea that technology is neutral or "value free." Every technology has inherent and identifiable social, political, and environmental consequences.

The fact that technology has a natural flash and appeal is meaningless. Negative attributes are slow to emerge.

Never judge a technology by the way it benefits you personally. Seek a holistic view of its impacts. The operative question is not whether it benefits you, but who benefits most? And to what end?

Keep in mind that an individual technology is only one piece of a larger web of technologies, "megatechnology." The operative question here is how the individual technology fits the larger one.

Make distinctions between technologies that primarily serve the individual or the small community (e.g., solar energy) and those that operate on a scale outside of community control (e.g., nuclear energy). The latter kind is the major problem of the day.

When it is argued that the benefits of the technological lifeway are worthwhile despite harmful outcomes, recall that Lewis Mumford referred to these alleged benefits as "bribery." Cite the figures about crime, suicide, alienation, drug abuse, as well as environmental and cultural degradation.

Do not accept the homily that "once the genie is out of the bottle you cannot put it back," or that rejecting technology is impossible. Such attitudes induce passivity and confirm victimization.

In thinking about technology within the present climate of technological worship, emphasize the negative. This brings balance. Negativity is positive.

RIGHTS OF THE CHILD

The United Nations Convention on the Rights of the Child says, in part:

All children have the right to life, a name, and a nationality.

All children's opinions shall be given careful consideration, and their best interests shall be protected.

All children shall be educated in a spirit of understanding, peace, and tolerance.

Disabled children shall have the right to special treatment, education, and care.

All children have a right to health care.

All children shall be cared for, by their parents if at all possible, by others if necessary.

Children shall be protected from forced labor, drug trafficking, kidnapping, and abuse.

Children exposed to war should receive special protection. No child under fifteen shall go to war.

Children of minority populations shall freely enjoy their own culture.

All children have the right to rest and play, and the right to equal opportunities for cultural and artistic activities.

A Prayer / Pledge of Responsibility for Children

Ina J. Hughs

We pray (accept responsibility) for children
who sneak Popsicles before supper,
who erase holes in math workbooks,
who can never find their shoes.

And we pray (accept responsibility) for those
who stare at photographers from behind barbed wire,
who can't bound down the street in a new pair of sneakers.
who never "counted potatoes,"
who were born in places in which we wouldn't be caught dead,
who never go to the circle,
who live in an X-rated world.

We pray (accept responsibility) for children
who bring us sticky kisses and fistfuls of dandelions,
who hug us in a hurry and forget their lunch money.

And we pray (accept responsibility) for those
who never get dessert,
who have no safe blanket to drag behind them,
who watch their parents watch them die,
who can't find any bread to steal,
who don't have any rooms to clean up,
whose pictures aren't on anybody's dresser,
whose monsters are real.

And we pray (accept responsibility) for children
who spend all their allowance before Tuesday,
who throw tantrums in the grocery store and pick at their food,
who like ghost stories,
who shove dirty clothes under the bed and never rinse out the tub,
who get visits from the tooth fairy,
who don't like to be kissed in front of the carpool,
who squirm in church or temple and scream in the phone,
whose tears we sometimes laugh at and whose smiles can make us cry.

And we pray (accept responsibility) for those
whose nightmares come in the daytime,
who will eat anything,
who have never seen a dentist,

who aren't spoiled by anybody,
who go to bed hungry and cry themselves to sleep,
who live and move, but have no being.

We pray (accept responsibility) for children
who want to be carried
and for those who must,
for those we never give up on
and for those who don't get a second chance.

For those we smother
and for those who will grab the hand
of anybody kind enough to offer it.

Additional Resources

Earth Prayers from around the World. Edited by Elizabeth Roberts and Elias Amidon. New York: HarperCollins, 1991.

Gandhi on Nonviolence. Edited by Thomas Merton. New York: New Directions, 1965.

Roger, John, and Peter McWilliams. *You Can't Afford the Luxury of a Negative Thought.* Los Angeles: Prelude Press, 1988.

The Seventh Path

THE WAY OF CHANGE

MAKING IT SO

I am of the opinion that my life belongs to the whole community and, as long as I live, it is my privilege to do for it whatever I can. I want to be thoroughly used up when I die, for the harder I work the more I live. I rejoice in life for its own sake. Life is no brief candle to me. It is a sort of splendid torch which I've got to hold up for the moment, and I want to make it burn as brightly as possible before handing it on to future generations.

—George Bernard Shaw

S OME DAYS MY LIFE SEEMS IRREVOCABLY OUT OF BALANCE—TOO MUCH WORK, too little time and energy for family and friends. I neglect the practices that enhance my well-being. Meditation and exercise are replaced by fast food and rushing. Sunsets pass without notice, and I don't smile much. On these days I contribute to the spread of violence. While doing "good work," I model and reinforce destructive patterns of living.

Always there is a dynamic tension between taking care of oneself and being of service to others. This tension gives way to awareness and change. Indeed, midway between the seemingly disparate polarities of self and other, they become harmonized. Then we see that it is impossible to decrease the levels of societal violence until we are able to increase our own peace.

FROM DOING TIME TO DOING PEACE

Mark Twain once said, "Never put off till tomorrow what you can do the day after tomorrow." He, along with many others, recognized that change is one of the constants of the universe. It occurs everywhere, incessantly. Sometimes it comes slowly and steadily, like a welcome breeze on a hot day. At other times it sweeps in like a whirlwind, catching us by surprise. Though we may resist its influence, we sense its inevitability. We eventually learn to ask each day, in our own way, that "God grant us the courage to change the things we can."

An old Sufi tale portrays a wise woman who disturbs her neighbors while rummaging around outside her small hut. She has lost her needle. Soon her neighbors are helping her, looking up and down the village path. Finally someone asks, "Rabiya, where exactly did the needle fall?" She responds that she dropped it inside her hut. "Then why are we searching out here?" the villager asks. She replies that it is easier to see outside, where there is more light. The people berate her for her foolishness, whereupon she begins to laugh and explains, "You are so wise about little things, yet you keep searching for your happiness in the outside world. Is that where you have lost it?"

We have all been caught searching the streets for happiness. Yet, when it comes to exploring inner landscapes, we behave like model prisoners. The violence we do to ourselves through our internal conversations keeps us in a state of captivity and creates enormous suffering. Trying to live up to others' shoulds further restrains us from exploring our personal values and needs. Fearful of both the darkness and the light within, we get stuck in our self-imposed attitude prisons. There, over time, the question "Who am I?" becomes covered over with layers of statements about "who I'm afraid I am."

The greatest tragedy is that many people die in misery, never knowing who they are. The more they have separated from themselves, the more unhappiness they have experienced. One woman I know recently confessed: "I often wonder what it will take to become willing to stop being miserable. A distressing life is all I've known. *How good can I stand it?*" She went on to explain that her pain and suffering were unavoidable, but her misery was optional. Then she added: "The only thing I need to recover from is my fractured sense of self, and the negativity and fear that arise from *that*. Peace really does begin with me."

To approach change effectively, we first need to relinquish the thought that we're not good enough, and accept the fact that we are all right *exactly as we are*. The password here is EWOP!—everything is working out perfectly . . . *and* there is room for improvement! Then change becomes a comrade worth seeking out because it can help us grow, rather than an adversary to avoid because it generates fear. Receptive to change, we embrace our authentic needs: to be good and care for our bodies and souls, to love and be loved in a mutually empowering exchange of affection and compassion, to express creativity, cultivate spirit, contribute, participate, and make a difference.

So how does one become an agent of change? How might you go about altering an unwanted aspect of your life? The following ABCDEs of change can serve as helpful guidelines:

Awaken. Begin by becoming aware of what you are hoping to change. Of all the problems you have, which one would you most like to solve? What would the world look like tomorrow morning if resolution were achieved overnight while you slept? What would be the first indication that things were different?

If you cannot think of an area in need of improvement, try using appreciative inquiry: while honoring all that is good in your life, heighten your curiosity about thoughts or behaviors that could be different, then focus on one at a time. Be an audience in your own theater. Take time for self-reflection, and listen to the secrets emerging at dawn. You may soon notice habitual patterns that do not serve you, that are making you uncomfortable. If you are not certain about the *direction* you wish to take, stay with your confusion, simply letting it be. As with the clearing of a muddy stream, time—and attention—will soon bring the clarity needed for taking the next step.

Believe. Whatever your desired change may be, believe you can accomplish it. Get your entire self behind it, with all the gates open. Intend the change fully, for in doing so you will generate "psychic gravity," attracting the elements needed to initiate it. To form an effective intention, begin with the phrase "I am willing to . . ." This wording will invite, rather than demand, assistance from yourself and others. Inviting acknowledges that the universe operates on a timetable of its own, whereas demanding, which is less participatory, brings on attachment and invariably leads to disappointment.

Also make sure your intention is clear. A clear intention is stated simply and directly, as in "I am going to write a song about creating peace. It will be helpful, memorable, and hence successful." If indecisiveness is keeping you from clarifying your intention, see if you are afraid of making a mistake or of failing. If you are, invite your fears and limiting belief systems to step forth and announce themselves. Learning to recognize them and move through them to set your intention will enable you to move through mistakes and failures as you change.

A bumper sticker I first saw on a nun's car reads, "Doo-doo happens!" That's certainly part of the tableau we must contend with as we embark on change. Actually, there are three aspects to the landscape of change: the *experiential* (that which happens to us), the *creative* (that which we bring into existence), and the *attitudinal* (our response to difficult circumstances). Each of these forces must be harnessed for change to proceed.

Believing in our ability to change resides halfway between accepting what life brings us and responding appropriately to that stimulus. It also rests on a firm belief in our freedom to choose by exercising self-awareness, imagination, conscience, and independent will.

Commit. With commitment comes an ability to focus energy and attention moment to moment on the desired change. The dominant question is, "What is happening *right now* that is helpful and instructive?"

If you know what needs altering, believe in your ability to create the change, but are unable to dedicate yourself to the process, you may be up against one of the following stumbling blocks:

✴ A secret attraction to victimhood. We all love to be victims. Nowhere, however, does the Good Book say, "Whine and you shall receive." To make a difference in our lives, we can take "slow" for an answer, but not "no." Be persistent, and *ask until* . . .

✴ A payoff for staying stuck in old habits. As always, discovering the source of your resistance is an important key to overcoming it. Do you really want this thought or behavior in your life, or are you holding on to it for someone else? What is your real incentive to change?

✴ Guilt. What exactly is stopping you from saying no, or from taking time to focus on your own well-being?

✴ Uncertainty. You can have *anything* you want, but not *everything* you want—a reality that can pose considerable vacillation. To commit, you must prioritize, organize, then get into action. In which arena do you have the most trouble?

✴ An attachment to the familiar. Only by embracing the fear of moving out of your comfort zone will you be able to fully commit your energy to the change.

Do It! Creating change begins by putting all one's energy into manifesting the new, rather than fighting the old. Amid acts of no resistance, old patterns wither from disuse.

So do not struggle against the old ways, or attempt to force the change you have committed to. Breathe deeply, and relax into it. Your greatest ally is not willpower, but rather constant attention—the ongoing consideration you give to the new reality you are creating. Also share your intention with friends, and ask for their support in specific ways. Although you have to effect the change yourself, you don't have to do it *alone.* Nurturing a supportive network of friends, neighbors, and relatives—a constellation Buddhists term a *sangha*—will significantly strengthen your capacity to enact the change.

Author and master Aikidoist George Leonard, in his book *Mastery,* says that opening doors to new skills requires five master keys: instruction, practice, surrender, intentionality, and the edge, or access to the terrain in which new habits emerge through a pool of fears. Loving the practice of each new skill is equally essential, for practice makes change permanent.

To have life be the way we want it, we have to give up the way it is—a renunciation that often brings about confusion and ambivalence. As the old pattern or identity dies and the new one emerges, we encounter "empty time," in which no change seems to be occurring. Accept this empty time, all the while continuing to hold your intention and focus your energy. Celebrate success, in whatever form it happens to appear.

Evaluate. While flying from Los Angeles to Hawaii, most airplanes are off course about 90 percent of the time. They reach their final destination by continually course correcting. So it is for humans en route to a new goal. To know if you are on track or not, you will need to evaluate each effort along the way: did it achieve the results you want, or an outcome you didn't want?

Accept all evaluative feedback. In the event of a failure, avoid beating yourself up. When breakdowns occur—as they are apt to do in the process of change—it is more helpful to return to your original intention, be patient with yourself, and learn from the mistakes. Above all, reward the efforts that bring you closer to your goal.

FORGING NEW TRAILS

Creating change on a personal level establishes a fertile seedbed for creating change in other contexts. Utilizing the knowledge gleaned on this path, you will be able to make a difference in family and community life, while helping to shift the mind-set of our culture. Remember, it takes only one person to change the nature of a relationship. Remember also that some of the most productive initiatives around the country are fueled by a handful of people with a vision and commitment to create positive change. So think globally, act locally, question vocally, and respond personally!

Violence is a relationship disorder, a communication failure. And people who pour time and energy into overcoming this disorder are not only forming more effective patterns of communication but are laying the groundwork for a more promising future. What focuses their energy is a combination of knowledge, skills, and desire. You, too, can help shape a less violent future. The knowledge and skills are available. You need only add the desire to do what requires doing in your little corner of the world.

Peace is not some rainbow at the end of a long journey. It is the moment-to-moment process of walking the roads of our lives with acceptance, trust, appreciation, creativity, and understanding. It is finding, in the midst of our pain and confusion, the courage to open our hearts, to extend a hand, and to take the hand of another when we are in need of support. In choosing peace, we begin creating peace.

Before us lies a landscape with a vast array of trails to travel in order to transform violence. These pages map out only some of them. The next steps are yours to take. May you sojourn in peace!

Additional Resources

Covey, Stephen. *The Seven Habits of Highly Effective People.* New York: Simon & Schuster, 1989.

Leonard, George. *Mastery.* New York: Penguin Books, 1991.

Maltz, Maxwell. *Psychocybernetics.* North Hollywood, CA: Wilshire Book Company, 1970.

TECHNICAL REFERENCES

Technical References to The First Path

1. Centers for Disease Control, "Homicides among 15–19 Year Old Males: United States 1963–1991," *Morbidity Mortality Weekly Report* 43, no. 40 (1994): 725–727.

2. US Department of Health and Human Services, *A Nation's Shame: Fatal Child Abuse and Neglect in the United States* (Washington, DC: National Clearinghouse on Child Abuse and Neglect, 1995).

3. The National Committee for Injury Prevention and Control, "Injury Prevention Meeting the Challenge," *American Journal of Preventive Medicine* (supplement) 5, no. 3 (1989): 216–217, 243–251.

4. Special Issue on Domestic Violence, *Journal of the American Medical Association* 267, no. 23 (17 June 1992).

5. "Children and Guns," a hearing before the Select Committee on Children, Youth and Families, House of Representatives, on 15 June 1989 (Washington, DC: US Government Printing Office, 1989).

6. Center to Prevent Handgun Violence, "Compilation of Handgun Fatality Statistics by Country."

7. M. L. Rosenberg et al., "Violence, Homicide and Assault," in *Closing the Gap: The Burden of Unnecessary Illness*, R. W. Amler and H. B. Dulls, eds. (New York: Oxford University Press, 1987), pp. 164–178.

8. Federal Bureau of Investigation, "Crime in the United States," *1993 Uniform Crime Reports* (Washington, DC: US Department of Justice, 1993).

9. National Institute on Drug Abuse Research, *Drugs and Violence: Causes, Correlates and Consequences*. Monograph #103.

10. D. Prothrow-Stith with M. Weissman, *Deadly Consequences: How Violence Is Destroying Our Teenage Population and a Plan to Begin Solving the Problem* (New York: HarperCollins, 1991).

11. *Street Gang Update* (Santa Fe, NM: NM Department of Public Safety, 1993).

12. A. Kellerman et al., "Gun Ownership As a Risk Factor for Homicide in the Home," *New England Journal of Medicine* 329, no. 15 (1993): 1084–1091.

13. Children's Safety Network, "Focus on Firearms," *BiblioAlert: New Resources for Preventing Injury and Violence* 1, no. 1 (1993).

14. R. J. Gelles and C. P. Cornell, *Intimate Violence in Families* (Newbury Park, CA: Sage Publications, 1990).

15. L. E. Walker, *The Battered Woman Syndrome* (New York: Springer Publishing Company, 1984).

16. *International Perspectives on Family Violence*, R. J. Gelles and C. P. Cornell, eds., (Lexington, MA: BC Health, 1983), pp. 1–22.

17. National Victim Center and Crime Victims Research and Treatment Center, *Rape in America: A Report to the Nation* (Arlington VA: National Victim Center, 1992).

18. *Note:* This discussion focuses largely on men battering women—a pattern that constitutes 98 percent of all domestic abuse. The remaining 2 percent pertains to men abused by women and violence occurring among gay and lesbian couples. American College of Obstetricians and Gynecologists, *The Abused Woman* (Washington, DC: American College of Obstetricians and Gynecologists, 1993).

19. Bureau of Justice Statistics, Federal Bureau of Investigation, *Murder in Families: Special Report* (Washington, DC: US Department of Justice, July 1994).

20. C. H. Zeanah, *Hurt Healing Hope: Caring for Infants and Toddlers in Violent Environments* (Washington, DC: Zero to Three National Center for Clinical Infant Programs, 1994).

21. K. A. Thornell, "My God, My God, Will They Hear My Cry?" *Cathedral Age* 63, no. 2 (Summer 1988): 31–32. .

22. "Welfare Reform Seen from a Children's Perspective," *National Center for Children in Poverty News and Issues* 5, no. 2 (Summer 1995).

23. Lisbeth B. Schorr and D. Schorr, *Within Our Reach: Breaking the Cycle of Disadvantage* (New York: Doubleday, 1988).

24. Children's Defense Fund, *Wasting America's Future: Children's Defense Fund Report on the Costs of Child Poverty* (Boston, MA: Beacon Press, 1994).

25. *Violence and Youth: Psychology's Response,* vol. 1 of *Summary Report of the American Psychological Association Commission on Violence and Youth* (Washington, DC: American Psychological Association, 1993), pp. 32–35.

Additional Sources of Information

Bureau of Justice Clearinghouse, 800-688-4252.
Children's Defense Fund Reports, 202-628-8787.
Clearinghouse on Child Abuse and Neglect, 800-394-3366.
National Center for Children in Poverty, 212-927-8793.
National Center for the Prevention and Control of Rape, 301-443-1410.
National Coalition against Domestic Violence, 202-638-6399.
National Committee for Prevention of Child Abuse, 312-663-3520.

Technical References to The Second Path

1. *Kids Count Data Book: State Profiles of Well-Being* (Baltimore, MD: The Annie E. Casey Foundation, 1995).

2. National Institute of Medicine, *The Best Intentions: Unintended Pregnancy and the Well-Being of Children and Families* (Washington, DC: National Academy Press, 1995).

3. Kelly L. Burrowes et al., "Research on the Biological Aspects of Violence," *Psychiatric Clinics of North America* 11, vol. 4 (Dec 1988): 499–509.

4. Bruce Perry, *Maltreated Children: Experience, Brain Development and The Next Generation* (in press).

5. C. Spatz Widom, *Victims of Childhood Sexual Abuse: Later Criminal Consequences* (Washington, DC: US Department of Justice, March 1995).

6. US Department of Health and Human Services, *Report of the Secretary's Task Force on Youth Suicide* (Washington, DC: US Government Printing Office, 1989).

INDEX

ABOUT THE AUTHOR

Victor La Cerva, MD, has been actively working in violence prevention for more than ten years. He is currently medical director of the Family Health Bureau of the New Mexico Department of Health, and holds a clinical faculty appointment with the Department of Pediatrics at the University of New Mexico Medical School.

In 1984 Victor co-created the New Mexico Men's Wellness movement to promote an exploration of the physical, emotional, mental, and spiritual needs of men in our society. As a result, years before the national men's movement became known, annual gatherings, hundreds of small support groups, a statewide newsletter, and support groups for young men were activated in New Mexico. In 1989 he organized four statewide workshops on violence, in collaboration with the New Mexico Public Health Association.

His first book, *Let Peace Begin With Us*, was released in 1990 and updated in 1993 and 1996, highlighting levels of homicide, suicide, child and elder abuse, domestic violence, and sexual assault on a county-by-county basis. Both editions have served as catalysts for community involvement. Victor continued to "build the movement" as the New Mexico co-chair for the September 1994 and 1996 Silent Marches on gun violence in Washington, DC, and the establishment of the New Mexico "Not Even One Team: Not One Gun Death in Any Young Person." He was recently interviewed by Bill Moyers as part of the "Solutions to Violence" series that was broadcast nationally.

Victor holds the rank of shodan in Aikido, a Japanese martial art that accepts and then redirects aggressive energy so that neither the defender nor the attacker is injured. The father of two daughters, he cares deeply about preventing violence in America. He believes that solutions emerge in the process of strengthening all that is good within ourselves, our families, our communities, and our culture.

Humans
Everywhere
Allied in
Love

HEAL

"The mission of the HEAL Foundation is to promote positive change and progress in understanding and improving human relationships through educational and peacemaking information, materials, and programs, in the hope of establishing a more common ground for all people to interact in peace and prosperity."

Stephan McLaughlin Jr.
HEAL Foundation
Executive Director

FOUNDATION GOALS

HEAL is an organization of people, who care about people, and who are committed to:

- Exploring fundamental elements and dynamics of human relationships;
- Identifying tools and techniques for encouraging healthier, happier relationships between individuals and themselves, their families, their friends, and their communities;
- Promoting healthier relationships by increasing people's awareness and use of these tools and techniques;
- Creating positive change by utilizing knowledge and understanding of relationships to assist in conflict resolution, community building, and addressing social issues and problems.

We believe all humans have the desire to increase their own health and happiness and to decrease their suffering. HEAL seeks to affirm and stimulate each individual's capacity to live in healthy relationships. Our work is based on the assumption that human relationships have similar dynamics and commonalties. People's lack of loving and nurturing relationship skills is at the heart of many pressing and disturbing problems that trouble our society.

We hold the belief that an improved understanding of our basic human characteristics and relationships are essential ingredients in understanding and dealing with many of the problems and challenges faced by individuals, families, societies, and even nations in the world community.

It is not our goal to present some form of ultimate truth. It is our hope that our work will help identify certain aspects of the human family that can be used to increase

Humans
Everywhere
Allied in
Love

HEAL

positive, harmonious human interaction while reducing negative, harmful human interaction.

Relationship formation and maintenance play major roles in defining us as people. In fact, a vast majority of our time is spent interacting in an incredible number and variety of relationships. Failure to form and sustain healthy relationships frequently leads to abusive relationships, which pose fundamental challenges to our individual and communal health.

Relationships are part of all aspects of our lives. We are involved in them at home, on the job, in the car, in our spiritual groups, even when we are alone. Looking at these activities and seeking to understand them better could open a new approach to living life, to connecting and communicating with people, to loving and nurturing those we care about, and to reducing and resolving conflicts with others.

Your interest and support of HEAL and its efforts are greatly appreciated. For more information, or to tell us about your important work in this area, please contact us at:

HEAL Foundation
Stephan McLaughlin Jr., Executive Director
1770 North Germantown Parkway
Suite 3-162
Cordova, TN 38018
(801) 947-0317
Or visit our web site: www.healfoundation.org

To Order Additional Copies of *Pathways to Peace*, call 1-800-472-0438.